THE BEST
SPIRITUAL
WRITING
2002

THE BEST
SPIRITUAL
WRITING
2002

EDITED BY
PHILIP ZALESKI

INTRODUCTION BY
NATALIE GOLDBERG

HarperSanFrancisco
A Division of HarperCollinsPublishers

Page 275 constitutes a continuation of this copyright page.

FIRST EDITION

Library of Congress Cataloging Card Number 98–12368

ISSN: 1525–5980

ISBN 0–06–050603–2

02 03 04 05 06 RRD(H) 10 9 8 7 6 5 4 3 2 1

Contents

Preface

When the dead have been buried, the rubble removed, the sirens silenced, the requiems sung, the innocent avenged, the guilty punished, when memories of the event have cracked and faded, what will remain of September 11? I've put this question to a hundred people and received as many answers. The responses all translate into one: *memento mori*. Remember death. Remember that I too shall die. From this answer flows a second: not *carpe diem,* but *carpe deum.* Hold onto God, truth, goodness. Remember that my life counts; that time, that incomprehensible coin, possesses a moral dimension, and that how I spend it will lead to corruption or sanctity; that within all human suffering lies the seed of divine hope. From this second answer flows a third: that with God's help, I can make a difference.

Ambitions such as these surge in our hearts; but ambition is one thing, execution another. How can we translate these fine sentiments into reality? One clue emerged in Assisi, Italy, in late January, when scores of religious leaders of every faith, invited by John Paul II, gathered in the Umbrian home of the great thirteenth-century saint, Francis *il poverello,* to pray for peace. The world marveled at the sight of Muslims and Jews, Christians and Hindus standing shoulder to shoulder in friendship. The gathering was, to be sure, testimony to the pope's spiritual leadership: "Only you, John Paul II, could put this together. Only you could make this happen," said Israel Singer, president of the governing board of the World Jewish Congress. Mr. Singer is right, but a second element also made this gathering possible: the urgent sense, felt as acutely in Africa and Asia as in the Americas and Europe, that after September 11 a new beginning was necessary, that new efforts must be made to recall the world to universal truths, above all the sacredness of human life and the dignity of human fellowship, by placing love before anger, humbleness before pride, and others before self.

Of the testimony and prayers—all of them helpful, few of them dull—offered that day at Assisi, I would like to quote from the presentation by Chief Amadou Gasseto, representative of Avelekete Vodou, an African tradition rarely, if ever, encountered in fashionable religious circles (and, for that matter, never before heard in *The Best Spiritual Writing* series). Chief Gasseto, who hails from Benin, had this to say:

> *I recognize in the first place that peace is a gift of God to us. However, this gift is left to the responsibility of man, called by the Creator to contribute to the building up of peace in this world. This is a universal responsibility which concerns all creation. . . . We must begin by achieving mastery over ourselves, so as not to speak words that lead to feelings of opposition, exclusion, or violence. We must be responsible for the spirit that our words produce. This should be a spirit that gives rise to harmony, friendliness, and fraternity. Peace will then have a favorable ground in which to grow among people.*

Chief Gasseto's words may serve as a guide to all spiritual writers. He crisply identifies the two critical stages that lead to the best work in the genre. First, the creative ground must be prepared through years of careful cultivation and seeding: "We must begin by achieving mastery over ourselves." Spiritual writing that emerges from self-mastery has an unmistakable quality about it. It rings true. This sense of lived experience cannot be counterfeited. Second, "we must be responsible for the spirit that our words produce." Spiritual writing has a thousand themes and a thousand styles, but it can have only one aim: to bring forth truth, beauty, and goodness. In some measure, although one or another quality may predominate, all three will be present in any successful work of spiritual writing (and, one might add, in any successful spiritual enterprise). Writing without beauty coarsens rather than refines; writing without truth hides rather than reveals; writing without goodness hurts rather than helps.

I am often asked what I look for in the essays and poems considered for publication in the Best Spiritual Writing series. I can do no better than to say that I am looking for what Chief Gasseto is looking for: words that indicate mastery over the self; essays and poems that radiate the three platonic virtues of beauty, truth, and goodness. One can learn much, too, by looking at shadows, and so the question is often put to me like this: what keeps an essay or a poem out of the collection? The obvious answer is lack of beauty, truth, or goodness, but I can offer a more concrete reply. There are two absolute vetoes: bad writing, and writing that attacks other people or their spiritual or religious beliefs.

The latter is of particular concern, for I run across it, while compiling this collection, more often than you might think, and I often suspect that the writer, hypnotized by cultural norms, is unaware of what he or she has done. Fifty years ago, when anti-Semitism ran rampant among intelligentsia (including, alas, many who worked in the spiritual writing genre), the guilty parties often claimed innocence; their prejudice was invisible to them, as prejudice usually is to its perpetrators. Cultural trends change, and while anti-Semitism remains a very serious problem, the favorite targets for religious bigotry, at least among the cultural elite, now also include Muslims, Catholics, and evangelical Protestants. Terrorist attacks by a handful of extremists on September 11 have triggered an outpouring of attacks against Muslims, decrying the Qur'an and Islam with little regard for the realities of this great tradition. Sexual scandals involving a tiny percentage of Catholic priests have unleashed an unprecedented wave of Catholic bashing, demonstrating once again the truth of the saying that "anti-Catholicism is the anti-Semitism of the intellectual." As for evangelical Christians, it remains business as usual; this group continues to receive a steady stream of contempt and scorn from those who certainly should know better.

The religious bigotry that I am describing is hardly limited to extremist newsletters or the tabloids; it turns up, at a disconcertingly regular rate, in many of our leading newspapers and magazines. One wonders about the true motives for these attacks. It seems no accident that Muslims, Catholics, and evangelicals, all of whom retain a strong sense of the sacred, stand in firm opposition to many of the values—on issues ranging from sexual ethics to care of the poorest of the poor—held dear by the dominant secular culture. Perhaps some soul-searching is in order. It may be that these traditions, which have flourished with such great vitality over so many centuries, possess secrets that the modern world would do well to discover. In any case, whenever I run across such biases while assembling these annual volumes, I place the offending piece aside.

Happily, the great majority of spiritual writing avoids such prejudice, and while a much smaller percentage of the material that passes across my desk can be called good writing (for literary skill remains a rare commodity), when the winnowing process is complete an ample bounty of work remains from which to select the gems that make their way into this collection. So let us rejoice and dig in. In these pages you will find the best that the genre has to offer; and the best, as I discover to my delight year after year, is very good indeed.

Many people helped in the production of this volume. My thanks to Gideon Weil, Calla Devlin, and the entire crew at Harper San Francisco; to Kim Witherspoon, David Forrer, and everyone at Witherspoon Associates; to Natalie Goldberg; to all others who contributed in ways large and small; and, as always, to my beloved Carol, John, and Andy.

NATALIE GOLDBERG

Introduction

The best job I ever had was as poet-in-residence for two years at a large inner-city elementary school in Minneapolis, Minnesota. By the end of my first year my respect for the students was so immense, I'd share poems I'd just written—complicated, dense poems—and I trusted their responses. Third graders I'd found were the most open and frank, still untainted but with the ability to read and write—a perfect combination. It's remarkable to think of this now, but I remember in May, daffodils at long last breaking the surface in that northern climate, I read to a group of them a lengthy lament of all the people I had known, loved, and lost.

At the end of the reading, I shook my head. "I can't think of a title. Any ideas?"

From the front-row corner, a sincere, slight nine-year-old in a white T-shirt and beige trousers cocked his head and raised his hand. I strain sometimes to remember his name and have finally given him one I almost can imagine as correct: Raphael Lamar James. He spoke in a clear and measured way—the elms outside the window full of the first ache of green—"Miz Goldberg, how about 'The World Come Home to Me?'"

"Where did you get that?" I must have fallen backward.

He held up his open palms and shook his head. "Just thought it might work."

"Raphael Lamar, I will never forget you," I declared as the school bell punctuated my last word and half-lie.

In truth, I fully remembered him. It's the name that eluded me, though that bell has continued to ring in my head these twenty years. It tells me over and over: that third grader got it right. We stop rushing around and, as we say in Zen, finally "settle the self on the self."

Writing can be the vehicle that narrows the distance between who we think we are and who we are, closes the gap between ourselves and what is around us. No illusion. Right here: twenty pounds overweight, cheeks sagging, a scar on our chin from six stitches we got in the emergency room after a bike accident, divorced twice, the third one working, tired and occasionally happy at the end of our day. Here is that sunset, those sycamores, this salt, the first kiss, the last good-bye, the rain, the lilac, the snow, door, step, corner. Her hand, his shoulder. At last we see our world. Arms full, we offer up our words.

No matter what our condition or what we write about—alcoholism, theft, rape, dancing, dying—the act of speaking, of bringing something out of shadows and darkness and into the realm of light and human consciousness, is a kind, generous, and powerful act. We are made known to ourselves.

And what could that possibly be like? We already know our names, the street we live on, the color of our hair and eyes, our favorite flavor of ice cream. But what is it we hunger for? There are layers upon layers to being human—yearnings that we live out unaware, that we are dedicated to for no apparent reason. That high school English teacher—where is he now? The old woman on the corner who makes us ache—who is she in us, how do we know her? We can down a cup of tea and dash out the door or drink it with the knowledge of water, meeting the seeping tea leaves, the sun, the rain, the land that grew them. Where do we end? At the tips of our fingers? At the end of our lives? Who dies with us?

The great thing about writing is that it is egalitarian; we only need pen and paper. Just sit down where we are and begin. Where do memories, words, thoughts come from? Look over your shoulder. Where is the past? We carry it now. It is in us. Only I know the sound of that drip off the roof lip in that town on the Japanese Sea. Or the black dog of loneliness when I think of the curl behind her ear or my father buried under the ground in a Hebrew cemetery across from a racetrack. To write the particular is also to sink deeper into the vast unknown, to become intimate with the huge life we take in, that our lungs hold for a moment, then release. Somewhere we have always known our own nature; we have met it over and over, it races through us and everyone around us. Now we are stopping at this table, sitting in this chair, and speaking it.

My old Zen teacher once interrupted me as I was about to complain about my worn-out marriage: "I see you're Buddha. You don't see it. You look around and see the goodness in others. When you see it in yourself, that's what being awake is."

Writing assists us in sealing that circle, in understanding the truth about ourselves. Not as good or bad people but just as we are, with the dirt under our nails and the grease in our hair.

No one can truly write without some degree of that acceptance, of acknowledging things as they are. And acceptance ushers in peace. I've heard it said that peace is the greatest pleasure. We learn to embrace it all, and not just the human, but rocks, mountains, chairs, floors, clouds. Our minds expand. Nothing is not worthy of our respect. Who says this lamp or doorknob or book isn't alive? But this is not a passive acquiescence. This is a dynamic confrontation, diving deeply so we can utter a resounding yes to our ordinary presence on this earth.

Human beings know something is afoot, some mystery, some hidden secret. We have a desire to wake up, and many intuit that writing may be the path. I have found that no one is excluded from this yearning. I have received letters from quarry workers in Missouri, blue-collar workers in Detroit, a vice president of an insurance agency in Florida, lawyers, doctors, housewives, architects, cooks, physical therapists—all wanting to put pen to paper. Writing has become the new religion, a chance to meet the world before we die.

One Vietnam vet from Southern Minnesota wrote, "Bob Dylan saved my life," and with that statement he broke down and life flooded back into him. A factory worker in his fifties from North Platte, Nebraska, wrote me a beautiful letter, full of longing to be a writer. I cajoled him into coming to a workshop I was teaching at a monastery. He showed up on a motorcycle with a black T-shirt imprinted with a flaming dragon. He was nervous. I told him, "Write everything you know, go for ten minutes," and the scared man released years of heartache. After a few days he and the student in her early twenties with bleached white hair and high-laced black boots, who was a singer in the off-Broadway show *Nunsense,* became best friends, eagerly reading to each other. Only writing would have cracked open the distance between their two worlds. A middle-aged upper-class socialite from Baltimore endured three weeks of sleeping in the lower bunk with creaky springs and not enough space in the room to fit her two large gold suitcases at Ghost Ranch in Abiquiu, New Mexico, an hour's drive from anyplace, so she could learn to tell the story of her dead son. People who have spent years shooting up, drinking; prisoners from Texas and Illinois write to me, wanting writing to help them find their way home.

How good that we now have someone—an advocate, a friend, an enthusiast—Philip Zaleski, who lives in a small hidden town in New England, who cares enough and who diligently peruses magazines, reviews, monthlies, quarterlies, weeklies to compile a collection of this country's best expression of the seen and unseen, the solid and ethereal, the hope, the trust, the belief and deep experience of what we call holy.

How wonderful that there is now an anthology that recognizes this need, pays tribute to the best in spiritual writing, honors the spirit as a genre of American letters.

How splendid that with this edition we celebrate the fifth year of this anthology, that it has taken root in our literary awareness and has helped us to recognize as readers and writers our own hunger for the ineffable, encouraging us to serve the world more fully with our words, our deeds, our dreams.

THE BEST
SPIRITUAL
WRITING
2002

John Luther Adams

Winter Music: A Composer's Journal

from Music*Works*

Winter Solstice 1998

For much of the year, the world in which I live is a vast, white canvas. In the deep stillness of the solstice, I'm profoundly moved by the exquisite colors of the sub-Arctic winter light on snow. Reading art critic John Gage's essay "Color As Subject," I'm struck by a parallel between the view out my window and Mark Rothko's use of white underneath the colors in his paintings. Like Rothko's translucent fields, the colors on the snow suggest to me broad diatonic washes suffused with gradually-changing chromatic harmonies.

Slowly, faintly, I begin to hear it: music stripped to its most essential elements—harmony and color floating in space, suspended in what Morton Feldman called "time undisturbed."

Christmas 1998

A life in music is a spiritual practice. As in many disciplines, my practice sometimes involves fasting. From time to time there are periods in which I listen to no music at all. I feel this as a physical need.

During busy periods of performance and teaching I hear a great deal of music. And just as I might feel the need to fast following a period of feasting on rich foods, after several months of intensive listening my ears tell me they need a time of rest from music. As I begin new work, my hope is that fasting may help me to hear sounds I haven't heard before, and to hear familiar sounds with new ears.

In her life and work, Pauline Oliveros practices an extremely difficult discipline: "Always to listen." I admire this very much. And though fasting from music might seem to be a retreat from listening, I experience it as a time for listening to silence. Most of us are inundated with music and other sounds, these days. I feel very fortunate to live in a place where silence endures as a pervasive, enveloping presence.

New Year 1999

Beginning to sketch a large new orchestral piece, I'm studying the paintings of Mark Rothko and Jackson Pollock. Like Cage in music, Pollock made a radical new beginning in the middle of the twentieth century. Both artists opened territories they could only begin to explore during their lives. The questions posed by their work will continue to occupy others for a long time to come.

By contrast, Rothko and Feldman were endings. They both explored intensely private, self-contained worlds. And what Brian O'Doherty said of the one could apply just as well to the other: "Rothko was the last Romantic. But the last of something is usually the first of something else."

Which makes me wonder: Is it somehow possible to live and work in that timeless intersection between endings and beginnings?

January 20, 1999

For me, composing is not about finding the notes. It's about losing them. Although I'm still involved in writing scores, knowing what to write down is not the most difficult thing. It's knowing what *not* to write down.

I hope to discover music that sounds and feels elemental and inevitable. And before beginning to write, I want to hear as much of the new piece as I can, as it begins to take shape in my mind's ear. This is a slow, sometimes difficult process. But over the years I've learned to trust it—even to savor it. I spend a lot of time thinking, reading, looking at art, walking, listening, sketching, trying to understand the essence of the new piece.

After six weeks in this mode, I now have several pages of notes for the new piece. But I've yet to start writing out the score.

JANUARY 22, 1999

Over the years, I've moved away from working with audible compositional processes—an inheritance of minimalism— toward an increasing focus on the fundamental materials of music: sound and time. My work is less and less a process of performing operations on notes, imposing compositional processes on sounds, or working within a syntax of musical ideas. I now concentrate primarily on asking questions about the essential nature of the music—what it wants from me, and what it wants to be.

JANUARY 23, 1999

Today, I'm forty-six years old. By this time in his life, Ives had lost his physical health and had virtually stopped composing. But Feldman was leaving the dry cleaning business and moving into his more expansive "middle" period.

Pollock was gone. But Rothko was poised on the verge of his major breakthrough into his signature style. That happened in 1950, when he was forty-seven.

Among my gifts today: The new score is under-way.

JANUARY 24, 1999

What is line in music? This is a question I've pondered for many years.

In Pollock's poured paintings, long, fluid lines are multiplied into layered fields of perpetually-moving stasis and perpetually-frozen motion.

Much of my composition *In the White Silence* is composed of continuously rising and falling lines, layered and diffused into an allover texture of frozen counterpoint. In that piece it feels as though at last I may have discovered a sense of line that is my own. Now, in a new piece, I'm trying to take a leap I've contemplated for years: to let go of line and figuration altogether. But what will be left?

JANUARY 25, 1999

In the new piece, individual sounds are diffused in a continuous texture, always changing but always with a minimum of what the art critics call "incident." This won't be easy to sustain. James Tenney, Pauline Oliveros, and LaMonte Young have all found it. So has Glenn Branca in his recent music for orchestra. And Morton Feldman achieved it most fully in his late orchestral works, *Coptic Light* and *For Samuel Beckett*.

Listening to allover textures, it's difficult to concentrate for long on a single sound. The music moves us beyond syntactical meaning, even beyond images, into the experience of listening within a larger, indivisible presence.

JANUARY 26, 1999

Monet's haystacks and water lilies, Cezanne's Mont Saint-Victoire, Rothko's floating rectangles, Diebenkorn's Ocean Park landscapes . . . In the twentieth century, painters discovered (or rediscovered) working in series. By freezing a particular motive the artist is free to concentrate on deeper nuances in other dimensions of the work.

As Robert Hughes observes: "One sees how absolutely Cezanne despised repetition, and how working en serie was his strategy for avoiding it."

It occurs to me that the new piece is part of a series of extended orchestral works, with *In the White Silence* and *Clouds of Forgetting, Clouds of Unknowing*. Some of the sounds are similar, even identical to those earlier works. But this is very different music.

Even within itself, the new piece embraces a series of sorts. Identical formal structures recur, from section to section. The temporal relationships between sounds remain the same. Only the sounds themselves change. Rather than moving on a journey through a musical landscape, the listener sits in the same place as light and shadows slowly change.

The longer we stay in one place, the more we notice change.

JANUARY 27, 1999

It's forty-five below zero, and getting colder. But it doesn't matter how cold it is. We're moving toward the light.

A month after the winter solstice the days are still very short, but noticeably longer. (We gain another seven minutes each day.) The low arc of the sun over the mountains is slowly expanding in height and breadth.

I'm working steadily and savoring the stillness.

January 28, 1999

The cold deepens. So does the silence.

Down in the valley, Fairbanks is wrapped in a dense cloud of ice fog. Across the Tanana flats, the peaks of the central Alaska Range have disappeared. But out here in the hills the day is golden. The sun is rimmed in a spectral halo of ice crystals.

The temperature on my afternoon walk is forty below. The only sound not made by me is the brief whoosh of wings as a lone raven flies past, in a straight line to the south. On the hillside, I encounter a young moose browsing on brittle alder branches. I stop. Speaking softly to her, I bow from the waist and move on, giving her a wide berth. She has enough to contend with just staying warm and fed.

They're predicting fifty below or colder tonight.

Back in the studio at the writing table, I'm startled by a bright, metallic ringing—like a small bell. I look up to see a boreal chickadee at the feeder outside my window. In such deep cold and silence, the smallest sounds speak with singular clarity.

After all these years, I'm still deeply obsessed with landscape. But the resonance of my musical landscape now is more interior, a little less obviously connected with the external world.

In art and music, landscape is usually portrayed as an objective presence, a setting within which subjective human emotions are experienced and expressed. But can we find other ways of listening in which the landscape itself—rather than our feelings about it—becomes the subject? Better yet: Can the listener and the landscape become one?

If in the past the more melodic elements of my music have somehow spoken of the subjective presence, the human figure in the landscape, in the new piece there's no one present . . . only slowly changing light and color on a timeless white field.

I remember the Gwich'in name for a place in the Brooks Range: "In a Treeless Place, Only Snow."

JANUARY 29, 1999

The cold hovers in place. The ice fog thickens over Fairbanks. The sun still rises only a few degrees above the horizon, and today it's veiled in frozen mist. The snow is bathed in a strange slate blue-gray light.

Toward the end of a long day in the studio, I realize that one of the eight layers in the new piece may be a little too busy and unnecessarily detailed. As always, the hard part is knowing what to leave out.

For years, I've kept near the piano my variation on Thoreau's dictum, a reminder of how I try to work: "Believe. Concentrate. Simplify. Simplify. Simplify."

JANUARY 30, 1999

This deep winter weather has completely changed the acoustics of this place.

A couple of days before the heavy cold settled in, it snowed. Since then the wind hasn't blown at all. So those two inches of fresh powder still rest undisturbed on the branches of the spruce and birch trees. The ice fog has now enveloped the hills.

Snow and cloud mute the earth and sky. There's almost no ambient noise. No wind. Fewer people and animals are stirring. The air is less reverberant than usual. But sounds travel farther. On my afternoon walk, the few sounds I hear are vividly present. A distant dog team sounds nearby. My mukluks growl angrily in the soft snow.

FEBRUARY 2, 1999

The high temperature at the house today was minus fifty. But the clouds have thinned and the sun was back, so I went out for my afternoon walk. Even though I was wearing snow pants, polar mukluks, double mittens, insulated cap with earflaps, and heavy parka with the hood up and the ruff pulled forward, my toes and fingers got cold.

In this extreme weather, the air almost becomes a different element—like the vapors of dry ice, like liquid fire. I love it. It makes me feel alive. Down with global warming! Long live the cold and the dark!

Back at work on the new piece, I concentrate on the organ, the string orchestra, and the string quartet. Moving at relative speeds of 2, 3 and 4, these are the slowest of eight tempo layers. Relentlessly diatonic throughout, they are the sonic ground of the piece.

One white cloud slowly dissolves into another, tone by tone. This makes an unbroken diatonic field from beginning to end, over seventy-five minutes. To hear the individual tones changing will require very close listening. I think of these as the brushstrokes—the little discontinuities that articulate and emphasize the larger continuity of the whole.

The chromatic clouds—the colors floating on the diatonic ground—are played by three choirs of muted brass and wind instruments, moving in three different tempi. All the instruments within a choir change tones together. But many of the written notes are too long to be played in one breath. So the players are free to breathe individually, as they choose. Brushstrokes, again . . . Those breaths will impart a certain richness to the texture.

FEBRUARY 3, 1999

Writing about Rothko, Brian O'Doherty asks rhetorically, "Why all this blurring of edges?"

I'm asking myself the same question about the new piece. It might well be called *Colors on a Diatonic Ground,* or *Light On Snow.* Both light and snow have soft edges. But despite my obsession with sounding images, this isn't tone painting. It's music. The sounds don't grow out of the form. The form of the music grows out of the sounds.

The sounds of *Strange and Sacred Noise* were so complex—machine-gun snare drums, roaring tam-tams, howling sirens, thundering bass drums and tom-toms—that they lent themselves to the decisive articulation of hard-edged, geometric forms.

But this new piece is in equal-temperament. And tempered sounds are more definite and declarative than noise. So to evoke the atmosphere of continuity and expectancy that I'm after, these blurred edges and more diffuse textures seem right.

A good day in the studio. The thermometer holds steady at fifty-five below zero.

FEBRUARY 4, 1999

This evening I boarded a jet in Fairbanks at forty-five below and flew north—across the Yukon River, the Brooks Range, and the Arctic coastal plain—to Barrow, where it's a balmy thirty-three below. (Although with the wind chill it's more like eighty below!)

I'm here for Kivgiq, the Messenger Feast: three nights of traditional Iñupiaq drumming, singing and dancing. Groups from all the Iñupiat villages in Alaska and four villages in Arctic Canada have come to Barrow for this midwinter festival of feasting, gift-giving, and celebration.

Although I've listened for twenty years to this music, it still sounds wonderfully strange to me. Yet it's also strangely familiar. By now I know a few songs, at least roughly. And the angular melodic contours, asymmetrical rhythms, powerful unison choruses and deep, explosive drums have become integral parts of the soundscape of my life.

Once, passing through a crowded urban airport somewhere down south, amid the noise of rushing travelers, I thought I heard an Iñupiaq drumbeat. Instantly, I was transported home. The memory of the sound of those drums took me there.

These sounds can take us on all kinds of journeys. The high-impact, full-spectrum sound of the drums—reiterated all night long—has an inescapable effect on consciousness. In some ways, the effect is similar to rock music. But the rhythms in Iñupiaq music are always at least a little surprising. And even when the phrases are relatively predictable, the basic rhythmic cells—2+3 or 2+2+3—are asymmetrical. To my ears this Iñupiat "heartbeat" (as it's sometimes called) is both more sophisticated and more energizing than the steady 4/4 backbeat of rock 'n roll. After I've heard a hot dance group from the Arctic coast, even the best rock bands sound rhythmically square.

FEBRUARY 5, 1999

Just before noon, out across the tundra, a dirty yellow disc barely nudges itself above the horizon. Its outline is vague. It gives off no warmth.

Fairbanks is at latitude sixty-four degrees north. Barrow sits at the seventy-first parallel. The days up here are still considerably shorter than in Fairbanks. But within seven weeks, on the spring equinox, they'll be the same length. In Fairbanks, for the past few weeks we've been gaining seven minutes of light every day. Up here the rate of change is twice as fast. Although it's still dark most of the time, Barrow is rapidly spinning toward the light.

Sunrise turns out to have been the brightest moment of the day. In mid-afternoon, I walk the mile or so from the lodge to the new Iñupiat Cultural Center. A vague fog has drifted in from the Arctic Ocean, bathing everything in a soft, blue light.

The flatness of the light mirrors the flatness of terrain. The sky feels enormous, all-encompassing. In this blue haze, it's difficult to distinguish the distant horizon. Sky melds with Earth, into an enveloping sphere—the center of which is everywhere, the circumference of which is nowhere. (Isn't that the way a Christian philosopher-saint described God?) Standing, walking, being in such a place, one can easily feel the presence of the spirit world.

On my return walk, my mukluk breaks the crusted snow, sending shards sliding across the surface. They sing like broken glass.

Again, the dancing goes until 1 A.M. During the final performance of the evening, a woman from the audience walks up to join the dancers from Kotzebue. She doesn't notice that a small plastic bag has caught her mukluk, and she drags the bag with her into the dance area. The audience finds this quite amusing, especially when she finally notices the bag, shakes it free, and continues dancing.

At that moment, one of the young drummers puts down his drum, moves quickly out onto the dance floor, picks up the bag and stuffs it into his pocket. He returns to the drum line, picks up his instrument, and continues drumming.

All this happens amid smiles and good spirits. But it leaves no doubt about the fact that this is ritual space.

FEBRUARY 6, 1999

The day dawns (at 11-something A.M.) clear and colder. My friend Doreen Simmonds—one of my Iñupiat collaborators on *Earth and the Great Weather,* takes me out to the end of the road, to Point Barrow, the northernmost point in Alaska. The Iñupiaq name for this place is nuvuk: *"a point of land which juts into the ocean."*

Although the wind is fairly light and the thermometer probably doesn't read much below minus thirty, the cold feels intense. We scan for polar bears, but it would be difficult to see them even if they were there.

The low sun floods the ice and snow with a rich pink light. The feeling of endless space is exhilarating. This is what I want to find in music!

Kivgiq is not held every year. It occurs following a prosperous hunting season, when there is enough material wealth to allow for widespread gift giving.

At the heart of Kivgiq is Kalukak, the Box Drum Dance. This elaborate ceremony is grounded in the myth of the Eagle Mother, who gave the gift of music and dancing to the People.

Tonight is the final night of the festival, and the highpoint of the evening is the Box Drum Dance. Traditionally each community on the Arctic coast performs a different variation of the dance. Three years ago at the last Kivgiq, the Kalukak was performed by the dancers from the village of Wainwright. Tonight it's performed by the Barrow dancers.

Before the dancers enter, two men bring out a tall extension ladder. One of them climbs the ladder and lowers a rope that's already been hung in place. A third man brings out the box drum and ties it to the rope, where it hangs, swinging freely. The drum is made of plywood, about one-by-one-by-three feet in dimensions. It's painted bright blue and yellow. The top is finished with jagged edges (representing mountain peaks) and adorned with a single eagle feather.

The drummers, singers, and dancers enter, chanting in unison to the steady click of sticks on the rims of the drums. The box drummer sits on a chair, facing the wooden drum, his back to the audience. He wears a headdress made from a loon's head and wing feathers. Several young male dancers take their places, sitting on the floor, facing him.

The twelve frame drummers (all men) sit in a single, long row. They are dressed in bright blue qaspaqs. Most of the women, in vibrant red, sit in three rows behind the drummers. But several younger women stand facing the box drummer, holding long wands tipped with feathers.

When everyone is in place, as the chant continues the frame drummers begin playing full force, until the box drummer cuts them off with a wildly irregular beat.

In silence, he begins an elaborate series of gestures. He bows forward from the waist, extending his right arm above his head, full length on the floor. The male dancers do the same, and the young women extend their feathered wands.

The singers begin a new chant, accompanied by clicks on the drum rims.

Slowly, the box drummer pulls his arm backward, holds it there for a moment, then brings it forward rapidly, stopping just short of striking the drum. He does this many times, with stylized gestures of great formality.

When he finally strikes the drum, in a sudden unison with the frame drums, the sound is stunning. Tears come to my eyes.

As the dance proceeds, the box drummer begins to swing the drum on its rope. As he swings left, the male dancers move to his right, like puppets on a string. He performs an elaborate series of movements with the drum, which the dancers mirror in reverse.

Several minutes into the dance, another dancer appears, also wearing a loon headdress. On each drumbeat, he hops, two-footed, moving around the box drum. Gradually he closes the circle, moving closer and closer to the drummer.

Suddenly, in a marvelously fluid movement on his backswing, the box drummer hands the heavy mallet to the dancer, who becomes the new drummer. All this happens without missing a beat.

This drumming, chanting and dancing is not art. It encompasses what we usually call art. But it's more than that. This is not art for art's sake. It's not social or political commentary. And it's certainly not self-expression. It subsumes all those things into the larger fabric of life—the life of the individual, the life of the community, the life of the land, and the life of the animals and the spirits that inhabit this place.

This is what so many of us have lost in the twentieth century, and what we so desperately need and desire in our lives. This is authentic. This has meaning. This is ritual.

Although this is not my culture, I would rather be here at the Messenger Feast in the Barrow High School gymnasium than in any symphony hall, opera house, or church I can imagine.

About 2 A.M., the festival ends with a processional of all the dance groups and a few songs sung and danced by virtually everyone in the space. The sound of a hundred Iñupiat drummers playing in unison is a sound I'll never forget.

FEBRUARY 7, 1999

On the morning plane back to Fairbanks, reading the arts section of last Sunday's *New York Times,* I'm struck again by how remote and moribund the "classical" music world seems. The term and most of what it implies simply doesn't apply to the music of most of the interesting composers working today.

By about 1950 many composers in America had figured this out. But it's taken another fifty years for the full implications to sink in. And by now we can add postmodernism (whatever that was supposed to be!) to the casualty list.

The media of the cultural establishment will probably be next to last to know. The administrators of most symphony orchestras, opera houses, and foundations will be the last. They'll read about it in the paper.

But what a relief for composers! We can simply get on with our work.

A dense fog covers the Arctic Coastal Plain. But as we reach the northern foothills, the stark peaks of the Brooks Range rise up, clear in the pink morning light.

FEBRUARY 8, 1999

Back to work in the studio, feeling energized and inspired from Barrow.

It's still cold, but the light on my afternoon walk is exquisite. Fifty below, tonight.

FEBRUARY 9, 1999

Another productive and satisfying day in the studio, working until after midnight. The new piece seems strange and extreme to me. The textures are so lush and amorphous and relentless. But that's exactly what I had hoped to discover. And at this stage in the process the music is leading me wherever it wants to go. I'm just doing my best to follow.

February 10, 1999

The cold is slowly dissipating. After two weeks of forty below and colder, twenty below feels absolutely balmy. The air is softer now. The light is more intense.

The music continues to unfold almost effortlessly. I find myself a bit overwhelmed, even intimidated by it.

At evening, the progressive shades of blue—slate, indigo, midnight—are breathtaking. The aurora borealis begins dancing. If only I could find the sounds of those colors.

February 12, 1999

I'm studying Ellsworth Kelly. A couple of years ago, Cindy and I visited the Guggenheim retrospective of his work. The next day we took in the Jasper Johns exhibition at the Museum of Modern Art.

Both shows made strong impressions, but I was overwhelmed by the richly tactile surfaces and the sheer creative fecundity of Johns's work. Although the whole body of Kelly's work was impressive, I wasn't as immediately enamored of individual pieces. By now, though, it seems that my own aspirations in music have more in common with Kelly than with Johns.

The big Mondrian exhibit at MOMA several years back also engaged me. Seeing the paintings themselves gave me a completely different reading of Mondrian. In reproductions, his paintings appear hard edged and hypergeometrical (without the obvious painterly touch of, say, Barnett Newman's surfaces). But in person, Mondrian's canvases seemed so fragile, so awkward, so human. Still, I've still never been able to completely warm up to Mondrian.

With Kelly, the obvious differences between the reproduction and the actual painting are size and fidelity of color. Beyond that, what you see in one is pretty much what you see in the other. There's little of that tactile element that so appeals to me in art and in music. As John Coplans observes, Kelly is more sensory than sensual. Still, I find myself more taken with Kelly than Mondrian. Maybe it's simply that he's more modern, more "American," and more extreme.

Like Kelly's paintings, my new piece emphasizes only color, form, and space. When I read Coplans's book on Kelly, these words leaped off the page at me: "Since color and the canvas shapes are one and the same . . . color itself takes on spatial characteristics. 'Color' becomes both color and space."

I imagine that at some point I'll work with harder-edged forms and more uninflected sounds. *Strange and Sacred Noise* is extreme in its geometric formalism. But the sounds themselves are much too rich and complex to be equivalents to Kelly's hard, flat colors. My guess is that I may find those equivalents in large harmonic blocks of electronic sounds. Silence, too, is likely to be a structural element in such music.

But that's another world, very different from the one in which I'm currently immersed. While the new piece is rigorously formal, my hope is that it will sound organic, even formless.

FEBRUARY 14, 1999

This evening we attended a performance by musicians and dancers from Bali. The gamelan was Tirta Sari de Peliatan, modeled on the older Semar Pegulingan—appropriately for Valentine's day, the gamelan of the love god.

My trip to Barrow and tonight's performance have reminded me that too often I think of music only in terms of metaphor or image, forgetting the fundamental role of the body.

The memory of the bright, shimmering sounds of the gamelan warms and brightens the dark, subzero night.

February 16, 1999

I'm fascinated with equivalents, shared resonances between different phenomena: between landscape and mind, culture and ecosystem, painting and music.

Color and form, surface and texture, field and gesture: The equivalents between these elements of music and painting continue to fascinate me.

February 17, 1999

One of the defining currents of twentieth-century painting was the movement away from the detached viewpoint of perspective and its illusions of receding depth, toward a new emphasis on color and surface.

In music there's been a parallel movement away from the sequential development of relationships between sounds, to a new emphasis on the inherent qualities of sounds heard in the present moment. In this new context, harmony becomes simply (in Cage's all-encompassing definition) "sounds heard together."

February 18, 1999

After all the innovations of the twentieth century, most Western music continues to exhibit a perplexing two-dimensionality of time. The barlines are little boxes containing precisely measured portions of time. Even when the rhythms within those boxes are relatively complex, they're still bouncing off the measured walls that contain them.

Stravinsky railed against the tyranny of the barline. By rapidly juxtaposing boxes of different dimensions (measures of different meters), he created a new illusion of depth in a flat temporal plane—much as Picasso and Braque did with cubist painting.

Ives was a pioneer of more truly multi-dimensional space. Although still narrative in conception, his music begins to move beyond the theatrical space of Berlioz and Strauss, toward a more complete physical space in which events occur with an independence more like that in nature. Varèse left the story behind entirely, constructing like an architect, in abstract geometries of sound.

It was Henry Cowell who first postulated a unified theory of temporal harmony (in *New Musical Resources*). But it wasn't until Conlon Nancarrow that complete temporal depth entered Western music. As the twenty-first century begins, we're just beginning to explore the possibilities inherent in Nancarrow's work with simultaneous dimensions of tempo.

FEBRUARY 20, 1999

What a joy it is to listen with curiosity and fascination as this strange music unfolds, each new sonority emerging from the last! The experience of working on a piece of this scale is like taking a journey through large, open country. I hope the experience of hearing it will be even more absorbing.

I want this music to be a wilderness. And I want to get hopelessly lost in it.

FEBRUARY 21 TO MARCH 4, 1999

We're moving into late winter. It's still quite cold, but the light is back. The arc of the sun is higher and wider. It no longer sets behind Ester Dome but farther to the west and north, behind the ridges of Murphy Dome.

Three days of soft snow falling, and dusty grey light are followed by several days of sparkling blue.

As I drive home from the Festival of Native Arts in the wee hours, the aurora is so beautiful I have to whoop out loud.

The animals are more active. The squirrel at the studio has emerged again. The redpolls have joined the chickadees at the feeder. The ravens seem to be more extravagant in flight, and even more vocal than usual.

The boreal owl has been calling since late January. And tonight, I hear the great horned owl for the first time this year.

Walking through the woods one afternoon last week, I flushed a snowshoe hare—a sudden apparition of white on white.

I feel fortunate to have wild animals as my neighbors.

MARCH 8, 1999

I'm back at work on the new orchestra piece, moving into the home stretch.

I want the sound to be lush and transparent at the same time. The danger is that all the colors will run together.

The physical space, the distance between the instrumental choirs, is an integral part of this music. But I also hope to find a full and purely musical space, in which each of the layers of time/harmony and timbre is distinctly audible.

The diatonic ("white") layers can be lush. But the chromatics need to be more transparent—like veils of color floating over the surface. As the manuscript nears completion, I'm thinning out the chromatic layers and re-spacing the harmonies as widely as possible.

MARCH 13, 1999

It's finished, this evening: *The Immeasurable Space of Tones*. Seventy-four minutes of continuous orchestral sound, it's the strangest thing yet to come out of my studio.

After six weeks thinking and sketching, actually writing the notes took only about the same amount of time. The piece really did seem to write itself. I'm exhilarated and exhausted.

Twelve years ago, after the premiere of my piece *The Far Country of Sleep*, my friend Leif Thompson made a prophetic observation: "I especially like that middle section," he said. "You know—the part where nothing happens. That's what you really want to do, isn't it?"

I've been trying to find the courage to do this ever since. My fear has been that by leaving everything out of the music, there'd be nothing left. Now that I've finally taken the leap and left everything out, my hope is that the only thing left is—the music!

Working on *Immeasurable Space,* I was continually amazed at how much is happening in the music all the time. What at first I thought was static and empty turns out to be remarkably active, full, and constantly changing.

We travel into new territory, and slowly we begin to locate ourselves, to understand where we are.

To Keep Alive

from *Parabola*

Why should I trust my heart, the organ of love, the threshold of light, the spirit's compass?

All four of my grandparents and both of my parents died of its affliction. Different paths, the same daunting destination.

Dirk Kruidenier, my maternal grandfather, was the nine-year-old son of pioneers from Holland who traveled eighteen weeks by packet, by iron horse and covered wagon from the docks of Rotterdam to Pella, Iowa, a religious refuge in the fertile fields of the New World's heartland. He made his fortune from the prairie, married the youngest, prettiest daughter of a Great Lakes ship owner, moved his family of six children to a fine house in the state capital, saw his favorite daughter married in his own garden.

Then, in his prime, at Sunday dinner he was struck down, surrounded by his horrified family—no preparation, no reckoning made, betrayed by his heart.

Grandmother Wilhelmina Kruidenier spent most of her widowhood in the Far West when it was still, compared to Iowa, an earthly paradise. For twenty years there were no brutal summers, no cruel winters. In San Diego, a small port city with a magnificent harbor, the coastal steamers, dazzling white by day, bright with jubilee lights by night, moved slowly up the channel past her veranda. Her yard was filled with fruit unknown back home: guavas, loquats, kumquats, apricots the size of tennis balls.

She returned at last to die in the bedroom across the landing from my brother's and mine. For months she battled her treacherous, suffocating heart, until its dry rattle finally declared through one blistering Iowa day and halfway into the humid night that it was giving up. Before we woke she was carried away, down the hall and the stairs, over the threshold, breathless, heartless, to lie eventually beside her husband in the shadow of oaks and hickories under the stained granite family monolith.

Father's mother, Letta Barrett, the eldest child of Des Moines's first blacksmith and his elegant Eastern bride, died, her daughters insisted, of a broken heart. It was that simple—a husband grown indifferent and ornery, the youngest of her five grandchildren, her favorite, suddenly gone before her. The doctors called it angina pectoris.

That husband, grandfather William Edwin Barrett, was a farm boy with an edge and a heritage. His grandfather, John Dolsen, a grunt in the Revolution, crossed the Delaware with Washington, was there at Trenton and Yorktown and whatever fell between. Helen, the youngest of John's twenty-seven children and Will's mother, orphaned and indentured at fourteen, went west from Painted Post, New York, to help worry a farm out of what was then the Michigan wilderness, to dip her own candles, weave her own cloth, stave off unfriendly Indians, raise nine children.

Will, field hand turned Iowa banker, half his life a widower, one day locked the vault for the final time, caught the Ingersoll trolley home, and took to his bed, my spinster aunt Ada assigned to be his caretaker. After long, complaining months in her best bedroom, his heart finally stopped, and Ada, past marrying, had her room back.

Then a decade or two more and it was coronaries for my parents, my father's third, my mother's first. They were gone in a minute from their cozy retirement bungalow on Point Loma, set in a garden that never stopped blooming.

As for me, no one has ever, even in my heartsore family, had such a reluctant heart as mine: reluctant to properly do its work, reluctant to give up. Two coronaries, one cardiac arrest, a quintuple bypass, congestive failure, pulmonary edema, a stroke. The compass wobbles, the light glimmers, love's labor seems lost, but the heart within the heart, the echo of the heart, weaker, dimmer, thumps on.

And yet I am convinced, perhaps with more justification than most, that the winding down of the heart, like the dimming of thought, the failure of breath, will drop me into or raise me up to the divine effulgence, as dry as tinder, as bright as day.

Any threat to the heart must be a reminder of this consummation, this ultimate consolation, the supernal light, the steady, universal pulse.

Its failure, my heart tells me, will be the victory of God. The fading beat will herald a new knowledge, steady, without a thump, without heat, without a surge. So I must believe, one by one, my grandparents, my parents in proper order, wherever they started, wherever they ended up, came, as I will, breathless, thoughtless, heartless into the Presence where inevitably we all will meet.

In that Presence, the heart that sustained and informed us is irrelevant. The silence, the speaking silence of the Godhead, prevails. The heart, so long our proprietor, our guide and teacher, our tormentor, our nemesis, will have finally failed—and triumphed. Where all is heart ours will no longer be needed.

As St. Augustine said, long before he could have confirmed its truth, "Thou hast made us for Thyself, O Lord, and our heart is restless until it rests in Thee."

The heart is the
number one killer
in the U.S.,
counting just short
of one million victims
in 1998,
the last year for which
statistics are available.

WENDELL BERRY

All, The Fact, The Answer

from *Ploughshares*

ALL

All bend
in one wind.

THE FACT

After all these
analyses,
the fact
remains intact

THE ANSWER

What's it all about?
Don't ask
and then you'll know.

HARVEY COX

Gamboling with God

from the *Harvard Divinity School Bulletin*

> *Let the Torah never be for you an antiquated decree, but*
> *rather like a decree freshly issued, no more than two or*
> *three days old. . . . But Ben Azzai said: Not even as old as*
> *a decree issued two or three days ago, but as a decree is-*
> *sued this very day.*
>
> —*Peskita* of Rab Kahana

It is a cool New England autumn evening. Black-and-yellow-striped police barriers have closed off traffic on Tremont Street in Cambridge. No wonder. In front of the old Tremont Street shul, a Conservative synagogue just off the avenue that connects Harvard with MIT, the road is jammed with two hundred people, young and old, whirling and jumping and holding hands in serpentine circles to the beat of blaring klezmer music. It is the holiday when Jews act most like Pentecostals. But look again. Scattered here and there, some of the prancers are hugging large, rolled-up scrolls encased in silk covers. On this night Jews dance with the Torah—sometimes into the wee hours—in near euphoria to thank God for the gift of the Law.

The Hebrew words *simhat torah* mean "the rejoicing of the Torah." The holiday comes just after the completion of the eight days of Sukkot and marks the end of the annual reading of the Torah (the first five books of the Bible). The service on Simhat Torah begins inside the synagogue with the reading of the last chapters of Deuteronomy, the last of the five books of Moses, thus completing the cycle. To celebrate the event, a procession with the scrolls snakes up and down the aisles, becomes more and more energized, and then, in many synagogues, spills out into the street.

Simhat Torah is one of the Jewish holidays I relish the most, and not just because I enjoy street parties and klezmer music. It is a holiday in which I catch a glimpse of something utterly fundamental to Judaism and realize how many of my stereotypes about "legalistic" Judaism have to be discarded. Simhat Torah also offers a splendid example of how my growing understanding of Judaism has helped enhance my appreciation for important elements of my own faith.

It takes awhile to dawn on Christians that for Jews the Law is not a burden, a hindrance, or an obstacle to living a fully human and vitally spiritual life. The Law (Torah) is a condition of being human. It is a generous gift that God bestows on his people simply out of love. But there is little wonder that many Christians have difficulty with this concept. It is true that Jesus says he has not come to change even one "jot or tittle" of the Law; yet he also frequently says, "You have heard it said of old . . . , but I say unto you. . . ." The Gospels often portray him debating with the scribes and Pharisees, the scholars who interpreted the Law in his day, but Christians are often unaware that these were not debates about the validity of the Law itself. They were arguments, often spirited ones, on how the Law was to be applied. Much Christian Sunday school material still wrongly suggests that while Judaism is a severe religion of the Law, Christianity is the religion of love, but this is an uninformed and erroneous comparison. So here I am, whirling in a circle with my wife and son and what appear to be hundreds of other people, to celebrate God's gift of the Law.

I have not just been swept up in the heady exhilaration of the trombones, clarinets, and gyrating bodies. It is true that at first I took part in this holiday mainly out of curiosity and familial loyalty. But now I have come to the conclusion that most Christian theology has unnecessarily given the Law a bad name (not helped, perhaps, by the low estate to which lawyers have slipped in today's popular jokes). A more accurate grasp of the enormous but subtle significance of the Law in Judaism is the first and indispensable step Christians must take to end some of the suspicion and hostility that have divided the two communities. The Torah is utterly pivotal to traditional rabbinic Judaism, and it also plays a beguiling role in the mystical and esoteric tradition of Kabbalistic Judaism, in which God is envisioned consulting the Torah before creating the world. I am convinced that the false opposition that has often been set up by Christian theology between Law on the one hand and Gospel on the other is still one of the principal hindrances to dialogue and reconciliation. I only wish that those Christians who still picture Judaism as the image of a bent and burdened figure crushed into a slump by the excessive weight of the Law could spend one evening at a Simhat Torah street whirl. These buoyant dancers are anything but bowed down. They seem to be soaring.

One source of much Christian understanding is that we rarely, if ever, have heard that the Torah "speaks in two voices." Every informed Jew knows that there is not only the written Torah, there is also, and of equal importance, the oral Torah, the accumulated history of centuries of rabbinical interpretation and application of the written Torah. The Torah is not just a scroll. It is not just the tablets that, according to the biblical account, God gave to Moses on Mount Sinai. The Torah is a lively, continuing conversation, still going on at this moment. When a Christian comes to understand this (and not many do), it is hard not to think of an obvious analogy. The Torah is not only like Christ, the physical presence of God among the people, it is also a bit like what Christians say about the Holy Spirit. It is God's spiritual presence in the midst of his people today, teaching, sustaining, and inspiring.

I think I am a little closer today to understanding the significance of Torah to Jews than I once was. But my head was not originally turned by reading books and articles. It happened in an unexpected and memorable episode that took place at the B'nai Jeshurun synagogue just a few years after Nina and I were married. B'nai Jeshurun is a conservative congregation on the Upper West Side of New York City, not far from where Nina grew up. At that time a new rabbi assumed the leadership of the synagogue, a rabbi who, by chance, I already happened to know, Marshall Meyer. I had met him many years earlier in Buenos Aires, where he had spent much of his career serving a Jewish congregation and leading a seminary. When the military regime came to power in Argentina, he quickly became one of its most fearless and outspoken opponents. Jacob Timerman later dedicated his moving testimony, *Prisoner Without a Name, Cell Without a Number,* to Meyer, "a rabbi who brought comfort to Jewish, Christian and atheist prisoners in Argentine jails." When Marshall came to New York, he and I renewed our acquaintance and quickly became fast friends. A few years later, I arranged for him to continue his research and do some teaching with me at Harvard. But it was long before that, during the first year of his service at B'nai Jeshurun, that my most formative encounter with Torah took place.

Whenever we visited Nina's family, we made it our custom to attend a Friday evening or Saturday morning service at B'nai Jeshurun. It was always enlivening. A congregation that had been declining fast was, under Marshall's leadership, growing by leaps and bounds. The music, drawn in part from Rabbi Meyer's Latin American years and in part from many other sources, infused both the Hebrew and the English prayers with melodic magic.

Marshall made many changes. Instead of giving a sermon, he instituted the practice of a congregation-wide open discussion of the Torah passage of the week. After it was read and Marshall made a brief commentary, ushers roamed the aisles with portable microphones while anyone who had anything to say about the text was invited to speak up. Many people did, and every time we were there, an animated discussion brought even the most obscure passage to life. People puzzled over what it could possibly mean, chewed on it, agreed with it, and disagreed with it. They often spoke about how a text did or did not intersect their lives as active New Yorkers. Marshall handled what might have become pandemonium with diplomacy and tact. Whatever else those discussions proved, they demonstrated that Torah is anything but a fossil, a code of outmoded regulations rolled up in a fancy scroll. This was the living Torah at its liveliest.

But, interestingly, my moment of truth did not come during the discussion. At every service, the Torah scroll is reverently removed from its place in the ark at the front of the synagogue and carried in procession up and down the aisles. The worshipers reach out and touch it with their prayer books or the corners of their prayer shawls. I was always impressed by this display of reverence for the scroll and what it stands for. Then, one Saturday morning, just before the procession began, Marshall beckoned me to come forward to where he was standing. When the Torah was removed from the ark, without saying a word he held it out to me and indicated that I was to bear it around the synagogue.

I was nearly overwhelmed, not just with surprise but with a powerful sense of affection for him, for the congregation, and for this precious scroll I was cradling. As people reached out to touch it with their prayer shawls and books, I could sense their heartfelt attachment to it and to the millennia of history and tradition it symbolized. In the first century C.E., the Roman governor Apostomus publicly burned the Torah in Jerusalem to signal its extinction as the Jews were driven into exile. During the medieval period, Christians often insisted that only they could give authoritative interpretations of the scriptures, and they periodically seized Torah scrolls from Jews and burned them. The Nazis regularly desecrated Torah scrolls, sometimes pouring filth and refuse on them.

Still, here I was, a gentile and a Christian, granted the privilege of carrying this sacred scroll while the Jews in B'nai Jeshurun caressed it. It is a moment I will never forget, and when I eventually returned to my seat, I knew that my attitude toward Torah could never be the same again. As Abraham Joshua Heschel says, I had an experience of awe and wonder, and it was now inextricably fused with the scroll of the Torah. I later learned that I was not the first non-Jew to have this privilege. It happens rarely, but on occasion, that a special guest or visitor can be asked by the leaders of the synagogue to carry the Torah in procession. For a short time afterward I was annoyed at Marshall for not at least warning me that it was going to happen. But I have since changed my mind about that. First of all, Marshall Meyer was a famously impulsive person whose impulses were almost always right. This one—at least for me—was certainly right. Also, if I had been warned (or even invited), I might have steeled myself and could even have slipped into a pose. I might have acted out the "honored guest carries Torah" scenario. But because of Marshall's impetuosity (or was it calculation?), I had no time for that, which made the experience even fresher and more compelling.

However, I soon came to realize that even an indelible encounter with a Torah scroll was not enough to change my intellectual understanding of the Torah itself; so I began to read both the Jewish editions, with their commentaries on it, and articles written by Jews about the meaning of the Torah in Jewish life. I found many useful sources. The most informative, however, was a chapter entitled "The Joy of Torah" in a book by Rabbi David Hartman. I had met Rabbi Hartman during one of my visits to Jerusalem, where he heads a study and research center (the Shalom Hartman Institute) named for his father, which is dedicated to trying to develop the classical Orthodox Jewish tradition and its relationship to religious pluralism and contemporary life. Hartman's ideas are important for the current Jewish-Christian conversation because as Christians finally become a little more familiar with Jewish thought, some respond more favorably to the Judaism of Martin Buber and the more effervescent, mystical Hasidic tradition of the Baal Shem Tov. For some Christians, these Jewish masters seem to lack the "legalism" they expect in Judaism. This was certainly true of me in my earlier years, and I have met many Christians, including scholars, who have never read any Jewish thinker but Martin Buber.

David Hartman's writings demonstrate what they have been missing. An Orthodox rabbi, he shows how a spiritual life based on studying and trying to follow halakah, the law that is derived from the study of the Torah, can also be joyful. Furthermore, he is a daring thinker. He holds that God himself is learning from his experience with human beings. Although Adam and Eve may have been created to be perfect and placed in a paradise, it quickly became evident that God had been a bit unrealistic in imagining that they would stay that way. It was clear that they would need some help, lots of help in fact, given their inclination to self-centeredness and their hankering to "become as god," which they immediately displayed. True, it was God's first inclination to wipe the slate clean, go back to the drawing board, and start over, possibly with a new design. He came close to doing so in the story of Noah and the great deluge. But then God, having learned something from his experience, decided on another tactic. God gave humanity the Torah, which might be thought of as a gift of love for an imperfect—all-too-human—people.

The gift of Torah suggests that God is becoming a realist, no longer expecting perfection but seeing us human beings as we are, a mixture of good and evil inclinations and impulses with both attractive and distinctly unattractive features. The great experiment of creating a truly free being who would return God's love and would love his and her fellow creatures was not a complete failure. But it was not turning out as well as God had apparently anticipated. The Torah is an expression of love, not of romantic indulgence or sentimental self-delusion. It is the kind of love that sometimes eventually ripens between parents and children, and between spouses when they become aware of each other's faults and limitations but do not stop loving. Rather, their love deepens into a more mature kind, one that takes the reality—rather than the idealized image—of the loved one into consideration. Living with the Law, therefore, for Hartman, is "inherently related to the joy of feeling accepted and confirmed by God. Not only are realism and responsibility not antithetical to love and joy, they are their very grounds."

Nothing in Rabbi Hartman's chapter on the joy of Torah suggests that he is searching for correlations to Christianity. But I could not help noticing some, especially in his discussion of the relationship of the divine to the human. It has often been said, by Christians and Jews alike, that Jews recoil from what appears to be a mixture of the human and the divine in the Christian understanding of Jesus. He was, according to classical Christian teaching, both fully human and fully God. But is this really such an impossible thought? Hartman, discussing what he calls "the experience of the love of God" that is characteristic of the "Halakic way of life," inspired and based on Torah, says that here "the distinction between what is the Word of God and what is humanly derived loses all significance." This claim is at least reminiscent, if not almost identical, to what Christians say about Jesus. It is not that part of him is divine and part human. In him these two seemingly incommensurable elements meet in such a way that making the distinction "loses all significance." Later, when describing Torah, Hartman says, "The Word that mediates divine love becomes integrated with the human response." I see here a clear parallel to at least one classical Christian explanation of how Jesus could be thought of as divine, namely, that he became the complete human receptor of God's love, the one who, more than any other person we know, was so totally open to God's love that he became its bearer and its vehicle.

Even when Hartman discusses what he describes as the legal minutiae of the endless rabbinical arguments about the meaning of the Law for everyday life, he reveals—perhaps unintentionally—further parallels. Why is the Torah full of so many discussions of what we do when someone's ox gores someone else's or when a fungus growth appears on the wall of a house or where one may safely defecate? These seemingly humdrum affairs are all discussed by the rabbis in the Talmud and elsewhere. But why are they in the sacred books? Because, Hartman says, they all have to do with "a God who is involved in the world of ordinary human beings." This is exactly what Christians say about Jesus. Even the tempestuous discussions that have sometimes raged between Christians and Jews fade several decibels for me when Hartman cites a certain Rab Kahana. It seems that this legendary rabbi wanted to assure his students that although God appears at different times in history and in different roles, it is indeed one and the same God. Speaking for God, Rab Kahana says, "Come to no false conclusions because you see Me in many guises, for I am He who was with you at Sinai: I am the Lord thy God."

Jews and Christians could ponder for a long time how much this statement of Rab Kahana about the different guises in which God appears resembles Christian language about the Trinity. Personally, I do not think the two are all that far apart. When Rab Kahana's Jewish pupils began to wonder whether all these different manifestations of God—as Creator, Redeemer, Lawgiver, Teacher of Wisdom—could be of the same God, he reassured them that they were. The idea of the Trinity arose from a similar puzzlement of the early Christians over their experience of the different faces of God. The Trinity is described as "one God in three persons," understandably causing Jews (and many Christians) to wonder whether monotheism was being endangered. But Paul Tillich explains that this is not really the case. The Greek *persona,* first used by the early Christian theologian Tertullian (c. 160–c. 230) to describe the different faces of God, does not mean the same as *person* does now. Today the word stands for a human being who can reason and decide. "Such a concept of person," Tillich says, was not applied to the three ways God had been experienced, the three hypostases in God. He continues: "Persona, like the Greek word *prosopon,* is the mask of the actor through which a special character is acted out. Thus we have three faces, three countenances, three characteristic expressions of the divine self-explication."

In light of this clarification, it is not so difficult to imagine how the early Christians hit on the idea of the Trinity. They believed God had created the world, called Israel, given the Ten Commandments on Sinai, and spoken through the prophets. But they also believed they had met the same God in the person of the rabbi from Nazareth, and they still felt his Spirit to be alive in their midst even after his death by torture under the Romans. Was this really the same God? Their answer was phrased in the metaphorical language of theater masks, through which one actor could play different roles. But it could just as easily have been expressed in the words of Rab Kahana: "Come to no false conclusions because you see me in many guises. . . . I am the Lord thy God."

Discovering these parallels has convinced me that the Trinitarian language nearly all Christians use to describe God need not pose an insurmountable barrier between Christians and Jews. Rab Kahana with his "guises" and Tertullian with his "personae," had they ever met, would have had many issues to disagree about, but that the one God has many "faces" would have been acceptable to both.

But what about the alleged opposition between Law and Gospel? How big an obstacle is that? Usually the responsibility for inventing the opposition is laid at the feet of Saint Paul, and there are indeed parts of some of his writings that could be read to support such an opposition. In recent years, however, scholars who investigate Paul have suggested a more fruitful way to understand him. The newer approach—although it does not resolve all the difficulties—at least throws into question some of the harsh opposition between law and grace that characterized the old one. This important shift in Pauline studies was largely begun by E. P. Sanders twenty years ago and has won wide acceptance since then. It suggests that throughout the whole of Saint Paul's adult life—both before and after his experience on the Damascus Road—his driving motivation was twofold. First, he wanted to persuade gentiles to become a part of the Commonwealth of Israel and therefore to escape the inevitable approaching judgment of God, which he believed would not be long in coming. Second, he wanted to convince Jews that the time for gentiles to be welcomed into the household of Israel, long foreseen by the Hebrew prophets, had now come. There is indeed some evidence that Paul (who in his earlier years called himself Saul) had this dream even before his famous mystical confrontation with Christ.

This encounter has usually been referred to as the conversion of Saint Paul. But that is hardly the right word for it. It was more a calling than a conversion. Paul never stopped thinking of himself as a Jew, a Hebrew, and a Pharisee; he continued to take fierce pride in this heritage. But like earlier Hebrew prophets, he now believed God had sent him on a specific prophetic mission, like Jeremiah's or Jonah's. What had changed in his mind was the means by which this ingathering of the gentiles should proceed. Before his Damascus Road vision, the only way he could see its happening was by the gentiles undergoing a ritual purification bath and circumcision and endeavoring to study and observe the Law. Now, however, God—by enlarging the covenant through Jesus—had made it possible for gentiles to become a part of Israel without a "circumcision of the flesh." What was now required was a "circumcision of the heart." He still expected Jews to be circumcised, and gentiles were expected to observe the moral laws of the Torah but not its ritual requirements, such as keeping kosher. Through Jesus, gentiles could begin worshiping and serving the God of Israel without any prerequisites. In other words, it was not—as I sometimes heard in my seminary training—justification by faith versus the Law that was the central impulse of Paul's theology. This is a partial reading of Saint Paul, which Luther, who had his own peculiar agenda, passed on to almost all subsequent Protestant theology. But it turns out to be misleading. Rather than faith versus law, the pivotal point for Saint Paul was the new relationship God had made possible between the people of Israel and "the nations" (gentiles).

Terence L. Donaldson, in *Paul and the Gentiles: Remapping the*

Apostle's World, helps explain why the misreading of Saint Paul became so widespread. He says we have tended to generalize from specific segments in his writings. But, he adds, we should not be misled by the way Paul responds to particular situations in the early churches, at Corinth or Galatia or Philippi, where one or another of his basic teachings was being questioned. In such situations, obviously anyone emphasizes a corrective element. But in these epistles Paul was putting out brushfires, not composing a coherently organized theology. Only in Romans does he try to be systematic. Therefore, what Donaldson calls Paul's convictional world must be seen as a kind of substratum under what consists mainly of ad hoc writings. This substratum begins with God the creator of all humanity, then includes the calling of Israel and the gift of Torah, and goes on to the special role of Jesus Christ and to Paul's belief that he himself had been called by God to carry God's message to the gentiles.

But Paul's underlying motive remains the same. He knows the earlier prophets had promised a time when "the nations" would be gathered into the people of God. He believes this time has come, and he desperately wants these gentile nations to take advantage of it and to become a part of the family of Abraham. He is not calling on Jews to abandon the Law. For those who are children of Abraham "according to the flesh," the Torah continues to be authoritative. It is simply no longer the only gateway for the outsiders to enter the family circle. This is why he is so adamant that gentiles have absolutely nothing to boast about. God has made this adoption possible solely because he loves the gentiles as well as the Jews, not to reward them for something they have done. In short, until the final culmination of history, which Paul believed—at least in some of his many changing moods—was not far off, Jews would continue to be Jews, and gentiles would become a part of the Covenant community through a different entrance. In short, Law is for the Jews, and Gospel is for the gentiles. God has called both into one family.

I have no illusion that the blissful young people—and some not so young—who are gamboling with God on a warm autumn night on Tremont Street know, or even care, about the intricacies of either God's many guises or the mysteries of Law and Gospel. Why should they?

And as I look over the crowd I can recognize some of my non-Jewish students skipping in the circles as well. They no doubt have been invited to this frolic by their Jewish friends. They are obviously having what the younger ones would call an "awesome" evening, and if anyone ever tries to tell them that for the Jews, Torah/Law is nothing but burden, bother, and bad news, they will know that it just isn't so.

SARA DAVIDSON

The Making of an American Swami

from *My Generation*

It's 8 A.M. on New Year's morning and I'm sitting in the darkened hall of the Siddha Yoga Meditation Center in Los Angeles, staring at the swamis in red sitting cross-legged on the floor. There's a slender woman with short blond hair. Is that Sally? That's what she looked like thirty years ago, but I've heard that she's gained weight and I'm sure her hair has signs of gray.

She's called Swami Durgananda now, but I knew her as Sally Kempton: the brilliant, icily beautiful writer who was the daughter of the celebrated newspaper columnist Murray Kempton and who wrote the purest, most lethal and eloquent statement of feminist rage published in the seventies—an essay called "Cutting Loose," which appeared in *Esquire,* the premier male magazine of the time. I'd last seen her in 1974, when she became a follower of Swami Muktananda. To the surprise of many who knew her, she took vows of celibacy, became a swami herself, and has stayed in the order for twenty-seven years. While I'd thought about her from time to time, we'd had no contact until the fall of 2000, when I heard she'd written a book called *The Heart of Meditation.*

I called her to suggest an interview on the occasion of her book's publication, which is set for 2002. She was pleased to hear from me but said, "I don't get to make my own decisions." I was floored that Sally, whom I'd known as a gutsy, irreverent young woman who wouldn't be cowed by anyone, had surrendered her ability to make her own decisions. She explained that she makes her decisions on personal matters, but any question affecting the Siddha

Yoga Foundation, which has about 250 centers and ashrams throughout the world, has to be referred to a committee. A month later she informed me the decision was no, but three months later she said, "Amazingly enough, the people here have decided it *would* be a good idea." We arranged to meet in Los Angeles where she would be teaching at the group's Winter Love Retreat.

I was eager to see her and sense the effects of a twenty-seven-year commitment to rigorous Hindu practice. I was also curious because she'd followed a road I couldn't have imagined taking. We'd started at the same place in our twenties: We were journalists in New York, married and writing for magazines such as *Esquire* and *Harper's* as well as the *Village Voice* and *Rolling Stone*. We became caught up in the women's movement and eventually divorced. In the early seventies we started to pursue what was then called "the path," seeking answers to life's essential questions. But while Sally committed herself entirely, I kept one foot on and one foot off. I married again and had two children, wrote books and TV shows, studied Judaism, Hinduism, Buddhism, and Christianity, and now it's twenty-seven years later and we're meeting at the Siddha Meditation Center.

The master of ceremonies says, "Here to guide us is Swami Durgananda. She makes the difficult easy. She makes the complex simple." The slender blond woman stands. It is Sally, wearing a fitted red tunic, a long red skirt, and red stockings. Her face—unmistakable, with large blue eyes and prominent cheekbones—appears on two large video screens, because the retreat is being broadcast live to Siddha Yoga centers around the world.

Anyone expecting her to be spacey or robotic would be immediately disabused. The intelligence, ironic wit, and elegance of language I remember are in full display—only they're being used to explicate the principles of Kashmir Shaivism, a philosophy whose bottom line is that God both creates and dwells within all beings.

Because Gurumayi, the young woman who succeeded Swami Muktananda after he died, is in India, Durgananda is about to deliver the guru's message for the New Year. She reads the words as they flash on-screen: "Approach the present with your heart's consent. Make it a blessed event." When I repeat this later to a friend, he says, "It sounds like a Chinese fortune cookie." I laugh. The words of someone else's guru invariably sound like a cookie fortune, but Durgananda later deconstructs them. "You know how it is," she says. "Most of the time, whatever we're doing, we're sort of half there? I keep asking myself: Am I giving my heart's consent to what I'm doing in this moment? Am I fully anchored in the present? Because the present is the only moment we have, in terms of making choices, acting, transforming. It's all there is."

At the first break, I walk toward her and we hug, assuring each other that we appear little changed.

"Your hair is still blond," I say.

"The women in my family don't turn gray till they're seventy," she says. There's a quality about her, however, that I don't recollect: a gentleness, an active sympathy, a sense that with her, one will be in safe hands.

When we'd been friends before, I'd been intimidated and guarded in her presence. I knew she might seem sympathetic, but she could skewer people with a look or a single phrase that would pierce their pose and reduce them to an object of ridicule. One reporter called her a "dangerous woman," and for certain men she was an object of erotic obsession. She was also warm and fun and game for anything.

The week after New Year's, I'm having lunch with Swami Durgananda at Pradeep's, a nouvelle California-Indian restaurant in Santa Monica. Durgananda reads from the menu with mocking humor, "Create your own Indian-style burrito." She orders curry.

"I'm basically an ironist," she says, adding that when you commit yourself to a spiritual life and "everything gets stripped away, you're left with your soul and your natural personality. Mine is ironic."

I ask what caused her to move from militant feminism to spirituality. "That is a darn good question," she says playfully. She was a feminist for only a year, she says, when she realized she'd simply turned from "radical self-blame to radical blaming of others. The truth was, I was responsible for my life. It wasn't any guy's fault." She says feminism was the start of her spiritual quest. Despite her gifts and achievements, despite her cool exterior, she felt empty and fraught with anxiety. "To tell you the truth, I was looking for happiness, but since I was a political/intellectual/left-wing person, I couldn't go straight to God. The road was twisty."

She had also experienced LSD. "One time when I'd taken the drug, I saw the skin come off the world. I saw that everyone was playing a game. The rules were arbitrary. There was no reason for anyone to be doing anything because the rules were completely made up." On another occasion she felt an inrush of love and joy, but when she told her radical-activist boyfriend, "He thought I was crazy. He said, 'That's just an acid trip. That's not life.' At the time, I never believed in the reality of that joy or that my daily life could be like that." She takes a sip of juice. "And now it is."

I stop eating. "Are you serious?"

She nods.

"Joy is your basic state, every day? How long has this been true?"

"About ten years."

I tell her I've had interludes I would call happy, but mostly there's been pain from one sector or another. She nods in recognition. "I used to be in pain 98 percent of the time." Through her work in Siddha Yoga, she says, the pain diminished, and joy became her customary state. "And it's a juicy, vibrant feeling."

I press her to define this joy. "The closest analogy I have is the joy you feel when you're in love. That heart-melting feeling when you're happy and the world seems fascinating and you're aware of the life in yourself and the life in others. You find a lot of pleasure in simple things." She says there are degrees to this and sometimes she feels worried or frightened but can always bring herself back to that heartfelt happiness.

She does seem content, but I've seen her only one day and can't know how she is when alone. I'm inclined to believe, though, that years of meditation and cultivating love toward the self and others have brought her this equanimity.

Sally Kempton grew up with three brothers in Princeton, New Jersey. Her parents had met as young socialists while attending Johns Hopkins University and Goucher College. Her mother, Mina, was a social worker, and her father, Murray, was a beloved liberal columnist who won a Pulitzer Prize and a National Book Award. When she was young, Kempton was close to her father, but relations became strained as she grew older. In "Cutting Loose," she wrote that her father raised her with "a sort of eighteenth-century fantasy about our relationship, the one in which the count teaches his daughter to read Virgil and ride like a man and she grows up to be the perfect feminine companion, parroting him with such subtlety that it is impossible to tell that her thoughts and feelings, so perfectly coincident with his, are not original."

She chose to attend Sarah Lawrence over Barnard because her boyfriend said the former was more "feminine." While working as a freelance journalist she was introduced to the New York Radical Feminists in 1969. She took part in the sit-in at the *Ladies' Home Journal* offices to protest the magazine's sappy portrayal of women. She appeared on *The Dick Cavett Show* with Susan Brownmiller to confront Hugh Hefner. When Brownmiller pointed at Hefner and cried, "That man is my enemy," Kempton sat draped in her chair exuding frosty disdain.

She was twenty-six when she wrote "Cutting Loose," which is still remembered and widely quoted. In writing it, she pushed literary confession to its extreme. She wrote that she'd had a "compulsion to seduce men" and needed to marry a father figure—Harrison Starr, who was thirteen years older and produced movies, including Antonioni's flawed take on the sixties, *Zabriskie Point*. She wrote that Starr insisted she was too young for him. "I would climb upon his lap, figuratively speaking, and protest that I was not. It was no more disgusting than most courtships."

The most famous image from the piece is of Kempton lying awake in bed beside her husband as he sleeps, wishing "I had the courage to bash in his head with a frying pan." She doesn't dare, she realizes, because she's afraid "that if I cracked his head with a frying pan he would leave me."

This image of rage and dependency melded in the frying pan shocked both men and women, ratcheting up the gender wars. She says, "I knew the writing came from the place that's the closest you can get to truth. But the downside was, I became a character in a public story that resembled mine but was a huge oversimplification of a complex life."

Partly as a consequence of the piece, she and Starr were divorced. "He'd read it in advance but didn't realize how bad it would make him look," she says. "When it came out and was so big, it was humiliating." Her father hated the essay. "First he called and said how great it was. Then he wrote me a nasty letter. Our relationship was complicated and full of misunderstandings for years." Both her parents, who'd divorced, were disheartened when she became a yogi monk. "They wanted me to be a New York writer," she says. But as time passed, they felt a softening, a kindness in her, which allowed them to become close again.

Kempton first met Muktananda in 1974. She'd taken courses in meditation and was having dramatic experiences of "energy rushing up from the base of my spine and exploding in my head. It scared me, and I thought, you don't want to do this without a guru." She says I was the one who connected her with Baba, as he was called, but I have no memory of this. I was living in Venice, California, writing *Loose Change,* and went to a weekend "intensive" with him during which I had to get up at 5 A.M. and Baba hit me on the head with peacock feathers. I thought some kind of mass hypnosis might be going on—people were laughing, crying out, and convulsing after being hit with the peacock feathers. Nothing like that happened to me and I never returned.

Kempton, however, walked into the mansion in Pasadena where Baba was staying, saw him sitting on a gold chair wearing an orange robe, a ski cap, and dark glasses, and had what she says William James would call a "classic conversion experience." She realized Baba was in a state of unity and felt herself flooded with love. "I had the thought: This is what I've been looking for. This is what I was born for."

I ask Durgananda how she explains the fact that none of her friends had a similar response to Muktananda. She says simply, "He wasn't their guru. Or it wasn't their time."

Shortly after meeting Muktananda, she flew to Denver and joined his tour across America, plunging into the strict discipline of his traveling ashram. They rose at 5 A.M., chanted, meditated, did seva—service to the guru. They were asked to be celibate, eat vegetarian, and give up stimulants including books, magazines, and social talk.

Those who heard from afar about Kempton's conversion were baffled. She'd jumped from being an iconoclastic rebel against authority—specifically male authority—to accepting a belief system and the authority of a male guru whose word was literally God's. How was this possible with the mind she owned? She asked herself similar questions: "Am I running away from my unresolved problems? Taking the easy way out? Am I handing my power to someone outside myself? The way I resolved it was deciding that my life is about service and this was training for that service."

She says she became celibate "two minutes after I met Baba. The inner experience became so delightful and consuming—it was more interesting than anything going on with another person. It wasn't a sacrifice." Before joining Muktananda, Kempton had been in love with one man and having an affair with a second. I was less surprised by her celibacy than her willingness to surrender to Muktananda. The idea of finding a guru who would guide one's life was appealing, and I understood the premise—that by giving up external liberty one might gain inner freedom—but it was impossible for me. When I ask Durgananda about this, she says, "Surrender is impossible without love. When I met Baba, a huge love was kindled, and with it came the desire to serve. I wasn't in a state of surrender, I was practicing surrender." If the ashram leaders made a decision she opposed, she resisted it. If the decision wasn't changed, she had to go along with it or leave. "It's the same in marriage. When you have a disagreement, if your commitment is to your marriage rather than the issue you're disagreeing on, you stay with the marriage."

Kempton did not think she was making a commitment for life. "I was thirty-one, I didn't have a husband or kids, so I was free to live as a yogi." After she'd been with Muktananda six months, an editor called and offered her an assignment for the *New York Times Magazine*. She decided it was time to put her career back on track. "Then it came to me. I was in the middle of an important process. Baba was sixty-six, and I wanted to stay with the process. Whatever I was leaving unfinished in the world—my writing career, intimate relationships—I would go back to and finish someday."

During her early years with Baba, Kempton was in a frequent state of bliss, which she says is typical of the first arc in the devotional path. "You fall in love with the guru and have experiences you attribute to the guru, some of which are quite spectacular." In *New York* magazine she described an experience when she felt she was floating in a soft, warm pool. "It was the most intensely sensual feeling I'd ever had. It felt so good that my first reaction was a sharp pang of guilt, a feeling that I had stumbled into some forbidden region, perhaps tapped a pleasure center in the brain."

She developed a missionary zeal, wanting to make Baba's teaching and spiritual power available to many. Baba had said that his goal was to start a "meditation revolution—to create a world full of saints." Durgananda says she'd always been shy and anxious about speaking on the phone, but she became Baba's press secretary and had to do that continually.

In 1976, she went to India with Baba and stayed in his ashram for two years. "I had absolutely no money." She explains that the disciple offers service to the guru and the guru will feed and clothe the disciple, but the disciple is not supposed to ask for anything. "I became extraordinarily austere. It was humbling and physically hard—sleeping in a room with forty other women and all my stuff under the bed." She became withdrawn and unavailable to people. She thought her real relationship was with the guru and any other relationship was a distraction. She believed the personality of Sally Kempton was not acceptable spiritually. "I felt I had to cut off whole parts of myself—the bohemian, rebellious, intellectual, ironic radical."

In the late seventies, when Baba created an order of monks who would be teachers, Kempton put her name on the list. She was ambivalent about the commitment and wearing yellow clothes. "The whole uniform thing went against the artistic individualist in me." She withdrew, but Baba talked her into it. He gave her the name Durgananda, which means the bliss of Durga, the divine mother. Kempton thought of herself as Saraswati, goddess of learning, art, and music. "Durga wasn't my favorite goddess, and I don't like the sound so much. In America, it's pronounced 'dir-ga,' like 'dirty.' On the other hand, Durga is a warrior, and it's great to have a new name because it forces you to drop your identification with the old persona. I couldn't use my old byline anymore."

She found she was suited for monasticism. "A simple life works best for me, one without a huge amount of emotional entanglements." After five years, she was ordained a swami, which set off waves of consternation among her family and old friends. "I'd crossed the guru curtain," she says. "How many swamis do we know? It's like you're not a regular person anymore." As a swami, she'd taken vows to renounce worldly ambition and to give her life to the pursuit of knowing God, serving the guru, and helping others. She wears red or orange exclusively—a custom-made *punjabi* when she's teaching and red slacks and sweaters when she's not. There are currently fourteen swamis in the Siddha Yoga organization but only one guru, who takes responsibility for all the disciples' progress. After her ordination, Durgananda ran into a classmate from Sarah Lawrence who wrote in the alumni newsletter, "Saw Sally Kempton, '64, who is now married to an Indian man and is Mrs. Durgananda."

In April of this year, I take the bus from Manhattan to South Fallsburg, New York, to visit Durgananda at the Shree Muktananda Ashram, the center of Siddha Yoga. The sprawling compound, valued at an estimated $17 million, feels like India in the Catskills: statues of Shiva and Lakshmi stand before elegant remodeled buildings that were once borscht-belt hotels but now have Hindu names. When I tell residents I'm an old friend of Swami Durgananda, they look at me with awe. It feels like being an F.O.B. (friend of Bill) during the Clinton administration. "We appreciate her intellect," one woman says. "She's a great being."

There are two subjects Durgananda does not feel at liberty to discuss: the struggle for the throne after Baba died in 1982 and the allegations reported in the *New Yorker* and elsewhere that Baba had sex with young girls in the ashram. "It's impossible to say what happened or didn't happen, because Baba isn't around," she says.

During the turmoil following Baba's death, Durgananda questioned whether she could open herself to another guru. While many swamis left, she stayed because, to her surprise, she began to feel an inner link to Gurumayi, who was then twenty-seven. "What I learned is that the guru is not Baba or Gurumayi but an energy that's present in the guru and lives in you as well." She says this was the second stage of the devotional path, "when you realize the energy is there when the guru isn't present and you internalize it more. In the final stage, you own it."

Durgananda spent the early eighties teaching in Oakland and Los Angeles. She found teaching rewarding but realized that she still had psychological issues to deal with. Feelings of sadness rose in her—from her childhood, from relationships, from sources she couldn't even define. "For two years, I cried and cried." She felt it was part of the cleansing or purification that takes place on the yogic path. "Old feelings like anger or sadness come up, and if you allow yourself to be with the feelings, if you don't try to squash them or turn away, they eventually dissolve."

Around 1989, she reached an equilibrium and felt she could be a "regular person" again. She began to reclaim parts of herself she'd tried to disown. "For a long time, I believed that the critical, doubting part of my mind was the enemy and discounted everything it said. Then I saw that the doubting mind was part of the divine. Everything in life is part of the divine."

She began to spend time with old friends, read novels, and go to movies. "I stopped having to keep the fence so tight. I could be with people without worrying they'd clutter up my mind and ruin my meditation." In 1995, she wrote her father a letter saying she knew he'd been angry with her, she was grateful for all he'd taught her and sorry for anything she'd done to engender his anger. "We became quite close," she says. When her father contracted pancreatic cancer, Durgananda was with him every day until he died. "There was a lot of love at the end."

She also started writing intently. She meditated for three to four hours a day, experimenting with techniques, exploring and mapping her own consciousness. "Even if you have a guru, there's no guarantee you'll get anywhere until you take responsibility for the inner drilling," she says.

As a result of her work, she wrote *The Heart of Meditation,* a guide for people starting to meditate or wishing to go deeper. The words are precise, the tone humble. She writes, "You might want to try . . ." instead of "You must do this." The book is rich with anecdotes about how she was able to quiet her mind and become "radically more positive" and suggestions aimed at inspiring readers to create a practice of their own.

Durgananda is driving me to the bus stop in the 1990 red Toyota her mother gave her. On the spiritual path, it's said that one can go deep or one can go wide—deep by staying with one master or tradition, wide by gleaning what's of value from different traditions. It occurs to me that Durgananda has gone deep and I've gone wide and we've each reaped benefits and paid a price. I wouldn't give up what I've had: my children, certain love affairs, the exaltation of the creative process. But these experiences haven't brought me the sustained inner joy she claims to own. I ask if there's anything she wishes she'd done, any experience she missed by being a monk. "Yes," she says and falls silent. I wait. "I feel I still have writing to do. There are ways of experiencing

Leap

from *The American Scholar*

A couple leaped from the south tower, hand in hand. They reached for each other and their hands met and they jumped. Jennifer Brickhouse saw them falling, hand in hand.

Many people jumped. Perhaps hundreds. No one knows. They struck the pavement with such force that there was a pink mist in the air.

The mayor reported the mist.

A kindergarten boy who saw people falling in flames told his teacher that the birds were on fire. She ran with him on her shoulders out of the ashes.

Tiffany Keeling saw fireballs falling that she later realized were people. Jennifer Griffin saw people falling and wept as she told the story. Niko Winstral saw people free-falling backwards with their hands out, as if they were parachuting. Joe Duncan on his roof on Duane Street looked up and saw people jumping. Henry Weintraub saw people "leaping as they flew out." John Carson saw six people fall, "falling over themselves, falling, they were somersaulting." Steve Miller saw people jumping from a thousand feet in the air. Kirk Kjeldsen saw people flailing on the way down, people lining up and jumping, "too many people falling." Jane Tedder saw people leaping and the sight haunts her at night. Steve Tamas counted fourteen people jumping and then he stopped counting. Stuart DeHann saw one woman's dress billowing as she fell, and he saw a shirtless man falling end over end, and he too saw the couple leaping hand in hand.

people—a kind of vulnerable intimacy that I've been protected from. I guess I feel that in one way or another I'll have those things before I leave this world."

In the seventies, she wrote that she wanted to become like Muktananda, a saint. I ask if she still wants that. "At times I've felt that state of oneness," she says, "and I hope I'll experience it more fully in this lifetime."

We arrive at the dreary corner of town where the bus stops, and I start my customary worrying: Did we miss it? Has it passed yet? An aging car rolls by with a sign, Ronnie's Royal Car Service, and Durgananda can't resist observing dryly, "He's come up in the world. 'Royal Car'—he used to be 'Ronnie's Taxi.'" Then she returns to the issue of sainthood. She says what Baba meant by saint was a realized or enlightened being, and "there are many levels of enlightenment. As you enter certain states, the ante goes up. You realize there are deeper levels of equanimity, freedom, and love. The bar is always being raised."

The bus lumbers down the street and I gather my bags, preparing to board. She says no state is trustworthy until you hold it during a crisis, such as death. "If it's there at your death . . ." she smiles, "then you have it."

On June 15, 2002, after twenty-eight years as a yogi nun, Swami Durgananda left the Siddha Yoga organization and reassumed the name Sally Kempton. She said that she wants to write and teach meditation with more autonomy, and realized that "it's time for me to face the challenge of living a spiritual life outside the protected atmosphere of the ashram."

Several pedestrians were killed by people falling from the sky. A fireman was killed by a body falling from the sky.

But he reached for her hand and she reached for his hand and they leaped out the window holding hands.

The day of the Lord will come as a thief in the night, in which the heavens shall pass away with a great noise, wrote John the Apostle, *and the elements shall melt with a fervent heat, the earth also and the works that are therein shall be burned up.*

I try to whisper prayers for the sudden dead and the harrowed families of the dead and the screaming souls of the murderers but I keep coming back to his hand and her hand nestled in each other with such extraordinary ordinary succinct ancient naked stunning perfect simple ferocious love.

There is no fear in love, wrote John, *but perfect love casteth out fear, because fear hath torment.*

Their hands reaching and joining are the most powerful prayer I can imagine, the most eloquent, the most graceful. It is everything that we are capable of against horror and loss and death. It is what makes me believe that we are not craven fools and charlatans to believe in God, to believe that human beings have greatness and holiness within them like seeds that open only under great fires, to believe that some unimaginable essence of who we are persists past the dissolution of what we were, to believe against such evil hourly evidence that love is why we are here.

Their passing away was thought an affliction, and their going forth from us utter destruction, says the Book of Wisdom, *but they are in peace. They shall shine, and shall dart about as sparks through stubble.*

No one knows who they were: husband and wife, lovers, dear friends, colleagues, strangers thrown together at the window there at the lip of hell. Maybe they didn't even reach for each other consciously, maybe it was instinctive, a reflex, as they both decided at the same time to take two running steps and jump out the shattered window, but they did reach for each other, and they held on tight, and leaped, and fell endlessly into the smoking canyon, at two hundred miles an hour, falling so far and so fast that they would have blacked out before they hit the pavement near Liberty Street so hard that there was a pink mist in the air.

I trust I shall shortly see thee, John wrote, *and we shall speak face-to-face.* Jennifer Brickhouse saw them holding hands, and Stuart DeHann saw them holding hands, and I hold on to that.

pager to read it for myself. Then came the confusion and rumors on the street: "The Capitol's been attacked!" "The State Department has been bombed!" "The Supreme Court is in flames!" "Camp David is burning!" "A plane is on its way to the White House!"

During all this, the fire trucks had been racing past on their way to the towers. I must have seen twelve of them rush past our corner. In the coming hours and days, I often wondered how many of the men on those trucks died just minutes later.

Soon the NYPD asked us to evacuate the area. It was only a minute after we began to walk uptown and away from the towers that the sound of several claps of thunder began to rip through the air just over my shoulder. I turned around and saw with my own eyes a sight of pure horror, as the left-hand tower began to collapse into a massive white cloud. Our walk quickly became a run, and then a stampede.

Eventually, as we got farther away from the cataclysm, our pace slowed back down. I caught my breath, trying to absorb what I had just witnessed, when an olive-skinned man with a mustache and briefcase walking to my right began to intone: "You see what happens! All the Palestinians want is a place to call home, a small piece of land. We continue to fund the Israelis, we supply them with money and weapons, we support the persecution of a people for decades, and you see what happens! It should not have come to this. It didn't have to come to this! They have had enough, and you see how they respond—they've got our attention now."

Letting him push on without me, I paused with several hundred others at the Manhattan Bridge to watch the lone burning tower. We had outrun the smoke and dust unscathed, but now thousands of others followed behind us. They were in groups of three or four, marching toward midtown, some sprinkled with ash, many others caked with a dust that had hardened on their

VINCENT DRUDING

Ground Zero: A Journal

from *First Things*

September 11 was to be my first day of work at a new job in downtown Manhattan. Though New York was still very new to me, it was immediately obvious that something was terribly wrong. As I climbed the stairs of the subway just a few blocks from the World Trade Center, there was a palpable feeling of panic in the air as people stared, horrified, into the sky. I followed their gaze upward and I instantly understood. Smoke and fire were gushing from a gaping hole in the smooth, silvery surface of the right-hand tower.

I asked someone nearby if he knew what had happened, and he said it was a bomb. Another man walked over and declared, "No, it was a plane, a plane flew right into building. . . ." Then an enormous explosion drowned out his words. Above our heads, an orange fireball swallowed the top of the second tower, as clouds of paper filled the sky above us. Hundreds of people began scattering. I ran across the street to the Municipal Building and up to a shrieking woman who stammered through her sobs that she had seen a large blue and white plane slam into the building. We stared slack-jawed as sections of the building's metallic facade fell in chunks to the ground. It took a few moments until we realized that some of those falling pieces were not metal at all, but rather human beings leaping eighty or more stories to their deaths— right before our eyes. All I could think to do was make the sign of the cross.

As I stood there in disbelief, a man next to me with a messaging pager said that the Pentagon had just been hit. I grabbed at his skin as it mixed with sweat and traces of blood. They passed by like ghosts—grayish white figures carrying bags, suitcases, and purses. Extras from the set of a horror film, quietly walking home.

As I followed them uptown, a businessman from Atlanta who was in New York on business told me that he couldn't get through to his wife on his cell phone; he knew she'd be scared as hell. "I was on the eighty-first floor, and we were probably the last to get out, but the firefighters kept coming in, heading up as we headed down. They just kept filing up the stairs."

Then, a sudden gasp from a group of Chinese men and women on the corner, and we turned to watch the second tower follow the fate of the first. After a few seconds, I continued my dazed trek to my apartment on Nineteenth Street.

I'm not sure why I went back. The morning of the twelfth I heard a homily at Mass imploring Christians not to yield to the pain and evil but to overcome adversity with faith. That message stuck with me.

The van of volunteers drove us through the smoking and dusty streets of lower Manhattan, cluttered with countless thousands of sheets of paper; all around us, cars and emergency vehicles looked like they were made of papier-mâché. Fruit and bagel stands stood abandoned on empty sidewalks, the apples and bananas sitting in undisturbed rows, coated with a layer of pulverized concrete half an inch thick.

For someone raised in peaceful and prosperous America, Ground Zero itself was simply astonishing to behold. In the center of the street south of the World Trade Center, a crater 60 feet deep and 120 feet across. On each side of the pit, the mangled remains of the towers themselves. They say that each floor of each massive 110-story building was an acre in size. Spread before me were 220 acres of pure destruction crammed into a 16-acre plaza.

Stringy steel rods cut like irregular staircase steps—the skeleton of the building facade—surrounded two six-story piles of debris. Twisted red steel. Windows. Carpets. Toilets. Bits of copy machines, computers, file cabinets, desks. And of course, hidden somewhere within the mountainous piles, the mutilated remains of over three thousand human beings. And then there was the noxious smoke, streaming from a thousand cracks and fissures in the piles from hundreds of hidden fires beneath them. It was a smoldering mound of hell on earth.

No one seemed to be in charge. Hundreds of firefighters crawled around on the piles in small groups. Several pockets of twenty or thirty of them labored with torches, shovels, wire cutters, jackhammers, electric saws, oxygen canisters, hoses, dogs, and their bare hands. At the fringe of the pile—near the Brooks Brothers store that had been transformed into a makeshift morgue—stood several long lines of emergency workers who handed off buckets of debris, one by one. Spontaneous order emerged from the chaos.

So, for example, a New York City fire captain in the pit who needed forty welding tips phoned a friend in New Jersey who has a boat. His friend calls the local union, and in an hour a couple boxes of welding tips are loaded onto a ship, along with several boxes of food, clothes, medical supplies, and fifteen guys looking to lend a hand. An hour later the captain docks the boat at the Cove, east of the American Express building directly adjacent to the site. Ten minutes later, a motley group of construction workers, police officers, volunteers, FBI agents, and National Guardsmen arrive to unload the boxes and pass them down a 150-man work line. Linda and Jackie, two nurses, organize the unloading at the end of the supply line: "Medical supplies, here! Clothes, there! Construction supplies, here!" The captain radios that the welding tips are off the boat. Twenty minutes later, a retired veteran named Rich makes his way into the makeshift supply store on the second floor of the AMEX building, finds the welding tips, and hauls them in a golf cart across the plaza to an equally makeshift transfer station. Half an hour later, the captain who "ordered" the welding tips from his friend in New Jersey not more than two hours earlier walks over to pick up his supplies.

Much of my time was spent directing materials around the site. The supply triangle between the dock, the AMEX building, and the piles ran nonstop for several days and nights. In the days following September 11, similar operations were repeated throughout lower Manhattan, as thousands of people spontaneously found and contributed to the supply chain.

There was much goodness and bravery at the site, but there was also fear, as frayed nerves frequently conspired to induce instantaneous panic. When something shifted unexpectedly on one of the piles, for instance, a firefighter would run, sending the team around him leaping from the huge mound, thereby inspiring hundreds of workers in that quadrant of Ground Zero to scatter. Within seconds several hundred workers would be "running for their lives" down the nearest street, tossing their tools, kicking up dust behind them, tripping over live fire hoses.

Then, as people began to realize that it had been a false alarm, the explanations would begin. "The Millennium Building was gonna come down." "I smelled natural gas." "There was a fire on the pile." After twenty minutes or so, people would slowly creep back toward the site. This cycle repeated itself several times in the first few days, until a system of bells and bullhorns replaced leaping bodies as the official evacuation call.

I would never have predicted it beforehand, but one of the most helpful and generous groups on-site were the Scientologists, who, as I learned, take great pride in being the first to respond to the scene of disasters and crises. When you state your need to a member of the Church of Scientology, the entire group enters what they call the "cycle of action." Anyone who answers a request must do everything in his power to satisfy it and return directly to the person who issued the request to report the results. Ask a Scientologist for a respirator, for example, and your request immediately echoes out from your location in concentric circles. "You need a respirator?" "Respirator!" "We need a respirator up here!" "Okay, who's got the respirators?" "Bring out the respirators!" It was extremely efficient, if also slightly comic.

The Scientologists were not always so helpful, however. They also provided what they called an "assist"—an odd procedure during which a worker runs his hands over your arms and legs in order to "center your energy." It didn't so much resemble a massage as a child petting a small dog before he has acquired complete motor coordination.

At a time when so many people seemed to be at their best, it was sad, although hardly surprising, to learn that a few took advantage of the breakdown of law and order in the vicinity of Ground Zero. Some of the looters did their damage in the shadows, late at night, while others were bolder, dressing up as construction or utility workers. They pilfered through the AMEX supply area, filling up bags and buckets with donated jeans, shoes, sweatshirts, socks, and underwear. They made their way into people's homes and businesses, taking advantage of the mass evacuations in lower Manhattan to take what they wished.

One day an off-duty officer from the Department of Justice took me on a golf cart tour of the businesses that had been looted shortly after being boarded up by the authorities. He was particularly incensed that a nearby National Guardsman had been so in-

effective in preventing the damage. Moreover, a number of apart-
ments in Battery Park City—the high-rise residential buildings
that abut the Trade Center—had been broken into, and a number
of supplies down at the dock had been stolen, both while suppos-
edly under watch by the National Guard officers. A few days later,
the military police and the NYPD stepped in to clamp down on
the crime.

President Bush arrived at Ground Zero on Friday, September
14—the first day in my twenty-four years of living that I experienced genuine patriotism. When word got out that the president
might pay us a visit, eyebrows lifted and smiles cracked on faces.
Twenty minutes before he arrived, the NYPD cleared the area at
the northern edge of the site, and several work crews that had
been on their way to work began to congregate around the area
where Bush would arrive. As soon as he stepped out of his black
Suburban, the workers dropped their shovels and scurried around
to welcome him. Many of us stood on overturned buckets behind
a few rows of people to catch a glimpse, and those behind us
stood on two or three buckets. Scores of workers climbed on top
of the trucks, cranes, and emergency vehicles in the area to watch
and listen. Some just climbed higher on the rubble, or stood on
an overturned I beam to catch a glimpse.

I thought to myself that this scene must be reminiscent of
some bygone time in America's political history when a White
House staff did not plan every presidential visit weeks in advance.
I thought of Lincoln at Gettysburg, stepping out of a train to
make a speech, and spontaneous crowds of people, some climbing
into trees or on walls, gathering around to watch and listen. Here
was our commander-in-chief, faced with unprecedented destruction on American soil, to rally men and women in hard hats at the
center of a wounded city, at the center of a stunned nation.

As he passed in front of our section, his hand met mine, and he looked me in the eye for more than a moment to hear me stammer what I believe was something like, "God bless, Mr. President, we're behind you." He was in no hurry to speak to us as a group but rather took his time meeting us individually. The crowd around the rubble was growing fast, reaching at least a thousand. There was clearly an enthusiasm in the air for the first time since September 11.

When the president finally grabbed a bullhorn and began to speak, it was hard to hear him at first. When someone behind me shouted, "We can't hear you!" the president proclaimed loudly, "But I can hear you! And the rest of the country hears you! And soon, the people who did this . . . are going to hear from all of us!" At that moment, a shot of electricity surged through the crowd. Cheers erupted and echoed off the surrounding buildings, each draped with a tattered American flag. "U.S.A.! U.S.A.! U.S.A.!" It went on and on.

Then—at the corner of West and Vesey Streets in New York City, on the edge of a mass grave, at the feet of the commander-in-chief of the world's mightiest nation—I was overwhelmed with an unexpected sense of fraternity and love of country. Not fifty feet away lay the remains of three thousand innocent people, and here, at their side, a band of their brothers stood before their leader, united in an unconditional love of justice. I really do think that is what it was.

One night at 2:00 A.M. I was on my way through the rain to pick up supplies in the AMEX building, which, among other things, was being used as a transfer station for the bodies and parts of bodies we had recovered from the site. From there they were packed onto trucks to be taken to the morgue at Bellevue Hospital. As I entered the atrium of the building I saw scores of workers holding their hard hats over their chests. Fifty yards away a dozen firefighters proceeded slowly in my direction carrying a body bag. I removed my hard hat and stepped to the side. As they approached, I could read their red, swollen eyes. Their uniforms were dark with mud and soot. Raindrops dripped from everyone's gear. A priest wearing a raincoat, a hard hat, goggles, a respirator, and a headlamp came forward with a book and oils. The men carrying their fallen friend cried quietly as the priest rolled back the bag and anointed the body, administering what appeared to be last rites. In the atrium, heads bowed and no one moved. I don't remember how long we stood there, but time seemed to stop as profane space became as sacred as a shrine. Eventually, the priest stepped away, and the firemen walked slowly forward, out the doors, and into the truck waiting outside. Without a word, we went back out into the dark rain to work.

Before the rainstorm, nearly everything at Ground Zero was covered with a layer of dust, which became the parchment for the messages of rescue workers. On windows or walls, you could find short compositions: "God Bless America," "Engine company 6," "Give us Justice," "Revenge is a bitch," "We miss you Johnny," and the like. But one message stood out. Written with a black marker on a flier posted on a pillar of the AMEX building, "RIP Fr. Mike." Father Mike Judge, a Franciscan priest and chaplain of the FDNY, died while praying in the South Tower on September 11. In the days since September 11, working around the clock with little to no rest, I lost track of time. But this message reminded me that it was Sunday.

Sunday was my fifth day working at Ground Zero. I was exhausted. After making my rounds at the supply area, I walked up North End Avenue to the support center at Stuyvesant High School. I had heard earlier in the day that St. Patrick's Cathedral was going to hold a 5:30 Mass, and I wanted to attend it. As I entered the building, I saw a man dressed in a white habit walking slowly but deliberately down the hall. The tip of his Roman collar peeked out of the robe. He looked and spoke like James Earl Jones and his face was very serious. It occurred to me later that he was probably a Franciscan and had likely just come from attending to the dead at Ground Zero.

All around us, the Scientologists and volunteers buzzed back and forth, and police officers and workers passed by. I asked the priest whether there would be an evening Mass around the site, and he told me that the only one had been held at 9:00 that morning. I told him that I was hoping to attend the memorial Mass at St. Patrick's, which I instantly realized had started six minutes earlier. He then said very deliberately, "I can offer you the Holy Eucharist. Would you like that?" And then, with five days of chaos in my head and my body fatigued, a nameless priest in a white robe, almost invisible in the white hallway were it not for his dark complexion, put his hand on my head, said a blessing, and placed the Body of Christ in my mouth. My eyes remained closed for a long time.

Here, amid the nonstop movement and clutter of bodies and buildings, amid the constant acrid smell of smoke and smog, amid the signs reading "Warning, high levels of asbestos here!" amid the dozens of workers who seemed always on the verge of breaking down in tears, amid the steady flow of sobbing civilians who toured the place where their loved one lay entombed, amid the constant sounds of machines, crashing metal, and sirens, amid all of the destruction and death—here was a pocket of peace. Here, Christ was present, not only among us, but now, again, inside me. And then this angel in the whirlwind sent me on my way and resumed his slow but deliberate walk through the horror, looking to dispense solace to any and all who would accept it, passing through the tumult, almost as though he were from another world.

ROBERT EDDY

Writing: The Interpreter of Desires

from *Writing on the Edge*

It is mid-October 1981 at Tanta University, Egypt. I am an American in my first semester at this university in the center of the Nile Delta. I am teaching a graduate course called American and Arabic Theories of Writing. It is a few minutes after 2:00. The sky is clear, and the temperature is approaching 100 degrees. The room has a very high ceiling. All the windows are open; there is no air conditioning. There are hints of sand on all surfaces, even though they are cleaned once a day. The room has whitewashed walls, with no decorations. We sit around the one table in the room, approximately six by twelve feet. There are twelve chairs. It is about two weeks since President Sadat was assassinated, and the air is electric with fears of a national conspiracy against the government.

There are six students in the room, including two women. The topic for today's class, selected by the students, is "Why write?" One of the men, Gamal, is presenting the ideas of Muhyiddin Ibn Arabi, who died in 1240. Gamal has just read the following lines from Ibn Arabi's *Tarjuman al-Ashwaq* (*The Interpreter of Desires*):

> She said, "I marvel at a lover of such conceit
> To walk so proud among a garden's flowers";
> I answered, "Do not wonder at what you see—
> It is yourself, in the mirror of a man."

Gamal is explaining his general interpretation of Ibn Arabi on style in writing, as an answer to the question "Why write?" He promises that after he finishes his general remarks, he will talk with us about the quotation.

"For Ibn Arabi," says Gamal, "style is not a mere religious or poetic adornment; it is everything. Style doesn't simply embody content; it is content."

There is a commotion in the inner courtyard. The graduate students in the room start to listen to the voices outside. An undergraduate woman outside in the courtyard, Jehan, who has helped me to navigate in my new culture, shouts out in Arabic. "Dr. Eddy, danger! There is a bomb!" The six students in the room, including the two women, rush to cover me with their bodies, knocking over chairs, including mine, as they do so.

I'm experiencing the strange consciousness of facing life and death direct, with eyes involuntarily open, wide and unblinking. Time becomes different and slow. I notice I'm staring at a small section of the ceiling that is peeling away, which I somehow can see through the jumble of bodies on top of me. The small of my back pushes against the back of the chair, on the cement floor. My left elbow and forearm are pressed against the seat of my chair, which is facing upward. My right arm, positioned almost directly above my head, is pinned to the floor under the body of Noor, one of the university's most highly regarded graduate students. With the thumb of my right hand, I perceive what I believe is her right hipbone. What must be her left arm is pressed against the right side of my body from just under my armpit down to the outside of my thigh. Her left armpit is close to my right ear. I smell her fear and her protection. Noor's body is pressed down under Gamal's. Most of the rest of my body is being protected by the other woman taking the course, Fatimah, who is on her hands and knees, bearing the weight of the three other men, just as the ancient Egyptian goddess Nut bears the weight of the universe in countless temple paintings, protecting the land of Egypt.

Time is passing. We hear no explosions. Could this be a false alarm? A small explosion, which seems little more than a thud, comes from the far corner of the building. We wait. We hear no voices, no movement, no other explosions. The silence is calming; it is an opening, a space to crawl through.

I am starting to get very hot, and my unplanned visual concentration on the peeling section of the ceiling is broken. I am now acutely aware of the two women and four men covering my body.

I begin to wonder what I should do or say. I feel, somehow, that we are one being. I begin to notice that I am trembling, but not in fear. I don't want the silence to be broken, or the time of connection to end. I become aware that I am silently repeating a slight rephrasing of one line of the quotation from *The Interpreter of Desires:* "It is yourself, in the mirror of a woman." Fatimah, as the goddess Nut, holding up the heavens, is the first to move our seven-bodied personhood. She turns her head, at great effort, toward me and I see her full face. "Doctore, are you all right?" Unable to speak, I shake my head yes.

The men begin to talk quietly in Arabic. I cannot follow what they are saying. I perceive the three men variously above Fatimah move away. They walk to the window. Fatimah maintains her position exactly. She is close to me but without any physical touching. Jehan shouts from outside, "Dr. Eddy. All is safe."

Fatimah looks at me, nods her head, and Gamal, Noor, and Fatimah rise up seemingly at once. The three of them lift me briskly yet gently to my feet, with little effort. My feet are steady, but my right arm is completely asleep. My trembling is disappearing. Gamal lifts my chair and helps seat me. The two women reclaim their seats at the far end of the table, while the four men disappear for a minute or two. Fatimah and Noor are reciting a prayer in audible but quiet voices. As they are finishing, the men return.

"Doctore, all is safe now, thanks to God," said Gamal. "Would you permit us to continue?"

All I want to do is talk to them about what has just happened, to find some way to thank them for shielding me with their bodies. I am overwhelmed by what they have given to me. I look at each of them. They seem to have no shyness, self-consciousness, or need to talk. They look as if what they did was routine rather than remarkable. They appear to want no praise or thanks. The absolute physical closeness did not embarrass them, including the women. They want to get back to work, and so I answer Gamal, "Yes, certainly. Let us continue. But I have one question. How can I possibly thank you for what you have just done for me?"

"Doctore, it is not necessary to thank us. We have only God to thank that you are safe," explains Gamal.

"I thank God," I immediately reply, "but I also thank each of you for your spontaneous gift of life."

"Pardon, Doctore," adds Noor in a deep and richly modulated voice, "only God can give the gift of life. It was our duty to protect you. We could do no less."

"But it was also our honor, sir," Fatimah adds, with a brief smile.

Gamal, looking at Fatimah, and with some impatience in his voice, insists, "Doctore, please. May we continue? We have much work to do."

I accept that, especially by Gamal, I have been put back into my role as foreign professor, but for the first time, here in Egypt, I feel circumscribed. I can't help but ruminate about what American students might have done in a similar situation. A remarkable, indeed miraculous, event, at least in my life, has just occurred, and I am not going to be allowed to respond as a person. Gamal is anxious to reestablish comfortable and safe social roles.

But now Gamal returns to his analysis of a famous Arab writer and critic—Ibn Arabi—who had to leave Egypt to save his life, threatened by censors. Ibn Arabi's *The Interpreter of Desires* is the writer's answer to the attacks of the censors. This remarkable document, one of the most exciting and moving experiences of literature I have ever had, involves the writer himself adding a commentary to each poem. Usually the commentaries indirectly answer the charges of salaciousness in his poetry and pantheism in his presentation of religious experience. In this work we have a writer interpreting his desires, so as to add his critical voice to those of his censorious readers.

"The danger we just faced seems to have chased away my thoughts on Ibn Arabi's style," observes Gamal. "Allow me, Doctore, to move our discussion directly to the four-line quotation. Could I ask one of my male colleagues and one of my female colleagues to please recite these lines for us? Then I want to lead a discussion about these troubling lines, and what they imply about writing and religion."

Uncharacteristically, compared to earlier classes, no man volunteered to read and discuss the lines, and so Gamal read them himself. "What I want to say about these lines, with their beautiful images and atmosphere, especially the image of the mirror of love, is that they involve a man making overstatements to the girl he loves. For a girl to compare a man to flowers is funny, since men usually refer to girls as flowers. But that's okay. Love makes us do crazy things. And when the man tells the girl that she sees herself in the man's face, I think he sees her as his reflection. Critics have said these lines are part of a poem that contains blasphemous ideas, but I don't see any trace of religion here. Could we please have a female's reading and analysis?"

Fatimah reads the lines once quickly, and in her second reading, slowly, and with exuberance. Everyone, especially Gamal, is taken by the power of her reading. "Let me start with Ibn Arabi's own commentary on these lines, which my colleague, Gamal, seems to ignore for some reason. Here is what the poet as commentator wrote, directly addressing his beloved, Nizam:

> I am like a mirror to thee, and in those Qualities with which I am invested thou beholdest thyself, not me—but thou beholdest them in my human nature which has received this investiture."

In her analysis of the Arabic word translated as "investiture," Fatimah says that since it has clear religious associations, the lines from the poem must be read with their religious implications. Several of the men interject that they see nothing of religion in the passage. Fatimah responds quietly but firmly. "But the poet's own commentary affirms the religious dimension of the poem:

> This is the vision of God in created beings, which in the opinion of some is more exalted than the vision of created things in God."

The men suck in their breaths, in amazement and nervousness. Noor seems stunned. Gamal, whose face is turning angry, stutters, "Th, th, th . . . this is blasphemy! He did deserve the fate the censors had in mind for him here in Egypt. I am sorry he escaped."

The students were clearly afraid of what could happen next. Blasphemy was not to be discussed. "Doctore, please give us your expert opinion on this crucial point. Is it not blasphemy to see the infinite God of the Koran in the girl you love?" Gamal has finished his question, and all eyes are on me.

"Earlier, when the six of you were willing to give your lives to save mine, you called me your 'guest' and 'foreign expert.' I do not feel like either. Our lives are now too closely connected for me to see myself as simply your guest. I feel more like you are my brothers and sisters. Forgive me if my words break any rules of etiquette. I mean no offense."

"Certainly no offense is taken, sir, at the words from your heart. It is our honor to take you as a brother," says Gamal, whose eyes are shining. Everyone's seemingly unblinking eyes are on me, and they nod in agreement at Gamal's words. "Sir, please continue," he adds.

"I certainly, also, do not feel like an expert of any kind, foreign or otherwise, when we are talking about Arabic literature. Let me remind you of what you are too polite to admit: that when it comes to this passage in particular, or Arabic literature in general, the six of you are much more expert than I. Since there is just one minute left in our class today, we must finish. But your question is too important for me to miss any aspect of it. Please state it again, Gamal."

"Is it not blasphemy, sir, to see the infinite God of the Koran in the girl you love?" Gamal has repeated his question in a loud, insistent voice.

I ask for a copy of the Koran. Fatimah hands me hers, which includes an English translation. I turn to chapter fifty-five, verse thirteen, and read, in a clear but quiet voice, a line I have always loved: "Which of thy Lord's blessings will you deny?"

Joseph Epstein

What Are You Afraid Of?

from *Notre Dame Magazine*

Courage isn't so easily defined. As splendid a mind as that of Socrates, in the early dialogue called *Laches,* is rather disappointing at the job. He tells us the kinds, or realms, of courage, which include courage in war, on sea, in disease and poverty, in politics, against pain, and—here's one you might have overlooked—in contending against desires and pleasures. He later tells us that we need to know a great deal about good and evil, to distinguish between what is and is not to be feared, if we are to know where the exercise of courage is required. Then, just when things begin to get interesting, the old boy knocks off for the afternoon, perhaps returning to his famously nagging wife, Xanthippe, which no doubt took a certain grim courage of its own.

Better perhaps to go at things the other way round, attempt to understand courage by taking up the subject of fear. Fears, taken at a fairly high level of generality, seem to me four: fear of death, of loss, of pain, and of humiliation. Over a respectable number of years, I have felt them all, in varying degrees of intensity, and am even now not through with them, with only the fear of humiliation having attenuated, or thinned out, a bit. I don't think of myself as perpetually living with fear. But, then, it occurs to me that I arranged a fair portion of my life in a way that has enabled me to play around these fears and fear generally.

If I am guilty of acts of outright cowardice, I do not remember them. I can say that I never backed out of a physical fight, but only when I add that one of the organizing principles of my quotidian life is not to look for fights. My last fight, at age eleven, was against a kid named David Netboy and ended in a dreary draw. I do not think myself, in the old playground word, a chicken, yet, as a boy playing baseball and football and (later) basketball, style not aggressiveness was my specialty, smooth moves not brutal strength on the playground gave me the keenest pleasure.

I might not have known about my want of physical aggressiveness but for the presence of a friend named Marty Summerfield, with whom I grew up and played on the same playgrounds. Marty didn't seem to mind pain. He would back into brick walls to catch fly balls, crash into the line without a helmet to pick up important short yardage. He was a catcher in hardball, a job that no one squeamish should ever consider, and in close plays at the plate would give up his body without a second thought. ("I'm glad my son is going into boxing," Rocky Marciano's mother, Pasqualina Marchegiano, is alleged to have said. "I didn't raise the boy to be a catcher.") In later life, when the occasion called for it, Marty would get into fights with guys fifty and seventy pounds heavier than he. In case you think Marty was a brute and a blockhead into the bargain, I had better report that he is five feet nine inches tall, weighing maybe 150 pounds, and went on to teach university mathematics.

Possibly Marty had a little jingeroo: sometime early in life the fear button fell off his panel of emotions. We now know that there are people who not only are fearless but need to court danger, live on the rim, rev themselves up with such delightful pastimes as rock climbing, bungee jumping, and skydiving. Mention of the last reminds me that, when I was in the army, one morning our company was marched over to learn about going to jump school and becoming a paratrooper. As I sat listening to the youthful sergeant, in beret and ascot, recount all of the glories of being a paratrooper, including an additional $55 in "danger" pay, I thought, why not, let 'er rip, jumping out of a plane would at least expose me to a new experience. Before I got round to considering how I might spend the extra $55 in monthly salary, I said to myself, Yo, hold it there, kid, it's tough enough getting up in the morning as it is without the prospect of a sergeant screaming at you to jump out of a plane. Today, I shouldn't mind *having* jumped out of a plane; it is only the thought of doing it now that appalls me, using the word in its root sense of causing one to go pale.

I am no courage junky. I feel no regular need to prove myself, if only to myself.

I require absolutely no false fear stimulants. I watch no horror movies, ride no roller-coasters, answer no serious dares. I steer clear of all this in the firm belief that life, left to its own devices, is sufficiently fear laden on its own. No need to lay on extra ones.

I have no phobias, in the accepted psychological sense of irrational fears. I don't worry unduly about flying. Heights bring me no especial terrors. Close spaces, within reason, provide no problem. I think here of poor Kingsley Amis, the novelist, whose son reports that he "refused to drive and refused to fly, couldn't easily be alone in a bus, a train, or a lift (or in a house, after dark), wasn't exactly keen on boats. . . ." I have a small terror about rats, one George Orwell seemed also to have had, but then I've read somewhere that humankind divides in its loathing for either rats or snakes. In short, I seem to be nearly nauseatingly normal.

Public speaking is said to be the second greatest fear among Americans (acquiring a fatal disease is first). I have known this fear, the extreme nervousness before standing up in front of a large crowd and, through one's intrinsic power to bore or through ill preparation or by dint of simple ignorance, making a great purple-bottomed baboon of oneself. But I have conquered this fear to the extent that I now do a fair amount of such speaking, ever ready to risk making a serious fool of myself for the right fee.

Along with taking the check, I find myself also pleased that I have won through what was once a real fear, though I still feel a certain stomach churning, of a kind I prefer to think athletes feel before a big game begins, until I begin gassing away from the podium.

I have been lucky in that history has thus far seen fit to steer me clear of the larger fearful possibilities. Chief among these has been war. Born in 1937, I was a child during World War II, still too young for Korea, then too old for Vietnam. My army days—from 1958 to 1960—were spent in the Cold War. A part of me wishes I had gone to war. I suspect that most men who haven't feel themselves, in some fundamental way, untested. I haven't any longing for war, mind you, but because war has always seemed a test of manhood, I should have been pleased to have passed it, even while perhaps disapproving of it. As things stand, I shall never know if I would have come through. I have, meanwhile, admiration for those who have.

Between the efforts of my father—who regularly and I think rightly reminded me when a little boy "to be a man"—and the ethos of the playground and playing field, I was brought up on a program of courage. Boys don't cry. Don't back down before bullies. Don't let a little pain throw you; shake it off. Play on through. I seem to have passed most of these minor tests. But could I have conquered the terror of confronting other men with genuine homicide in their eyes? Under the horror, the squalor, the full terror of war, would my legs have come unstrung, my bowels held themselves in check, my mind retained some measure of its lucidity, my senses not become entirely deranged? I can only guess, and because I'm reduced to guessing, it is impossible not to have doubts. I shall never know—and it bothers me that I won't.

The only society on historical record that ever used courage as an organizing principle was that of the Spartans in the fifth century B.C. It was, in the nature of the case, male dominated, a military society through and through. Brawling, running, silently absorbing punishment, eliminating all traces of effeminacy, sleeping with one's shield and spear—in Sparta acculturation meant the inculcation of courage, at least physical courage.

In Steven Pressfield's excellent *Gates of Fire*, a historically accurate novel about the three hundred Spartans (all with living sons) who led a troop of roughly six thousand Greeks that held off tens of thousands of Persians at Thermopylae, one gets a clear view of how stern the training of Spartan youth could be. In one scene, a Spartan knight and Olympic victor breaks the noses of all the youth under his training so that they learn the importance of their shields and of the seriousness of their training. Such tactics seem to work, but at what price?

How would a man with Spartan training have reacted the hot sunny afternoon when, entering my car in the middle of a fairly empty supermarket parking lot, I was approached by a young, muscular man who looked to have no sense of humor whatsoever and who, with nothing of the supplicant in his voice, said, "Hey, man, I just got out of jail and could use some help. Let me have a buck?" My policy in the matter of begging is to give only to beggars who look to be in deep trouble or those whose stories are dramatically witty. This guy satisfied neither condition. Would a man with Spartan courage have come up with the dollar? I hope you find this an interesting theoretical question. At the time, I didn't even find it a question but instead forked over the dollar, relieved to enter my car without a knife protruding from my stomach.

We live in an age, I fear, when paranoia has become the better part of valor. A writer in the *Wall Street Journal* not long ago wrote, "The American landscape of fear has been immutably changed by this era of success and affluence." Yet he allows that, despite this, the national anxiety level appears to have risen, judged by the increase in both the use of becalming drugs and the recourse to various psychotherapies, and he quotes a psychiatrist remarking that "anxiety is a condition of the privileged." Is this true? Do we really now have only to fear, as the man said, fear itself?

Statistically, true enough, there would appear to be less to fear in the world: Crime rates continue to drop, job security in most places seems to have risen, nuclear holocaust isn't for the most part on the public consciousness. Yet statistics about safety, however overwhelming, are never finally reassuring. Tell someone the chances of dying in a plane crash are many times fewer than dying in an automobile and that does nothing to relieve the worry of the sound of a juddering engine when one is aloft during a thunderstorm. The battle against certain cancers may be showing great progress, but that doesn't much ease the mind of the man who discovers blood in his urine.

Most serious fears are at bottom fears of death. "The real world is simply too terrible to admit," writes Ernest Becker in *The Denial of Death*. "It tells man that he is a small trembling animal who will decay and die." For a peek into my own quavering consciousness, let me list the five forms of modern death I—at one time or another, for one reason or another—have found worth fearing and see if they check out with your own:

1. Though I am able to put it from my mind when flying, let me begin with air crash, for the obviousness of which I apologize. The classicist Mary Lefkowitz described not long ago (on the op-ed pages in the *New York Times*) the experience of surviving what looked to be a certain crash landing, when the plane she was flying in was reported to be unable to get its landing wheels to descend. She ends by writing, "Are the passengers on the planes that actually crash as uncannily calm as we were—

silent, unlamenting, bracing ourselves in the dark cabin? Do they, before the last moments, experience, as we did, a terror so anesthetizing that it could pass for courage?"

2. Arbitrary violence: a drive-by shooting, muggings that get out of hand, meeting up with a maniac. An acquaintance recently told me about a student of hers who made the mistake of getting caught staring at a young man in a Kalamazoo bus station who turned out to be a schizophrenic and pummeled him to death. In the backs of the minds of all of us who live in large cities is the figure of that terrified—and terrifying—wretch, the drug addict who holds us up or breaks into our homes and, out of control, goes too far. Oddly enough, I once had someone try to break into my home, waking me while doing so at three in the morning. I discovered myself going over to the window that he was attempting to pry loose and yelling at him in a voice rather deeper than I usually possess. I was not in the least afraid, but of all things furious at the nerve of the man attempting to violate my home.

3. Death in a hospital, through picking up some nutty infection, bad blood work, being given the wrong meds by an incompetent nurse or orderly. I continue to believe that hospitals are frightening places; too many people don't emerge from them. "To believe in medicine would be the height of folly," said Proust, "if not to believe in it were greater folly still." It's true, damn it, too true.

4. Death by modern appliance, not least an automobile driven by a drunk driver falling asleep at the wheel at just that moment when he is coming at you, passing you, crossing in front of you. But not by automobile alone. My friend Sonya Rudikoff, an excellent literary critic, came down one morning to turn up the gas under the kettle in her kitchen in Princeton, New Jersey, and was blown apart by an explosion. Too easy to imagine

heating systems expelling gas into one's bedroom at night, being electrocuted by loose wires in one's refrigerator, and other delicious ways of going down in perfectly arbitrary, infuriatingly senseless death.

5. Death, finally, by that cause that I have already mentioned Americans fear even beyond public speaking: by an early, painful, and degrading disease. Lots of them out there, cause and cure unknown. I speak of "early" death, the way obituarists speak of "untimely" deaths, though few people seem to have died timely ones, unless quite aged or very ill.

Fears exist this side of death, of course. Tom Wolfe, who seems to me keenest among contemporary novelists in admiring physical courage and understanding fear, in his last novel, *A Man in Full,* neatly plays into the male heterosexual fear of homosexual rape in prison. I myself have always admired the physical courage of women who go through childbirth and, having done it once, are prepared to do it again. I hope I shan't be accused of male chauvinism when I say I am pleased that my masculinity has precluded my having to face that test in courage.

But I seem to have been talking almost entirely of fear and courage in the physical realm. Physical courage not only has its limitations but needs qualifications. "Well," says the father of the hero of Mary Renault's fine novel *The Last of the Wine,* "I am glad to see you not so wanting in courage as in sense. But courage without conduct is the virtue of a robber, or a tyrant. Don't forget it." There is a lot of foolish courage in the world. And lots in which people act on instinct, which is still courage of a kind, but perhaps not of the highest kind.

Most of us, with a bit of luck, will go through life without having their physical courage tested. But of course there is a courage greater than physical courage. I myself know of no deeper courage than that required of parents who raise a mentally damaged or emotionally deeply disturbed child. If heaven be a football stadium—and I hope it isn't—theirs ought to be seats on the fifty.

It takes courage to die with serenity, especially if it means feigning serenity to make your death easier for family and friends. I shall never forget the death of my dearest friend, Edward Shils, who, when my wife went up to his bedside for what both knew would be the final time, set *her* at ease by telling her he wasn't frightened; reminded her of how much he valued her friendship and all their time together; and, in short, did, as my wife said, all the work. To die well not only requires the courage needed at the close of a life but also suggests that one has learned a vast amount, really learned courage, from much that has gone before in life leading up to that close.

My friend Edward Shils also taught me to value intellectual courage, though I only heard him use that exact phrase on one occasion. I was standing near him after he gave the Jefferson Lecture in the Humanities at the University of Chicago, in which he dissected the various ways he thought the modern university was becoming corrupted. A woman came up afterward to congratulate him on his "intellectual courage" in saying the things he did. "Intellectual courage!" he exclaimed, genuinely surprised at the thought. "What I said in that lecture took no intellectual courage. It takes intellectual courage to speak one's mind in the Soviet Union or in South Africa. But here doing so takes no courage whatsoever—only the absence of intellectual cowardice, which isn't quite the same as intellectual courage."

And yet how few academics or intellectuals are willing to say what they think? Not many, I have found. They fear what they think of as retaliation, a greatly overdramatized word really meaning losing useful connections, chances for promotion, minor raises, pathetically small lifts in their status in what is called the profession. When a professor comes along who does show his hatred for the false—a Sidney Hook, say, or a Paul Oskar Kristeller, or an Edward Shils—the skies light up.

Courage also can be a quality of nations. In this realm, the United States has not really been tested. How lucky we are since our founding never to have been invaded. In the modern era one thinks, of course, of the English, who came through World War II showing such admirable courage. "So let us drink a toast," said Noel Coward of his countrymen's conduct in that war, "to the courage and gallantry that made a strange heaven [of that time of courage] out of a particular hell."

Would we Americans come through under such circumstances? Would our culture provide a figure of the courageousness of Winston Churchill? Would the great good fortune of our long prosperity leave us with sufficient inner strength to face sustained adversity? All have to be left as tantalizing, disturbing, yet finally unsettled questions.

On a less dramatic but not less significant plane, there is the courage that resides in doing one's duties, fulfilling one's obligations, day in and day out, without needing to be reminded by anyone else what those duties and obligations are. I speak here of the courage to carry on in the face of small but genuine setbacks, when one's dreams have been dashed, one's hopes rendered nugatory, all one's bets in life come up double zero. At such times who among us, man or woman, has not felt like chucking all life's onerous responsibilities, getting in the car, and driving away—for good? Courage of the most demanding kind can sometimes be required merely to hang in there.

In the words of Australian poet Adam Lindsey Gordon (1833–1870),

Life is mostly froth and bubble
Two things stand like stone
KINDNESS in another's trouble
COURAGE in your own.

Courage, then, consists in knowing—really knowing—what to fear, and in acting upon this knowledge. Saying this, I seem to have gotten no further with the subject of courage than Socrates, though, in my charming modesty, I suppose I am prepared to settle for that.

A Dream of Solstice

from *The Kenyon Review*

The sun's rays enter Newgrange—5000-year-old passage grave north of Dublin—on December 21 every year. A slot in the stone entrance, 70 feet away from the burial chamber at the core of the tumulus, admits the light.

> *Qual è colüi che sognando vede,*
> *che dopo 'l sogno la passione impressa*
> *rimane, e l'altro a la mente no riede,*
>
> *cotal son io . . .*
>
> Dante, *Paradiso,* Canto xxxiii

Like somebody who sees things when he's dreaming
And after the dream lives with the aftermath
Of what he felt, no other trace remaining,

So I live now, for what I saw departs
And is almost lost, although a distilled sweetness
Still drops from it into my inner heart.

It is the same with snow the sun releases,
The same as when in wind, the hurried leaves
Swirl round your ankles and the shaking hedges

That had flopped their catkin cuff-lace and green sleeves
Are sleet-whipped bare. Dawn light began stealing
Through the cold universe to County Meath,

Over weirs where the Boyne water, fulgent, darkling,
Turns its thick axle, over rick-sized stones
Millennia deep in their own unmoving

And unmoved alignment. And now the planet turns
Earth brow and templed earth, the crowd grows still
In the wired-off precinct of the burial mounds,

Flight 104 from New York audible
As it descends on schedule into Dublin,
Boyne Valley Centre Car Park already full,

Waiting for seedling light on roof and windscreen.
And as *in illo tempore* people marked
The king's gold dagger when he plunged it in

To the hilt in unsown ground, to start the work
Of the world again, to speed the plough
And plant the riddled grain, we watch through murk

And overboiling cloud for the milted glow
Of sunrise, for an eastern dazzle
To send first light like share-shine in a furrow

Steadily deeper, farther available,
Creeping along the floor of the passage grave
To backstone and capstone, holding its candle

To the world inside the astronomic cave.

PATRICIA HOOPER

Where I Was

from *Image*

I thought I was only watering a few trees
in the long drought of summer, on a cool morning.
A stranger came down the street, he was wearing sandals,
carrying a Bible, and I thought, oh no,
no escape to the house, he's already seen me.
But he was used to that, people having to rush
to the dentist or drugstore, refusing to open doors.
He had eyes like blue fire, skin like tan silk.
He was twenty, maybe thirty, and six feet tall.
He was walking down the street, and I was standing
in his path, moving the lawn sprinklers.
I had to say good morning to be polite.
He had to ask would I listen, about the Bible.
I said no, I was busy. The light stayed in his eyes.
I said I'd already read it. He said, good.
It could have been any novel, he just smiled
and went on walking, not even leaving the little books.
I thought, maybe that's how Jesus walked through the world.
People were always busy, but some just let go
of the bucket or the fishnet or the green hose.
I wanted to follow him all the way down the street.
I wanted to listen to the long story of his short life.
But I didn't, I kept watering the maples and the new oak
and went back to my garden and weeded among the phlox.
I thought, now I know: I would have been one of those who held
    back.

I would have said, show me the miracles, I need proof.
But I would have said, thanks for trying, for standing there like
   that
in your blue cotton shirt with the lit sky in your eyes.
I would have seen how the well water gleamed in the clay cup
and lain down in the grass and looked all day at the sky.
I would have seen how the fish and the loaves could have fed
   everyone.
All summer since then I've been listening for that voice,
every stranger a bright chance, every small word filling me up.
I might have been in the story, I was that close.
I kept waking with the birds, I kept looking down the green
   street.
I was fishing as he passed, I was sweeping in the small house,
I was at the banquet, kneeling in the fine dust,
pouring water from the pitcher, steadying the stone bowl.
I was drying with my hair the beautiful, tired feet.

LEON R. KASS

L'Chaim and Its Limits: Why Not Immortality?

from *First Things*

You don't have to be Jewish to drink *L'Chaim,* to lift a glass "To life." Everyone in his right mind believes that life is good and that death is bad. But Jews have always had an unusually keen appreciation of life, and not only because it has been stolen from them so often and so cruelly. The celebration of life—of *this* life, not the next one—from the beginning has been central to Jewish ethical and religious sensibilities. In the Torah, "Be fruitful and multiply" is God's first blessing and first command. Judaism from its inception rejected child sacrifice and regarded long life as a fitting divine reward for righteous living. At the same time, Judaism embraces medicine and the human activity of healing the sick; from the Torah the rabbis deduced not only permission for doctors to heal, but also the positive obligation to do so. Indeed, so strong is this reverence for life that the duty of *pikuah nefesh* requires that Jews violate the holy Shabbat in order to save a life. Not by accident do we Jews raise our glasses "*L'Chaim.*"

Neither is it accidental that Jews have been enthusiastic boosters of modern medicine and modern biomedical science. Vastly out of proportion to their numbers, they build hospitals and laboratories, support medical research, and see their sons and daughters in the vanguard wherever new scientific discoveries are to be made and new remedies to be found. Yet this beloved biomedical project, for all its blessings, now raises for Jews and for all humanity a plethora of serious and often unprecedented moral challenges. Laboratory-assisted reproduction, artificial organs, genetic manipulation, psychoactive drugs, computer implants in the brain, and techniques to conquer aging—these and other present and projected techniques for altering our bodies and minds pose challenges to the very meaning of our humanity. Our growing power to control human life may require us to consider possible limits to the principle of L'*Chaim*.

One well-known set of challenges results from undesired consequences of medical success in sustaining life, as more and more people are kept alive by artificial means in greatly debilitated and degraded conditions. When, if ever, is it permissible for doctors to withhold antibiotics, discontinue a respirator, remove a feeding tube, or even assist in suicide or perform euthanasia?

A second set of challenges concerns the morality of means used to seek the cure of disease or the creation of life. Is it ethical to create living human embryos for the sole purpose of experimenting on them? To conceive a child in order that it may become a compatible bone marrow donor for an afflicted "sibling"? Is it ethical to practice human cloning to provide a child for an infertile couple?

Third, we may soon face challenges concerning the goal itself: Should we, partisans of life, welcome efforts to increase not just the average but also the maximum human life span, by conquering aging, decay, and ultimately mortality itself?

In the debates taking place in the United States, Jewish commentators on these and related medical ethical topics nearly always come down strongly in favor of medical progress and on the side of life—more life, longer life, new life. They treat the cure of disease, the prevention of death, and the prolongation of life as near-absolute values, trumping most if not all other moral objections. Unlike, say, Roman Catholic moralists who hold to certain natural law teachings that set limits on what are permissible prac-

tices, the Jewish commentators, even if they acknowledge difficulties, ultimately wind up saying that life and health are good and
that therefore whatever serves more of each and both is better.

Let me give two examples out of my own experience. Four
years ago, when I gave testimony on the ethics of human cloning
before the National Bioethics Advisory Commission, I was surprised to discover that the two experts who had been invited to
testify on the Jewish point of view were not especially troubled by
the prospect. The Orthodox rabbi, invoking the goodness of life
and the injunction to be fruitful and multiply, held that cloning
of the husband or the wife to provide a child for an infertile couple was utterly unobjectionable according to Jewish law. The
Conservative rabbi, while acknowledging certain worries, concluded, "If cloning human beings is intended to advance medical
research or cure infertility, it has a proper place in God's scheme
of things, as understood in the Jewish tradition." Let someone
else worry about Brave-New-Worldly turning procreation into
manufacture or the meaning of replacing heterosexual procreation by asexual propagation. Prospective cures for diseases and
children for infertile couples suffice to legitimate human
cloning—and, by extension, will legitimate farming human embryos for spare body parts or even creating babies in bottles when
that becomes feasible.

The second example. At a meeting in March 2000 on "Extended
Life, Eternal Life," scientists and theologians were invited to discuss
the desirability of increasing the maximum human life span and,
more radically, of treating death itself as a disease to be conquered.
The major Jewish speaker, a professor at a leading rabbinical seminary, embraced the project—you should excuse me—whole hog.
Gently needling his Christian colleagues by asserting that, for Jews,
God is Life, rather than Love, he used this principle to justify any
and all life-preserving and life-extending technologies, including

those that might yield massive increases in the maximum human life expectancy. When I pressed him in discussion to see if he had any objections to the biomedical pursuit of immortality, he responded that Judaism would only welcome such a project.

I am prepared to accept the view that traditional Jewish sources may be silent on these matters, given that the halakhah could know nothing about test-tube babies, cloning, or the campaign to conquer aging. But in my opinion, such unqualified endorsement of medical progress and the unlimited pursuit of longevity cannot be the counsel of wisdom and, therefore, should not be the counsel of Jewish wisdom. *L'Chaim,* but with limits.

Let us address the question of *L'Chaim* and its limits in its starkest and most radical form: If life is good and more is better, should we not regard death as a disease and try to cure it? Although this formulation of the question may seem too futuristic or far-fetched, there are several reasons for taking it up and treating it seriously.

First, reputable scientists are today answering the question in the affirmative and are already making large efforts toward bringing about a cure. Three kinds of research, still in their infancy, are attracting new attention and energies. First is the use of hormones, especially human growth hormone (hGH), to restore and enhance youthful bodily vigor. In the United States, over ten thousand people—including many physicians—are already injecting themselves daily with hGH for anti-aging purposes, with apparently remarkable improvements in bodily fitness and performance, though there is as yet no evidence that the hormones yield any increase in life expectancy. When the patent on hGH expires in 2002 and the cost comes down from its current $1,000 per month, many more people are almost certainly going to be injecting themselves from the hormonal fountain of youth.

Second is research on stem cells, those omnicompetent primordial cells that, on different signals, turn into all the different
differentiated tissues of the body—liver, heart, kidney, brain, etc.
Stem cell technologies—combined with techniques of cloning—
hold out the promise of an indefinite supply of replacement tissues and organs for any and all worn-out body parts. This is a
booming area in commercial biotechnology, and one of the leading biotech entrepreneurs has been touting his company's research as promising indefinite prolongation of life.

Third, there is research into the genetic switches that control
the biological processes of aging. The maximum life span for each
species—roughly one hundred years for human beings—is almost certainly under genetic control. In a startling recent discovery, fruit fly geneticists have shown that mutations in a *single* gene
produce a 50 percent increase in the natural lifetime of the flies.
Once the genes involved in regulating the human life cycle and
setting the midnight hour are identified, scientists predict that
they will be able to increase the human maximum age well beyond its natural limit. Quite frankly, I find some of the claims and
predictions to be overblown, but it would be foolhardy to bet
against scientific and technical progress along these lines.

But even if cures for aging and death are a long way off, there is a
second and more fundamental reason for inquiring into the radical question of the desirability of gaining a cure for death. For
truth to tell, victory over mortality is the unstated but implicit
goal of modern medical science, indeed of the entire modern scientific project, to which mankind was summoned almost four
hundred years ago by Francis Bacon and René Descartes. They
quite consciously trumpeted the conquest of nature for the relief
of man's estate, and they founded a science whose explicit purpose
was to reverse the curse laid on Adam and Eve, and especially to

restore the tree of life, by means of the tree of (scientific) knowledge. With medicine's increasing successes, realized mainly in the last half century, every death is increasingly regarded as premature, a failure of today's medicine that future research will prevent. In parallel with medical progress, a new moral sensibility has developed that serves precisely medicine's crusade against mortality: anything is permitted if it saves life, cures disease, prevents death. Regardless, therefore, of the imminence of anti-aging remedies, it is most worthwhile to reexamine the assumption upon which we have been operating: that everything should be done to preserve health and prolong life as much as possible, and that all other values must bow before the biomedical gods of better health, greater vigor, and longer life.

Recent proposals that we should conquer aging and death have not been without their critics. The criticism takes two forms: predictions of bad social consequences and complaints about distributive justice. Regarding the former, there are concerns about the effect on the size and age distribution of the population. How will growing numbers and percentages of people living well past one hundred affect, for example, work opportunities, retirement plans, hiring and promotion, cultural attitudes and beliefs, the structure of family life, relations between the generations, or the locus of rule and authority in government, business, and the professions? Even the most cursory examination of these matters suggests that the cumulative results of aggregated decisions for longer and more vigorous life could be highly disruptive and undesirable, even to the point that many individuals would be *worse off* through most of their lives, and worse off enough to offset the benefits of better health afforded them near the end of life. Indeed, several people have predicted that retardation of aging will present a classic instance of the Tragedy of the Commons, in which genuine and sought-for gains to individuals are nullified or worse, owing to the social consequences of granting them to everyone.

But other critics worry that technology's gift of long or immortal life will not be granted to everyone, especially if, as is likely, the treatments turn out to be expensive. Would it not be the ultimate injustice if only some people could afford a deathless existence, if the world were divided not only into rich and poor but into mortal and immortal?

Against these critics, the proponents of immortality research answer confidently that we will gradually figure out a way to solve these problems. We can handle any adverse social consequences through careful planning; we can overcome the inequities through cheaper technologies. Though I think these optimists woefully naive, let me for the moment grant their view regarding these issues. For both the proponents and their critics have yet to address thoughtfully the heart of the matter, the question of the goodness of the goal. The core question is this: Is it really true that longer life for individuals is an unqualified good?

How *much* longer life is a blessing for an individual? Ignoring now the possible harms flowing back to individuals from adverse social consequences, how much more life is good for us as individuals, other things being equal? How much more life do we want, assuming it to be healthy and vigorous? Assuming that it were up to us to set the human life span, where would or should we set the limit and why?

The simple answer is that no limit should be set. Life is good, and death is bad. Therefore, the more life the better, provided, of course, that we remain fit and our friends do, too.

This answer has the virtues of clarity and honesty. But most public advocates of conquering aging deny any such greediness. They hope not for immortality, but for something reasonable— just a few more years.

How many years are reasonably few? Let us start with ten. Which of us would find unreasonable or unwelcome the addition of ten healthy and vigorous years to his or her life, years like those between ages thirty and forty? We could learn more, earn more, see more, do more. Maybe we should ask for five years on top of that? Or ten? Why not fifteen, or twenty, or more?

If we can't immediately land on the reasonable number of added years, perhaps we can locate the principle. What is the principle of reasonableness? Time needed for our plans and projects yet to be completed? Some multiple of the age of a generation, say, that we might live to see great-grandchildren fully grown? Some notion—traditional, natural, revealed—of the proper life span for a being such as man? We have no answer to this question. We do not even know how to choose among the principles for setting our new life span.

Under such circumstances, lacking a standard of reasonableness, we fall back on our wants and desires. Under liberal democracy, this means the desires of the majority for whom the attachment to life—or the fear of death—knows no limits. It turns out that the simple answer is the best: we want to live and live, and not to wither and not to die. For most of us, especially under modern secular conditions in which more and more people believe that this is the only life they have, the desire to prolong the life span (even modestly) must be seen as expressing a desire *never* to grow old and die. However naive their counsel, those who propose immortality deserve credit: they honestly and shamelessly expose this desire.

Some, of course, eschew any desire for longer life. They seek not adding years to life, but life to years. For them, the ideal life span would be our natural (once thought three-, now known to be) fourscore and ten, or if by reason of strength, fivescore, lived with full powers right up to death, which could come rather suddenly, painlessly, at the maximal age.

This has much to recommend it. Who would not want to

avoid senility, crippling arthritis, the need for hearing aids and dentures, and the degrading dependencies of old age? But, in the absence of these degenerations, would we remain content to spurn longer life? Would we not become even more disinclined to exit? Would not death become even more of an affront? Would not the fear and loathing of death increase in the absence of its harbingers? We could no longer comfort the widow by pointing out that her husband was delivered from his suffering. Death would always be untimely, unprepared for, shocking.

Montaigne saw it clearly:

> I notice that in proportion as I sink into sickness, I naturally enter into a certain disdain for life. I find that I have much more trouble digesting this resolution when I am in health than when I have a fever. Inasmuch as I no longer cling so hard to the good things of life when I begin to lose the use and pleasure of them, I come to view death with much less frightened eyes. This makes me hope that the farther I get from life and the nearer to death, the more easily I shall accept the exchange. . . . If we fell into such a change [decrepitude] suddenly, I don't think we could endure it. But when we are led by Nature's hand down a gentle and virtually imperceptible slope, bit by bit, one step at a time, she rolls us into this wretched state and makes us familiar with it; so that we find no shock when youth dies within us, which in essence and in truth is a harder death than the complete death of a languishing life or the death of old age; inasmuch as the leap is not so cruel from a painful life as from a sweet and flourishing life to a grievous and painful one.

Thus it is highly likely that even a modest prolongation of life with vigor or even only a preservation of youthfulness with no increase in longevity would make death less acceptable and would exacerbate the desire to keep pushing it away—unless, for some reason, such life could also prove less satisfying.

Could longer, healthier life be less satisfying? How could it be, if life is good and death is bad? Perhaps the simple view is in error. Perhaps mortality is not simply an evil; perhaps it is even a blessing—not only for the welfare of the community, but even for us as individuals. How could this be?

I wish to make the case for the virtues of mortality. Against my own strong love of life, and against my even stronger wish that no more of my loved ones should die, I aspire to speak truth to my desires by showing that the finitude of human life is a blessing for every human individual, whether he knows it or not.

I know I won't persuade many people to my position. But I do hope I can convince readers of the gravity—I would say, the unique gravity—of this question. We are not talking about some minor new innovation with ethical wrinkles about which we may chatter or regulate as usual. Conquering death is not something that we can try for a while and then decide whether the results are better or worse—according to, God only knows, what standard. On the contrary, this is a question in which our very humanity is at stake, not only in the consequences but also in the very meaning of the choice. For to argue that human life would be better without death is, I submit, to argue that human life would be better being something other than human. To be immortal would not be just to continue life as we mortals now know it, only forever. The new immortals, in the decisive sense, would not be like us at all. If this is true, a human choice for bodily immortality would suffer from the deep confusion of choosing to have some great good only on the condition of turning into someone else. Moreover, such an immortal someone else, in my view, will be less well off than we mortals are now, thanks indeed to our mortality.

It goes without saying that there is no virtue in the death of a child or a young adult, or the untimely or premature death of anyone, before they had attained to the measure of man's days. I do not mean to imply that there is virtue in the particular *event* of death for anyone. Nor am I suggesting that separation through death is not painful for the survivors, those for whom the deceased was an integral part of their lives. Instead, my question concerns the fact of our finitude, the fact of our mortality—the fact *that we must die,* the fact that a full life for a human being has a biological, built-in limit, one that has evolved as part of our nature. Does this fact also have value? Is our finitude good for us— as individuals? (I intend this question entirely in the realm of natural reason and apart from any question about a life after death.)

To praise mortality must seem to be madness. If mortality is a blessing, it surely is not widely regarded as such. Life seeks to live, and rightly suspects all counsels of finitude. "Better to be a slave on earth than the king over all the dead," says Achilles in Hades to the visiting Odysseus, in apparent regret for his prior choice of the short but glorious life. Moreover, though some cultures—such as the Eskimo—can instruct and moderate somewhat the lust for life, liberal Western society gives it free rein, beginning with a political philosophy founded on a fear of violent death, and reaching to our current cults of youth and novelty, the cosmetic replastering of the wrinkles of age, and the widespread anxiety about disease and survival. Finally, the virtues of finitude—if there are any— may never be widely appreciated in any age or culture, if appreciation depends on a certain wisdom, if wisdom requires a certain detachment from the love of oneself and one's own, and if the possibility of such detachment is given only to the few. Still, if it is wisdom, the rest of us should hearken, for we may learn something of value for ourselves.

How, then, might our finitude be good for us? I offer four benefits, first among which is *interest and engagement.* If the human life span were increased even by only twenty years, would the pleasures of life increase proportionately? Would professional tennis players really enjoy playing 25 percent more games of tennis? Would the Don Juans of our world feel better for having seduced 1,250 women rather than 1,000? Having experienced the joys and tribulations of raising a family until the last had left for college, how many parents would like to extend the experience by another ten years? Likewise, those whose satisfaction comes from climbing the career ladder might well ask what there would be to do for fifteen years after one had been CEO of Microsoft, a member of Congress, or the president of Harvard for a quarter of a century. Even less clear are the additions to personal happiness from more of the same of the less pleasant and less fulfilling activities in which so many of us are engaged so much of the time. It seems to be as the poet says: "We move and ever spend our lives amid the same things, and not by any length of life is any new pleasure hammered out."

Second, *seriousness and aspiration.* Could life be serious or meaningful without the limit of mortality? Is not the limit on our time the ground of our taking life seriously and living it passionately? To know and to feel that one goes around only once, and that the deadline is not out of sight, is for many people the necessary spur to the pursuit of something worthwhile. "Teach us to number our days," says the psalmist, "that we may get a heart of wisdom." To number our days is the condition for making them count. Homer's immortals—Zeus and Hera, Apollo and Athena—for all their eternal beauty and youthfulness, live shallow and rather frivolous lives, their passions only transiently engaged, in first this and then that. They live as spectators of the mortals, who by comparison have depth, aspiration, genuine feeling, and hence a real center in their lives. Mortality makes life matter.

There may be some activities, especially in some human beings, that do not require finitude as a spur. A powerful desire for understanding can do without external proddings, let alone one related to mortality; and as there is never too much time to learn and to understand, longer, more vigorous life might be simply a boon. The best sorts of friendship, too, seem capable of indefinite growth, especially where growth is somehow tied to learning—though one may wonder whether real friendship doesn't depend in part on the shared perceptions of a common fate. But, in any case, I suspect that these are among the rare exceptions. For most activities, and for most of us, I think it is crucial that we recognize and feel the force of not having world enough and time.

A third matter, *beauty and love.* Death, says Wallace Stevens, is the mother of beauty. What he means is not easy to say. Perhaps he means that only a mortal being, aware of his mortality and the transience and vulnerability of all natural things, is moved to make beautiful artifacts, objects that will last, objects whose order will be immune to decay as their maker is not, beautiful objects that will bespeak and beautify a world that needs beautification, beautiful objects for other mortal beings who can appreciate what they cannot themselves make because of a taste for the beautiful, a taste perhaps connected to awareness of the ugliness of decay.

Perhaps the poet means to speak of natural beauty as well, which beauty—unlike that of objects of art—depends on its *im*permanence. Could the beauty of flowers depend on the fact that they will soon wither? Does the beauty of spring warblers depend upon the fall drabness that precedes and follows? What about the fading, late afternoon winter light or the spreading sunset? Is the beautiful necessarily fleeting, a peak that cannot be sustained? Or does the poet mean not that the beautiful is beautiful because mortal, but that our appreciation of its beauty depends on our appreciation of mortality—in us and in the beautiful? Does not love swell before the beautiful precisely on recognizing that it (and we) will not always be? Is not our mortality the cause of our enhanced appreciation of the beautiful and the worthy and of our treasuring and loving them? How deeply could one deathless "human" being love another?

Fourth, there is the peculiarly human beauty of character, *virtue and moral excellence*. To be mortal means that it is possible to give one's life, not only in one moment, say, on the field of battle, but also in the many other ways in which we are able in action to rise above attachment to survival. Through moral courage, endurance, greatness of soul, generosity, devotion to justice—in acts great and small—we rise above our mere creatureliness, spending the precious coinage of the time of our lives for the sake of the noble and the good and the holy. We free ourselves from fear, from bodily pleasures, or from attachments to wealth—all largely connected with survival—and in doing virtuous deeds overcome the weight of our neediness; yet for this nobility, vulnerability and mortality are the necessary conditions. The immortals cannot be noble.

Of this, too, the poets teach. Odysseus, long suffering, has already heard the shade of Achilles' testimony in praise of life when he is offered immortal life by the nymph Calypso. She is a beautiful goddess, attractive, kind, yielding; she sings sweetly and weaves on a golden loom; her island is well ordered and lovely, free of hardships and suffering. Says the poet, "Even a god who came into that place would have admired what he saw, the heart delighted within him." Yet Odysseus turns down the offer to be lord of her household and immortal:

> *Goddess and queen, do not be angry with me. I myself know that all you say is true and that circumspect Penelope can never match the impression you make for beauty and stature. She is mortal after all, and you are immortal and ageless. But even so, what I want and all my days I pine for is to go back to my house and see that day of my homecoming. And if some god batters me far out on the wine-blue water, I will endure it, keeping a stubborn spirit inside me, for already I have suffered much and done much hard work on the waves and in the fighting.*

To suffer, to endure, to trouble oneself for the sake of home, family, community, and genuine friendship, is truly to live, and is the clear choice of this exemplary mortal. This choice is both the mark of his excellence and the basis for the visible display of his excellence in deeds noble and just. Immortality is a kind of oblivion—like death itself.

But, someone might reasonably object, if mortality is such a blessing, why do so few cultures recognize it as such? Why do so many teach the promise of life after death, of something eternal, of something imperishable? This takes us to the heart of the matter.

What is the meaning of this concern with immortality? *Why* do we human beings seek immortality? Why do we want to live longer or forever? Is it really first and most because we do not want to die, because we do not want to leave this embodied life on earth or give up our earthly pastimes, because we want to see more and do more? I do not think so. This may be what we say, but it is not what we finally mean. Mortality as such is not our defect, nor bodily immortality our goal. Rather, mortality is at most a pointer, a derivative manifestation, or an accompaniment of some deeper deficiency. The promise of immortality and eternity answers rather to a deep truth about the human soul: the human soul yearns for, longs for, aspires to some condition, some state, some goal toward which our earthly activities are directed but which cannot be attained in earthly life. Our soul's reach exceeds our grasp; it seeks more than continuance; it reaches for something beyond us, something that for the most part eludes us. Our distress with mortality is the derivative manifestation of the conflict between the transcendent longings of the soul and the all-too-finite powers and fleshly concerns of the body.

What is it that we lack and long for but cannot reach? One possibility is completion in another person. For example, Plato's Aristophanes says we seek wholeness through complete and permanent bodily and psychic union with a unique human being whom we love, our "missing other half." Plato's Socrates, in contrast, says it is rather wholeness through wisdom, through comprehensive knowledge of the beautiful truth about the whole, that which philosophy seeks but can never attain. Yet again, biblical religion says we seek wholeness through dwelling in God's presence, love, and redemption—a restoration of innocent wholeheartedness lost in the Garden of Eden. But, please note, these and many other such accounts of human aspiration, despite their differences, all agree on this crucial point: man longs not so much for deathlessness as for wholeness, wisdom, goodness, and godliness—longings that cannot be satisfied fully in our embodied earthly life, the only life, by natural reason, we know we have. Hence the attractiveness of any prospect or promise of a different and thereby fulfilling life hereafter. The decisive inference is clear: none of these longings can be answered by prolonging earthly life.

Not even an unlimited amount of "more of the same" will satisfy our deepest aspirations.

If this is correct, there follows a decisive corollary regarding the battle against death. The human taste for immortality, for the imperishable and the eternal, is not a taste that the biomedical conquest of death could satisfy. We would still be incomplete; we would still lack wisdom; we would still lack God's presence and redemption. Mere continuance will not buy fulfillment. Worse, its pursuit threatens—already threatens—human happiness by distracting us from the goals toward which our souls naturally point. By diverting our aim, by misdirecting so much individual and social energy toward the goal of bodily immortality, we may seriously undermine our chances for living as well as we can and for satisfying to some extent, however incompletely, our deepest longings for what is best. The implication for human life is hardly nihilistic: once we acknowledge and accept our finitude, we can concern ourselves with living *well,* and care first and most for the *well-being* of our souls and not so much for their mere existence.

But perhaps this is all a mistake. Perhaps there is no such longing of the soul. Perhaps there is no soul. Certainly modern science doesn't speak about the soul; neither does medicine or even our *psychi*atrists, whose name means "healers of the soul." Perhaps we are just animals, complex ones to be sure, but animals nonetheless, content just to be here, frightened in the face of danger, avoiding pain, seeking pleasure.

Curiously, however, biology has its own view of our nature and its inclinations. Biology also teaches about transcendence, though it eschews talk about the soul. Biology has long shown us a feasible way to rise above our finitude and to participate in something permanent and eternal: I refer not to stem cells but to procreation—the bearing and caring for offspring, for the sake of which many animals risk and even sacrifice their lives. Indeed, in all higher animals, reproduction *as such* implies both the acceptance of the death of self and participation in its transcendence. The salmon, willingly swimming upstream to spawn and die, makes vivid this universal truth.

But man is natured for more than spawning. Human biology teaches how our life points beyond itself—to our offspring, to our community, to our species. Like the other animals, man is built for reproduction. More than the other animals, man is also built for sociality. And, alone among the animals, man is also built for culture—not only through capacities to transmit and receive skills and techniques, but also through capacities for shared beliefs, opinions, rituals, traditions. We are built with leanings toward, and capacities for, perpetuation. Is it not possible that aging and mortality are part of this construction and that the rate of aging and the human life span have been selected for their usefulness to the task of perpetuation? Could not extending the human life span place a great strain on our nature, jeopardizing our project and depriving us of success? Interestingly, perpetuation is a goal that *is* attainable, a transcendence of self that *is* (largely) realizable. Here is a form of participating in the enduring that is open to us, without qualification—provided, that is, that we remain open to it.

Biological considerations aside, simply to covet a prolonged life span for ourselves is both a sign and a cause of our failure to open ourselves to procreation and to any higher purpose. It is probably no accident that it is a generation whose intelligentsia proclaim the death of God and the meaninglessness of life that embarks on life's indefinite prolongation and that seeks to cure the emptiness of life by extending it forever. For the desire to prolong youthfulness is not only a childish desire to eat one's life and keep it; it is also an expression of a childish and narcissistic wish incompatible with devotion to posterity. It seeks an endless present, isolated from anything truly eternal and severed from any true continuity with past and future. It is in principle hostile to children because children, those who come after, are those who will take one's place; *they* are life's answer to mortality, and their presence in one's house is a constant reminder that one no longer belongs to the frontier generation. One cannot pursue agelessness for oneself and remain faithful to the spirit and meaning of perpetuation.

In perpetuation, we send forth not just the seed of our bodies, but also the bearer of our hopes, our truths, and those of our tradition. If our children are to flower, we need to sow them well and nurture them, cultivate them in rich and wholesome soil, clothe them in fine and decent opinions and mores, and direct them toward the highest light, to grow straight and tall—that they may take our place as we took that of those who planted us and made way for us, so that in time they, too, may make way and plant. But if they are truly to flower, we must go to seed; we must wither and give ground.

Against these considerations, the clever ones will propose that if we could do away with death, we would do away with the need for posterity. But that is a self-serving and shallow answer, one that thinks of life and aging solely in terms of the state of the body. It ignores the psychological effects simply of the passage of time—of experiencing and learning about the way things are. After a while, no matter how healthy we are, no matter how respected and well placed we are socially, most of us cease to look upon the world with fresh eyes. Little surprises us, nothing shocks us, righteous indignation at injustice dies out. We have seen it all already, seen it all. We have often been deceived, we have made many mistakes of our own. Many of us become small-souled, having been humbled not by bodily decline or the loss of loved ones but by life itself. So our ambition also begins to flag, or at least our noblest ambitions. As we grow older, Aristotle already noted, we "aspire to nothing great and exalted and crave the mere necessities and comforts of existence." At some point, most of us turn and say to our intimates, Is this all there is? We settle, we accept our situation—if we are lucky enough to be able to accept it. In many ways, perhaps in the most profound ways, most of us go to sleep long before our deaths—and we might even do so earlier in life if death no longer spurred us to make something of ourselves.

In contrast, it is in the young where aspiration, hope, freshness, boldness, and openness spring anew, even when they take the form of overturning our monuments. Immortality for oneself through children may be a delusion, but participating in the natural and eternal renewal of human possibility through children is not—not even in today's world.

For it still stands as it did when Homer made Glaukos say to Diomedes:

> As is the generation of leaves, so is that of humanity. The wind scatters the leaves to the ground, but the live timber burgeons with leaves again in the season of spring returning. So one generation of man will grow while another dies.

And yet it also still stands, as this very insight of Homer's itself reveals, that human beings are in another respect unlike the leaves; that the eternal renewal of human beings embraces also the eternally human possibility of learning and self-awareness; that we, too, here and now may participate with Homer, with Plato, with the Bible, yes with Descartes and Bacon, in catching at least some glimpse of the enduring truths about nature, God, and human affairs; and that we, too, may hand down and perpetuate this pursuit of wisdom and goodness to our children and our children's children. Children and their education, not growth hormone and perpetual organ replacement, are life's—and wisdom's—answer to mortality.

This ancient Homeric wisdom is, in fact, not so far from traditional Jewish wisdom. For although we believe that life is good and long life is better, we hold something higher than life itself to be best. We violate one Shabbat so that the person whose life is saved may observe many Shabbatoth. We are obliged to accept death rather than commit idolatry, murder, or sexual outrage. Though we love life and drink *L'Chaim,* we have been taught of old to love wisdom and justice and godliness more; among Jews, at least until recently, teachers were more revered than doctors. Regarding immortality, God Himself declares—in the Garden of Eden story—that human beings, once they have attained the burdensome knowledge of good and bad, should not have access to the tree of life. Instead, they are to cleave to the Torah as a tree of life, a life-perfecting path to righteousness and holiness. Unlike the death-defying Egyptians, those ancient precursors of the quest for bodily immortality, the Children of Israel do not mummify or embalm their dead; we bury our ancestors but keep them alive in memory, and, accepting our mortality, we look forward to the next generation. Indeed, the mitzvah to be fruitful and multiply, when rightly understood, celebrates not the life we have and selfishly would cling to, but the life that replaces us.

Confronted with the growing moral challenges posed by biomedical technology, let us resist the siren song of the conquest of aging and death. Let us cleave to our ancient wisdom and lift our voices and properly toast *L'Chaim,* to life beyond our own, to the life of our grandchildren and their grandchildren. May they, God willing, know health and long life, but especially so that they may also know the pursuit of truth and righteousness and holiness. And may they hand down and perpetuate this pursuit of what is humanly finest to succeeding generations for all time to come.

Heaven and Earth

from *The Sun*

When I first arrive from Boston, L.A. looks to me like one giant garbage heap, a big emperor with no clothes. I can't believe that the rich and famous drive the same featureless freeways I do; that movie stars reach the zenith of their careers in the Dorothy Chandler Pavilion, with its Liberace-style chandeliers; that immigrants have come here from their unspoiled homelands to build cheesy Hindu palaces and Korean barbecues inexplicably designed to resemble the Parthenon. There are some pockets of town so choked with concrete and cars, so devoid of greenery, humanity, and charm, that a near-suicidal depression engulfs me each time I pass through them.

But slowly, over the course of months, small treasures begin to reveal themselves: Lilies of the Nile rise from litter-strewn medians. Along the curbs of turn lanes, men sell garnet cherries, roses the color of old ivory, and dusty bags of peanuts.

A few years after my arrival, I move with my husband to Koreatown, a colorful neighborhood where our jewel of an apartment gleams quietly amid a cacophonous welter of Salvadoran taco vendors, alley-cruising crack-heads, and ambulance sirens wailing the news that yet another Seoul-trained driver has merrily run a red light. Though still assaulted by billboards for Disneyland, Universal Studios, and Magic Mountain, I discover Huntington Gardens, the Hollywood Farmers' Market, the downtown library. I constantly remind myself that if the traffic is fiendish, the weather is paradisaical; that if the city is too crowded, all these people create an infectious level of creative energy; that if it is too noisy, it makes me that much more grateful for every moment of silence.

I start to discern an underground network of seemingly inconsequential acts of goodness: The guy in line ahead of me at the supermarket sees I have only three items and waves me through. My mercurial neighbor Emil pads upstairs with a bowl of minestrone in apology for his thousandth unjustified snit. When my father dies, my usually undemonstrative tennis partner brings me a copy of Jane Kenyon's *Let Evening Come.* I ponder the mystery of how the smallest human touch brings comfort all out of proportion to the size of the gesture. I start going to church again and find that all around the city are quiet sanctuaries, places of prayer, oases of dark tranquillity smelling of incense and wax. Night and day— during shoot-outs and stabbings, mud slides and earthquakes— candles burn in red glass above the body of Christ.

I do not go to Mass to make myself "better." I go because, in the dimmest reaches of my scattered, angst-ridden mind, there is something that wants me to get down on my knees and, in spite of my own suffering and all the suffering around me, give thanks. I go because I am beginning to believe that heaven is not in some other world, but shot through the broken world in which we live.

I notice another woman at morning Mass. She is pretty, with an angular face and short, curly hair. She carries a backpack and wears jeans, a heavy sweater, and a pair of faded blue Keds. And she is white, like me, a rarity in this neighborhood. I try to peg her. She's not rich, but not dirt poor either. A struggling artist? A social worker? A nurse? When we greet each other during the sign of peace, her hand is like sandpaper. A sculptor? A painter? Her name is Barbara, I find out, and she's gone to Mass daily for years. We chat now and then, and one day I ask her what she does. She pauses for a second, then says, "I dance."

"A dancer!" I exclaim. "Jazz, or ballet, or . . . ?"

"Come to Saint Thomas the Apostle on Sunday," she says, "and I'll tell you all about it."

Koreatown is bad enough, but Saint Thomas the Apostle is on the edge of Pico-Union, a Hispanic neighborhood so poor, noisy, and gang filled that when we Anglos pass each other on the street there, we exchange sickly smiles of relief, as if to say, "Isn't it amazing; nobody's shot *me* yet either." The fact that Barbara attends church and possibly even lives there intrigues me. I'm more curious about her than ever.

When I show up for Mass on Sunday, I spot Barbara in a pew down front, all dressed up in a gray beret, turquoise angora sweater, gray kick-pleated skirt, nylons, and spectator pumps. She's obviously a regular, talking a mile a minute with everyone in sight. When she rises to give a reading, I notice her turned-out, dancer's feet, the muscled calves her jeans usually hide.

"Come on. We'll have coffee," she says afterward, grabbing my arm. "But first, let's go to the rummage sale." Out back in the parking lot, she paws through heaps of used clothing and toys, greeting friends and keeping up a running commentary in her piercing New York accent. She holds up a flowered jacket ("Won't this be pretty for spring, and only a quarter!"); picks out an armload of stuffed animals ("I have friends with children"); rejects a two-dollar bottle of skin cream ("Too expensive"). The whole time I am thinking, *Where does she work? Does she have a boyfriend? How old is she—fifty? Older?*

Finally, she leads me to a pastry shop down the street, where the glass case holds pans of pink-frosted cake and the air smells of sugar and stale coffee. Barbara knows the owner, the owner's sister, and—it turns out after we settle at a table near the open door—every other person who walks down the sidewalk.

"Hey, Maverick, where are you living?" she calls out to a crew-cut gal in grease-stained fatigues, wearing a wreath of dog tags and a huge wooden cross around her neck.

"Still on the street," Maverick admits apologetically, and Barbara slips her a handful of change.

"So, how did you end up in Pico-Union?" I ask.

In between sips of weak coffee and bites of air-filled croissants, she fills me in: She grew up in New York City, moved to L.A. in the seventies, and converted to Catholicism almost twenty years ago. Then God took her "out of the world" for seven years, during which time she cooked for the priests and taught dance in a former seminary in Italy. "It was cold and damp, totally medieval," she reports cheerfully. "Stone walls four feet thick, and when you opened a door, bats might fly out." Now she lives in an apartment down the street, with six dogs, eleven cats, and her senile Armenian landlady. She takes the bus to Studio City five days a week for ballet classes.

"I've had the same teacher off and on for twenty-five years. He's always on my case," she says, laughing. "'Some people think they don't have to work!' he says. 'Some people think they can just light a couple of candles in church.'" Her eyes are lined with black, her head cocked like a bird's.

"So, do you dance professionally?" I ask. "I mean, do you put on shows, or what?"

"Not really," Barbara replies. "I don't dance for success or money or to be seen; I do it as a form of prayer. I think of it as offering up my time and pain and body to someone who needs it more than I do. I say the rosary all day, one Hail Mary for each plié."

"You dance . . . to pray?" I say.

"On weekends I shoo away the animals and set up a barre right in my room," she continues, while I stare at her callused hands. "When I'm really tired or lonely or discouraged, I try to think of Christ on the cross."

There is a long silence while I attempt to digest this scenario, to envision such a life. "What do you do for money?" I finally ask.

"Oh, I don't need much," Barbara says vaguely. "God provides. Of course, it hasn't been easy: for a long time I felt totally isolated and thought I was going crazy. But finally I learned how to integrate my dancing with the rest of the world, and now my life is so incredibly rich and abundant."

I study Barbara closely. The radiant smile is missing a tooth in the lower jaw; the angora sweater is lightly matted with dog hair. She is like one of those holograms that show a mountain at sunrise and, tilted a fraction of a millimeter, the same scene at sunset. Is she a nut case, or some kind of saint? Am I even capable of judging? Does sainthood require perfection, or just a willingness to surrender our entire selves, including our imperfections, to love?

She points across the street to a man collecting bottles in a shopping cart. "Do you know what hard work that is?" she says. "I always save my glass for them."

Then she leans in, puts a roughened hand on mine, and whispers, "Hard times are coming, and all over, God is planting seeds, preparing people—not showy people, but little people. You don't know: it could be that raggedy old lady over there begging for change who's going to save us all."

Walking home, past the brown faces whose secrets are concealed from my white one, I think, *How many people like Barbara can there be in L.A.? What are the chances of finding one of them?* I peer into storefronts as I pass by and see a world parallel to mine, familiar yet alien. A lone man browses a sparsely stocked record shop. Candles gleam from the dim interior of a botanica selling magic charms and herbs. Upside-down water glasses glint atop white tablecloths in a pocket-sized restaurant. The smells of spit-roasted chicken, soapy perfume, and overripe bananas drift into the street.

On the sidewalk in front of Doti's Bridal Shop, sandwiched between a nail salon and a video store, stands a mannequin in a satin wedding gown. From half a block away, her dress is as shiny as licked lips, so white it has blue highlights in it. The sequins along the breast sparkle like diamonds, and the billowing hem grazes two white satin high heels topped by lush bows. Her eyes are raised hopefully heavenward; one hand is lifted as if in song. In the background, the skyscrapers of downtown glow faintly green through the smog, like dollar bills.

As I come up beside her, I see the crooked garland of wax flowers, the brittle blond hair, the missing clump of fake eyelashes, the broken index finger of the raised hand clumsily glued back on at the middle joint, the satin rosettes, dingy and drooping, the flesh-colored plaster chest above the sweetheart neckline, veiled with a layer of gray grit.

And somehow the imperfection makes her more beautiful still. Because isn't that always the way it is? And isn't it always, in the end, somehow all right?

Gospel

from *The New Yorker*

The new grass rising in the hills,
the cows loitering in the morning chill,
a dozen or more old browns hidden
in the shadows of the cottonwoods
beside the streambed. I go higher
to where the road gives up and there's
only a faint path strewn with lupine
between the mountain oaks. I don't
ask myself what I'm looking for.
I didn't come for answers
to a place like this, I came to walk
on the earth, still cold, still silent.
Still ungiving, I've said to myself,
although it greets me with last year's
dead thistles and this year's
hard spines, early-blooming
wild onions, the curling remains
of spider's cloth. What did I bring
to the dance? In my back pocket
a crushed letter from a woman
I've never met bearing bad news
I can do nothing about. So I wander
these woods half sightless while
a west wind picks up in the trees
clustered above. The pines make

a music like no other, rising and
falling like a distant surf at night
that calms the darkness before
first light. "Soughing" we call it, from
Old English, no less. How weightless
words are when nothing will do.

BARRY LOPEZ

The Naturalist

from *Orion*

My home stands on a wooded bench, set back about two hundred feet from the north bank of the McKenzie River in western Oregon. Almost every day I go down to the river with no intention but to sit and watch. I have been watching the river for thirty years, just the three or four hundred yards of it I can see from the forested bank, a run of clear, quick water about 350 feet wide. If I have learned anything here, it's that each time I come down, something I don't know yet will reveal itself.

If it's a man's intent to spend thirty years staring at a river's environs in order to arrive at an explanation of the river, he should find some other way to spend his time. To assert this, that a river can't be known, does not to my way of thinking denigrate science, any more than saying a brown bear can't be completely known. The reason this is true is because the river is not a thing, in the way a Saturn V rocket engine is a thing. It is an expression of biological life, in dynamic relation to everything around it—the salmon within, the violet-green swallow swooping its surface, alder twigs floating its current, a mountain lion sipping its bank water, the configurations of basalt that break its flow and give it timbre and tone.

In my experience with field biologists, those fresh to a task—say, caracara research—are the ones most likely to give themselves a deadline—ten years, say—against which they will challenge themselves to know all there is to know about that falcon. It never works. More seasoned field biologists, not as driven by a need to prove themselves, are content to concentrate on smaller arenas of knowledge. Instead of speaking definitively of coyote, armadillo, or wigeon, they tend to say, "This one animal, that one time, did this in that place." It's the approach to nature many hunting and gathering peoples take, to this day. The view suggests a horizon rather than a boundary for knowing, toward which we are always walking.

A great shift in the Western naturalist's frame of mind over the past fifty years, it seems to me, has been the growth of this awareness: to get anywhere deep with a species, you must immerse yourself in its milieu. You must study its ecology. If you wish to understand the caracara, you need to know a great deal about exactly where the caracara lives when; and what the caracara's relationships are with each of the many components of that place, including its weathers, its elevations, its seasonal light.

A modern naturalist, then, is no longer someone who goes no further than a stamp collector, mastering nomenclature and field marks. She or he knows a local flora and fauna as pieces of an inscrutable mystery, increasingly deep, a unity of organisms Western culture has been trying to elevate itself above since at least Mesopotamian times. The modern naturalist, in fact, has now become a kind of emissary in this, working to reestablish good relations with all the biological components humanity has excluded from its moral universe.

Sitting by the river, following mergansers hurtling past a few inches off its surface or eyeing an otter hauled out on a boulder with (in my binoculars) the scales of a trout glistening on its face, I ask myself not: What do I know?—that Canada geese have begun to occupy the nests of osprey here in recent springs, that harlequin ducks are now expanding their range to include this stretch of the river—but: Can I put this together? Can I imagine the river as a definable entity, evolving in time?

How is a naturalist today supposed to imagine the place between nature and culture? How is he or she to act, believing as many do that Western civilization is compromising its own biology by investing so heavily in material progress? And knowing that many in positions of corporate and political power regard nature as inconvenient, an inefficiency in their plans for a smoothly running future?

The question of how to behave, it seems to me, is nerve-wracking to contemplate because it is related to two areas of particular discomfort for naturalists. One is how to keep the issue of spirituality free of religious commentary; the other is how to manage emotional grief and moral indignation in pursuits so closely tied to science, with its historical claim to objectivity.

One response to the first concern is that the naturalist's spirituality is one with no icons (unlike religion's), and it is also one that enforces no particular morality. In fact, for many it is not much more than the residue of awe that modern life has not (yet) erased, a sensitivity to the realms of life that are not yet corralled by dogma. The second concern, how a person with a high regard for objectivity deals with emotions like grief and outrage, like so many questions about the trajectory of modern culture, is only a request to express love without being punished. It is, more deeply, an expression of the desire that love be on an equal footing with power when it comes to social change.

It is of some help here, I think, to consider where the modern naturalist has come from, to trace her or his ancestry. Since the era of Gilbert White in eighteenth-century England, by some reckonings, we have had a recognizable cohort of people who study the natural world and write about it from personal experience. White and his allies wrote respectfully about nature, and their treatments were meant to be edifying for the upper classes. Often, the writer's intent was merely to remind the reader not to overlook natural wonders, which were the evidence of divine creation. Darwin, in his turn, brought unprecedented depth to this kind of work. He accentuated the need for scientific rigor in the naturalist's inquiries, but he also suggested that certain far-reaching implications existed. Entanglements. People, too, he said, were biological, subject to the same forces of mutation as the finch. A hundred years further on, a man like Aldo Leopold could be characterized as a keen observer, a field biologist who understood a deeper connection (or reconnection) with nature, but also as someone aware of the role wildlife science had begun to play in politics. With Rachel Carson, the artificial but sometimes dramatic divide that can separate the scientist, with her allegiance to objective, peer-reviewed data, from the naturalist, for whom biology always raises issues of propriety, becomes apparent.

Following Leopold's and Carson's generations came a generation of naturalists that combined White's enthusiasm and sense of the nonmaterial world; Leopold's political consciousness and feelings of shared fate; and Carson's sense of rectitude and citizenship. For the first time, however, the humanists among this cadre of naturalists were broadly educated in the sciences. They had grown up with Watson and Crick, not to mention sodium fluoroacetate, Ebola virus ecology, melting ice shelves, and the California condor.

The modern naturalist, acutely even depressingly aware of the planet's shrinking and eviscerated habitats, often feels compelled to do more than merely register the damage. The impulse to protest, however, is often stifled by feelings of defensiveness, a fear of being misread. Years of firsthand field observation can be successfully challenged in court today by a computer modeler with not an hour's experience in the field. A carefully prepared analysis of stream flow, migration corridors, and long-term soil stability in a threatened watershed can be written off by the press (with some assistance from the opposition) as a hatred of mankind.

At the opening of the twenty-first century the naturalist, then, knows an urgency White did not foresee and a political scariness Leopold might actually have imagined in his worst moments. Further, in the light of the still-unfolding lessons of Charles Darwin's work, he or she knows that a cultural exemption from biological imperatives remains in the realm of science fiction.

In contemporary native villages, one might posit today that all people actively engaged in the land—hunting, fishing, gathering, traveling, camping—are naturalists, and say that some are better than others according to their gifts of observation. Native peoples differ here, however, from the Gilbert Whites, the Darwins, the Leopolds, and the Rachel Carsons in that accumulating and maintaining this sort of information is neither avocation nor profession. It is more comparable to religious activity, behavior steeped in tradition and considered essential for the maintenance of good living. It is a moral and an inculcated stance, a way of being. While White and others, by contrast, were searching for a way back *in* to nature, native peoples (down to the present in some instances), for whatever reason, have been at pains not to leave. The distinction is important because "looking for a way back in" is a striking characteristic of the modern naturalist's frame of mind.

Gilbert White stood out among his social peers because what he pursued—a concrete knowledge of the natural world around Selbourne in Hampshire—was unrelated to politics or progress. As such, it could be dismissed politically. Fascinating stuff, but inconsequential. Since then, almost every naturalist has borne the supercilious judgments of various sophisticates who thought the naturalist a romantic, a sentimentalist, a bucolic—or worse; and more latterly, the condescension of some scientists who thought the naturalist not rigorous, not analytic, not detached enough.

A naturalist of the modern era—an experientially based, well-versed devotee of natural ecosystems—is ideally among the best informed of the American electorate when it comes to the potentially catastrophic environmental effects of political decisions. The contemporary naturalist, it has turned out—again, scientifically grounded, politically attuned, field experienced, library enriched—is no custodian of irrelevant knowledge, no mere adept differentiating among *Empidonax* flycatchers on the wing, but a kind of citizen whose involvement in the political process, in the debates of public life, in the evolution of literature and the arts, has become crucial.

The bugbear in all of this—and there is one—is the role of field experience, the degree to which the naturalist's assessments are empirically grounded in firsthand knowledge. How much of what the contemporary naturalist claims to know about animals and the ecosystems they share with humans derives from what he has read, what he has heard, what he has seen televised? What part of what the naturalist has sworn his or her life to comes from firsthand experience, from what the body knows?

One of the reasons native people still living in some sort of close, daily association with their ancestral lands are so fascinating to those who arrive from the rural, urban, and suburban districts of civilization is because they are so possessed of authority. They radiate the authority of firsthand encounters. They are storehouses of it. They have not read about it, they have not compiled notebooks and assembled documentary photographs. It is so important that they remember it. When you ask them for specifics, the depth of what they can offer is scary. It's scary because it's not tidy, it doesn't lend itself to summation. By the very way that they say that they know, they suggest they are still learning something that cannot, in the end, be known.

It is instructive to consider how terrifying certain interlopers—rural developers, government planners, and other apostles of change—can seem to such people when, on the basis of a couple of books the interloper has read or a few (usually summer) weeks in the field with a pair of binoculars and some radio collars, he suggests a new direction for the local ecosystem and says he can't envision any difficulties.

In all the years I have spent standing or sitting on the banks of this river, I have learned this: the more knowledge I have, the greater becomes the mystery of what holds that knowledge together, this reticulated miracle called an ecosystem. The longer I watch the river, the more amazed I become (afraid, actually, sometimes) at the confidence of those people who after a few summer seasons here are ready to tell the county commissioners, emphatically, what the river is, to scribe its meaning for the outlander.

Firsthand knowledge is enormously time consuming to acquire; with its dallying and lack of end points, it is also out of phase with the short-term demands of modern life. It teaches humility and fallibility, and so represents an antithesis to progress. It makes a stance of awe in the witness of natural process seem appropriate, and attempts at summary knowledge naive. Historically, tyrants have sought selectively to eliminate firsthand knowledge when its sources lay outside their control. By silencing those with problematic firsthand experiences, they reduced the number of potential contradictions in their political or social designs, and so they felt safer. It is because natural process—how a mountain range disintegrates or how nitrogen cycles through a forest—is beyond the influence of the visionaries of globalization that firsthand knowledge of a country's ecosystems, a rapidly diminishing pool of expertise and awareness, lies at the radical edge of any country's political thought.

Over the years I have become a kind of naturalist, although I previously rejected the term because I felt I did not know enough, that my knowledge was far too incomplete. I never saw myself in the guise of Gilbert White, but I respected his work enough to have sought out his grave in Selbourne and expressed there my gratitude for his life. I never took a course in biology, not even in high school, and so it seemed to me that I couldn't really be any sort of authentic naturalist. What biology I was able to learn I took from books, from veterinary clinics, from an apprenticeship to my homeland in the Cascades, from field work with Western biologists, and from traveling with hunters and gatherers. As a naturalist, I have taken the lead of native tutors, who urged me to participate in the natural world, not hold it before me as an object of scrutiny.

When I am by the river, therefore, I am simply there. I watch it closely, repeatedly, and feel myself not apart from it. I do not feel compelled to explain it. I wonder sometimes, though, whether I am responding to the wrong question when it comes to speaking "for nature." Perhaps the issue is not whether one has the authority to claim to be a naturalist, but whether those who see themselves as naturalists believe they have the authority to help shape the world. What the naturalist-as-emissary intuits, I think, is that if he or she doesn't speak out, the political debate will be left instead to those seeking to benefit their various constituencies. Strictly speaking, a naturalist has no constituency.

To read the newspapers today, to merely answer the phone, is to know the world is in flames. People do not have time for the sort of empirical immersion I believe crucial to any sort of wisdom. This terrifies me, but I, too, see the developers' bulldozers arrayed at the mouth of every canyon, poised at the edge of every plain. And the elimination of these lands, I know, will further reduce the extent of the blueprints for undamaged life. After the last undomesticated stretch of land is brought to heel, there will be only records—strips of film and recording tape, computer printouts, magazine articles, books, laser-beam surveys—of these immensities. And then any tyrant can tell us what it meant, and in which direction we should now go. In this scenario, the authority of the grizzly bear will be replaced by the authority of a charismatic who says he represents the bear. And the naturalist— the ancient emissary to a world civilization wished to be rid of, a world it hoped to transform into a chemical warehouse, the same uneasy emissary who intuited that to separate nature from culture wouldn't finally work—will be an orphan. He will become a dealer in myths.

What being a naturalist has come to mean to me, sitting my mornings and evenings by the river, hearing the clack of herons through the creak of swallows over the screams of osprey under the purl of fox sparrows, so far removed from White and Darwin and Leopold and even Carson, is this: Pay attention to the mystery. Apprentice to the best apprentices. Rediscover in nature your own biology. Write and speak with appreciation for all you have been gifted. Recognize that a politics with no biology, or a politics without field biology, or a political platform in which human biological requirements form but one plank, is a vision of the gates of Hell.

BRET LOTT

The Ironic Stance and the Law of Diminishing Returns

from *Image*

PART ONE, *in which the Author cites Opaque Examples of what he Thinks he Means in Giving this Essay its Title*

Maybe this:

Every time I see the bumper sticker *Question Authority!* I want to ask the owner of the vehicle, Who are you to tell me what to do?

Thus fulfilling his directive to empower myself, and in the same instant nullifying his authority to do so. We are both left, as a consequence, nowhere and with nothing.

There. That sums it up quite nicely.

Or, maybe, this will work:

My student comes into the office, winded as they all are at the climb up here, three flights to the attic of this old Victorian in the center of campus. The last flight is up a narrow staircase that shoots like a ladder to my office door, the door cut at an angle to allow for the pitch of the roof, so that in addition to the climb my students must also duckwalk past the threshold, then emerge into a room with a wonderful dormer that leads out onto the roof, a room with pitched ceilings plenty high enough to let them stand in, the short walls lined with books and more books.

Because of all this, I have the best office on campus: the students who come to see me *want* to come to see me.

Lee is one of them. He wants to be a writer, wants to be one with all his heart. He's told me this plenty of times while sitting up there in that office, the two of us talking about what it means to write and to be a writer.

I believe him. He wants to be writer.

Today we're going to talk about a story he dropped off in my mailbox downstairs last week. Even though his face is flushed from the climb up here, I can see as he finally stands up straight in the room that he knows this one didn't work. I can see it in the way he's already smiling, slowly shaking his head at me. He takes off his backpack, sets it in one of the two chairs opposite my desk, then sinks into the other. He stops grinning, looks at the carpet, then at the desk edge before him, then at me. Then he grins again.

I say, "What's wrong?" though I know precisely.

He says, "There's just no heart to it."

I reach out to the desk top, pick up a paper clip, and tap it, quietly, on the blotter. I say, "Why do you say that?" and now I am grinning too, because he and I both know. This is the third story he's turned in this semester with just the same problem.

"Yeah, yeah," he says. He shoots out a breath, seems to sink even lower into the chair. He's grinning even bigger now, slowly shaking his head. "I know exactly why," he says. He says, "I'm not happy with it."

"Why?" I say, tapping the paper clip. His bookbag is partway open on the chair beside him, and I can see in there copies of *Libra* and *White Noise*. Texts for the DeLillo special topics course he's taking.

Don DeLillo: his favorite writer this semester.

He shakes his head one more time, and, so chagrined it's as though he's confessing to a crime, he says, "I'm just so afraid of being cheesy."

Let's try this one on:

A couple of years ago I was a visiting writer at a low-residency MFA program where I gave a lecture on creative nonfiction. The lecture included several passages regarding my two children and made reference to my love for my wife; in it I confessed to knowing nothing about writing and that this not knowing was in fact my own key to trying to understand it all. Later that day I gave a reading of a personal essay in which I was revealed to be the fool at the center of my own life, a recurring theme in pretty much all of my essays.

But an odd thing persisted that day, while I spoke to people, while I shook hands after the reading, while I fielded questions after the lecture: I couldn't read the crowd. I couldn't gauge how I was doing, many of the students stone-faced, reticent, it seemed. Reserved at and in my presence.

Then, the next morning at breakfast in the cafeteria, a woman came up to me at my table, where I was eating alone.

Still as stone-faced as most everyone had been the entire day before, she said to me, "Several of the women in our program were talking last night." Her hands were together in front of her, her mouth a straight line. It seemed what she wanted to say was taking some effort, as though this were work. "Your lecture and the essay made you sound like a sensitive person. As though you knew what you were talking about." She paused, nodded at her words, her eyebrows together in what seemed a kind of bestowal of something important upon me.

I nodded, smiled, a little appreciative, a little apprehensive. "Thank you," I said.

"We decided that we believe you," she said then. "What you said about writing, and your sensitivity. We just wanted you to know we believe you." She nodded again, the bestowal accomplished.

"Thank you," I said, and I know I blinked a couple of times too many. "I'm flattered," I said, and smiled, nodded myself, blinked one or two more times.

I'd been believed through democracy. They had voted, and reached a consensus: the visiting writer really did know nothing. And their decision to believe so was a gift to me, they wanted me to know.

The woman gave a final, quick smile, then went to her table, where she sat down among several other women to finish her breakfast.

I still blink a couple times too many when I think of that morning, that breakfast, that belief reached by ballot.

PART TWO, *or The Law of Diminishing Returns*

(The tendency for a continuing application of effort or skill toward a particular project or goal to decline in effectiveness after a certain level of result has been achieved.)

"Irony," a Hollywood mogul once said, "is what goes over the heads of the audience."

Its etymological pedigree goes back to the Greek *eiron,* which means dissembler, or one who disguises or conceals behind a false appearance. The most famous dissembler, of course, was Socrates. In Plato's *Apology,* Socrates testifies to his systematically alienating everyone who is said to have wisdom by asking each a series of leading questions designed, according to Socrates, to find someone wiser than himself in order to disprove the oracle at Delphi's pronouncement that Socrates was indeed the wisest.

Those dissembled, though, saw all this differently. One student of Plato's, Tyrtamus, left his tutelage for Plato's greatest rival, Aristotle, who subsequently named him Theophrastos, or "divine speaker." Theo (if I may) was the first to synthesize and survey the beliefs and notions and philosophies of his predecessors, and in the following assessment of irony, written sometime around 300 B.C., we can see clearly the kind of bitterness engendered by the dissemblers in those who have been, as it were, Socratically ironized (one can almost see here as well the specter of a *proto*–Jerry Seinfeld):

> *The ironical man is he who approaches his enemies and desires to have talk with them and let all hatred cease. He praises people to their faces, and behind their backs inveighs against them, but when they lose lawsuits bewails their fate with them. . . . Never does he admit that he is doing anything: he is always considering. He will pretend he is just this moment come, or he was late or he has been ill. To borrowers or those calling for a subscription he gives a large sum and says he is not rich. When he has something for sale he says he never sells, and when he does not wish to sell declares he will. He will hear but pretend he did not, or see and say he never saw. If he has admitted something he declares he has forgotten all about it. He will say he will see about it or sometimes has no knowledge whatever, or again is quite amazed, or perhaps he had thought so, had he not? . . . Men so double and designing in character are more to be guarded against than serpents.*

There are further definitions of irony, further curlicues and eddies and tendrils that have evolved through the eons, from Webster's ("the use of words to express something other than and especially the opposite of the literal meaning") to the venerable Fowler's take on the subject:

> *Irony is a form of utterance that postulates a double audience, consisting of one party that hearing shall hear & shall not understand, & another party that, when more is meant than meets the ear, is aware both of that more & of the outsiders' incomprehension.*

But what happens when the party that is aware both of that more and the outsider's incomprehension becomes unable to extract himself from that cold-blooded cocoon of detachment that knowing all this can become?

What happens when Freud enters the picture, and we are suddenly and irrevocably shackled to Self-consciousness, all of us made to believe our emotions are generic, our dreams predictable, our neuroses placable, our imaginations hard-wired to nothing more than our fear of death and predilection for sex?

"Before Freud, our feelings belonged to us," writes the novelist and short story writer Roxana Robinson in an essay in the *New York Times Books Review* on the absence of passion, of powerful feeling in contemporary fiction. Before Freud, our feelings "were powerful, violent, necessary, but private. They were ours. Freud took our feelings over and taught us to analyze them, which turned us into the objects of our own dissection. The idea of passionate engagement came to seem naive and foolish as we moved from an innocent, 19th-century, pre-Freudian childhood to a 20th-century adulthood, detached and analytical."

What happens when art, like science (included in the latter the new psychoanalysis), finds modernity its siren call? The term *modern* meant, until quite recently, common, vogueish—what was not to be emulated, as it had no depth or purpose beyond its own presence as something "new." In 1506, when Michelangelo was a young man and ancient Rome was still being excavated and rediscovered, the statue *Laocoön* was uncovered and paraded through the streets as being a fantastic revelation of pure beauty, and even though Michelangelo had already sculpted what was to be his own most enduring and beautiful work of art, the *Pietà,* he was so genuinely moved by the dynamic emotion caught in *Laocoön* that, later in life, he went on record as saying he'd staked his entire artistic life on that particular statue, finished in the second century and lost for so many hundreds of years. The Pre-Raphaelite Brotherhood, in reaction to the industrialization of England, founded their own school on the artistic integrity of an artist dead and buried for a couple hundred years.

But it wasn't until the mid–nineteenth century that the term *modern* was accepted as a critical term, one that could be applied in a benevolent way to the creation of art. Jacques Barzun, writing in his monumental and indispensable history *From Dawn to Decadence: 1500 to the Present—500 Years of Western Civilization,* writes of the outbreak of Modern,

> *Thanks to this changed view of modernity, art joined science in spreading the 20C dogma that latest is best. Modernist Man looks forward, a born futureist, thus reversing the old presumption about ancestral wisdom and the value of prudent conservation. It follows that whatever is old is obsolete, wrong, dull, or all three. . . .*

And what happens when the Great War turns out to be only the first one, and the Second turns out to have been a kind of fragmentation bomb that leads to an array of wars and rumors of wars still blossoming around us to this day?

What happens when *news* becomes an element of our every waking moment, and politicians—liberal and conservative both—break apart words and their meanings before our very eyes and ears, no matter the smile all the while or the stern set of the jaw?

What happens when, now, a student walks up to you and says he's afraid of being cheesy, when what he means to say is, *I'm afraid of writing about love?*

What else can one do, other than deconstruct bumper stickers, stand fearfully *outside* of that ring that demarks one's heart open to the world, and wait to believe until you've consulted others?

Where else can our hearts be, save for hidden away in the cloak of our stance, our distance from others, our fear of appearing—oh, fate worse than death!—*impassioned?*

In the remarkable book *For Common Things: Irony, Trust, and Commitment in America Today,* Jedediah Purdy, a twenty-six-year-old wunderkind, writes,

> *Our leading cultural currency today is a version of the stubbornly flat skepticism that Toqueville observed. We practice a form of irony insistently doubtful of the qualities that would make us take another person seriously: the integrity of personality, sincere motivation, the idea that opinions are more than symptoms of fear or desire. We are wary of hope, because we see little that can support it. Believing in nothing much, especially not in people, is a point of vague pride, and conviction can seem embarrassingly naive. . . . So far as we are ironists, we are determined not to be made suckers. The great fear of the ironist is being caught out having staked a good part of his all on a false hope—personal, political, or both.*

I would here have to add artistic hope; that is, we don't want to be caught out having hope in art.

And as if to validate such a truth as this—that we don't want to be caught out having hope—another wunderkind has appeared on our literary scene almost simultaneously with Purdy's work. David Eggers's memoir, *A Heartbreaking Work of Staggering Genius,* is a book that purports to tell the tale of twenty-two-year-old Eggers himself whose parents both have died, leaving him to raise his kid brother, for the most part, alone. It's an interesting book, one that has been critically acclaimed for its innovative form and seemingly unflinching honesty, yet its author's ironic stance—the vantage point from which he coolly assesses his own aloofness—

makes one wonder, finally, what truth we have actually encountered in this story of a life visited so fully by tragedy.

This particular passage describes the devolution, as it were, of the magazine *Might* Eggers and his friend Moodie have founded; it's a funny passage—humor is a hallmark of the book as a whole—and I include it here as a means to show Eggers's dissembling of meaning itself, and so of himself as editor of what has become a meaningless magazine:

> *In the month or so since that first issue,* Might *has become something different. We are much less inspired than we were then, and going through with another one seems, on a certain level, more dutiful than impassioned. After all, the last thing we want from this, or at least the last thing I want from all this, is some kind of job. We have to avoid that kind of cruelly ironic [please note his use of the word* ironic*] fate—that we, the loud-mouths who so cloyingly espouse the unshackling of one's ideas about work and life themselves become slaves to something, to a schedule, obligated to advertisers, investors, keeping regular hours. . . .*
>
> *We begin a pattern of almost immediate opinion-reversal and self-devouring. Whatever the prevailing thinking, especially our own, we contradict it, reflexively. We change our minds about Wendy Kopp, the young go-getter we heralded in the first issue, and her much-celebrated Teach for America. Where we originally praised her gumption and her organization's goals—to bring young, enthusiastic, well-educated teachers into underprivileged schools for two years— now, in a 6,000-word piece that dominates the second issue, we fault the nonprofit for attempting to solve inner-city problems, largely black problems, with white uppermiddle-class college-educated solutions. "Paternalistic condescension," we say.*

"Enlightened self-interest," we sigh. "Noblesse oblige," we sneer. We quote a professor summing up: "A study of Teach for America tells us more about the ideological, even psychological needs of today's middle-class white and minority youth than it does about the underclass to whom the project is targeted."

Kaboom!

And yet the entire notion of irony's appearance in Eggers's book is denied by the author himself, as though being caught out even *having* a stance were some form of commitment. This passage is from the Appendix to *AHWOSG* that accompanies the paperback version, a cluster of pages and words that defend the young man's hardback edition from any misreadings by the masses. He writes,

You can't know how much it pains me to even have that word, the one beginning with i and ending in y, in this book. It is not a word I like to see, anywhere, much less type onto my own pages. It is beyond a doubt the most over-used and under-understood word we currently have. I have that i-word here only to make clear what was clear to, by my estimation, about 99.9% of original hardcover readers of this book: that there is almost no irony, whatsoever, within its covers. But to hear a few people tell it, this entire book, or most of it, was/is ironic. . . .

But irony isn't dead, despite the assertions by some that it is. Rather, as with the term *postmodern* ("a theory based on the belief that there can be no such thing as a single, or even a properly privileged point of view," to quote Mary Warnock in *Imagination and Time*), we are now inhabiting the *post-ironic* age, a term that posits we have gone beyond irony to a simple recognition of the absurd as our everyday, as our language, as the air we breathe.

Part Three, *in which the Author Breaks out into a Sermon, Dammit!*

So, I want to ask, is any of this news?

No. Art has reiterated the ironic, has dissembled and dissembled and dissembled humans in order both to entertain and instruct from day one.

A Sumerian proverb goes like this: "Build like a lord, live like a servant. Build like a servant, live like a lord." In these few and ancient words the hollowness of human ambitions and desires are revealed all at once.

In Gerard Bullett's novel *The Jury,* published in 1935, we find this desultory passage on the self-consciousness of words:

> *Every word was wrong; every word was Romantic, banal, probably used by the so-called poets of the 19th Century. He tried again: ochrecous residue, heart's dregs—that was sufficiently unlike Tennyson, but it wouldn't do. Heart was one of the bad old words. But why write about autumn at all—another prohibited word. It all shows how second-rate I am, he concluded.*

So, if none of this is anything new, what's missing? What are we to do in order to make our stories—our hearts—new?

We must, I believe, see that irony is in and of itself only a tool of illumination, and not the subject of what is to be illuminated. It's as though we have finally arrived at a time when, no longer believing there can be path out of the cave we are living in, we have become content to use the flashlight of irony simply to cast hand shadows—this one is *sarcasm,* this one *hypocrisy,* this next one *facetiousness,* and this one *ridicule*—across the walls of the craggy and wet darkness in which we believe we have no choice but to re-side, instead of using the flashlight—this tool that can and does reveal our folly as human beings—to limn a path out.

The poet Richard Hugo, writing in *The Triggering Town*, yet another book any artist needs to own, confesses to the folly of contemporary literature's self-consciousness by noting,

> *All art that has endured has a quality we call schmaltz or corn. Our reaction against the sentimentality embodied in Victorian and post-Victorian writing was so resolute writers came to believe that the further from sentimentality we got, the truer the art. That was a mistake. As Bill Kittredge, my colleague who teaches fiction writing, has pointed out: if you are not risking sentimentality, you are not close to your inner self.*

My text this morning is from the Gospel of Mark, and so if you would please turn with me to—

Sorry—I forgot. This isn't a sermon, though I know it sounds like one. But I'm not kidding about the Gospel of Mark being our text. In chapter 10, John Mark tells the story of Jesus and the rich young ruler, the brief moment of their meeting. He writes:

> *As Jesus started on his way, a man ran up to him and fell on his knees before him. "Good teacher," he asked, "what must I do to inherit eternal life?" "Why do you call me good?" Jesus answered. "No one is good—except God alone. You know the commandments: Do not murder, do not commit adultery, do not steal, do not give false testimony, do not defraud, honor your father and mother."*
>
> *"Teacher," he declared, "all these I have kept since I was a boy."*
>
> *Jesus looked at him and loved him. "One thing you lack," he said. "Go, sell everything you have and give to the poor, and you will have treasure in heaven. Then come, follow me."*

At this the man's face fell. He went away sad, because he had great wealth. Jesus looked around and said to his disciples, "How hard it is for the rich to enter the kingdom of God." The disciples were amazed at his words. But Jesus said again, "Children, how hard it is to enter the kingdom of God. It is easier for a camel to go through the eye of a needle than for a rich man to enter the kingdom of God." The disciples were even more amazed, and said to each other, "Who then can be saved?" Jesus looked at them and said, "With man this is impossible, but not with God; all things are possible with God."

There. Perhaps one of the most widely known passages in the Bible, especially that last part about the camel through the eye of the needle. But what makes this story so memorable, so important and vital—if you believe in Heaven and Hell—and yet so utterly *ironic?* The rich young ruler has been utterly *dissembled;* that is, through Jesus' exacting incision into the man's soul, revealing in a moment the source of the man's identity, his pride in his possessions, all his presumptions have been put aside. The rich young ruler knows well the technique by which living for God is found—he has kept the commandments since he was a boy!—but when faced with how *faith* is found, through the ultimate surrender of self and the consequent following of Christ without a clue where that might lead, the young man comes up short, for his identity as a man of God has been based on the *technique* of being a man of God, and not on the *surrendering fully of the self* the world tells us is of value.

It's not so much his earthly possessions but the way he's allowed them to distance himself from his fellow humans that keeps him from being the man of God Jesus sees him as capable of being. The wealth he has acquired while keeping the commandments is inextricably entwined with his notion of what being a man of God is, and it is Jesus who sees this mistaken notion, this chasm between the rich young ruler and those in need around him. Jesus knows and tries to get the young man to see that communion with God—eternal life—is not accomplished by the cleverness of attending to rules or the accumulation of material wealth. Communion with God is accomplished through loving others.

An irony that goes right over the heads of the audience, his disciples.

But Jesus isn't merely a Socratic ironist. He's not feigning ignorance as a means simply to reveal folly in others, or to refute what some oracle has said about him, though the news of who he was at his birth was enough to make the reigning Hebrew monarch and Roman puppet slaughter every Jewish boy under the age of two.

No, Jesus was different from any other ironist, though irony was his means so very often of explaining and illustrating and teaching and living. The difference here is that Jesus, in revealing the rich young ruler, "looked at him and loved him."

Jesus loves him, I believe, because he sees the truth that he may very well have followed the commandments since he was a boy. But it is that step away from self-consciousness and into grace that is the core and truth of salvation—and, I believe, the core and truth of the making of art—and it is a step the young man cannot make. And, finally, Jesus assuages his disciples—us—with the element of hope: "With man this is impossible, but not with God; all things are possible with God."

Irony's necessary partners, then, are hope and love.

But how, you might well ask, do we find the power to find hope in our work?

Here is J. D. Salinger, in "Seymour: An Introduction," one of the most powerful passages that I have ever read on how we might find purpose and meaning inside what we do as writers.

It's a definition that bears no resemblance whatsoever to any sort of ironic stance one can adopt; it is, in fact, so bereft of any sense of irony that its sincerity, earnestness, and honesty nearly shout, and might even seem to some, well, cheesy. Seymour writes to his younger brother Buddy, a struggling writer:

> *When was writing ever your profession? It's never been anything but your religion. Never. I'm a little over-excited now. Since it's your religion, do you know what you will be asked when you die? But let me tell you first what you won't be asked. You won't be asked if you were working on a wonderful, moving piece of writing when you died. You won't be asked if it was long or short, sad or funny, published or unpublished. You won't be asked if you were in good or bad form while you were working on it. You won't even be asked if it was the one piece of writing you would have been working on if you had known your time would be up when it was finished—I think only poor Sören K. will get asked that. I'm so sure you'll get asked only two* questions. Were most of your stars out? Were you busy writing your heart out? *If only you knew how easy it would be for you to say yes to both questions. If only you'd remember before ever you sit down to write that you've been a reader long before you were ever a writer. You simply fix that fact in your mind, then sit very still and ask yourself, as a reader, what piece of writing in all the world Buddy Glass would most want to read if he had his heart's choice. The next step is terrible, but so simple I can hardly believe it as I write it. You just sit down shamelessly and write the thing yourself. I won't even underline that. It's too important to be underlined. Oh, dare to do it, Buddy! Trust your heart. You're a deserving craftsman. It would never betray you.*

And although my understanding of the human heart is first that it is untrustworthy—"The heart is deceitful above all things and beyond cure. Who can understand it?" Jeremiah writes—my other understanding of the human heart, the understanding that saves me and allows me as a writer to, in fact, write from my heart just as Seymour exhorts Buddy Glass, is the truth of God's care to make whole that which is incurable. "I will give you a new heart and put a new spirit in you; I will remove from you your heart of stone and give you a heart of flesh," God speaks in Ezekiel, and it is only in residing in this promise, my old clever life surrendered, the new and alien one here inside me, that I have been able to trust my heart, and try to find hope in the act of writing.

David Foster Wallace, author of *Infinite Jest,* the ironist's iro-nist's ironist's novel, another wunderkind considered one of the premier new writers of our time, though merely the literary prog-eny of the dangerously chuckling Mr. Stanley Fish, writes in an article that appeared in *Review of Contemporary Fiction,* on televi-sion and the American novel:

> *The next real literary "rebels" in this country might well emerge as some weird bunch of anti-rebels . . . who have the childish gall actually to endorse and instantiate single-entendre princi-ples. . . . Too sincere. Clearly repressed. Backward, quaint, naive, anachronistic. Maybe that'll be the point.*

It's a strange passage for such a writer as he to pen, for inside these few words lurks an almost wistful longing, as though he himself, the point man for the post-ironic age, finds himself alone in the trench and dreaming of liberation, of a day when he might be allowed to taste cool water, see blue sky and green hills.

But as for his notion of who the next rebels might be, I'm banking on his being right. The scandalous move right now is to have hope, to look out at the world in love in order to discover it anew in whatever way you can, in whatever form you can—please note, this essay has not entertained even a moment's derision of metafiction—risking all the while cheese, corn, schmaltz.

The scandalous and radical move right now is to infuse our post-ironic age with hope, and with love, risking, as it always and ever should be, your own heart.

BILL McKIBBEN

The Muslim Gandhi

from *DoubleTake*

The story that follows may be no more than a curiosity—an outlier in the data. Since I am not a scholar of Islam or Afghanistan, I cannot judge, although it fits with little else we've heard in the news recently. I first came across it many years ago, and had forgotten it until the events of September 11, but since that time it has rattled around in my brain. The story concerns the Muslims of the Afghan-Pakistan border, a people with whom we suddenly find ourselves intimately engaged, but who are more remote to us than almost any other on earth.

In 1890, in the village called Utmanzai, not far from the Khyber Pass, a boy named Abdul Ghaffar Khan was born. The son of a prosperous landowner, he grew to be six foot three, a powerful and proud Pashtun tribesman, a devout Muslim. And he also grew to become, along with his dear friend Gandhi, one of the greatest nonviolent leaders of the twentieth century. At one point, his unarmed Islamic "army," the Khudai Khidmatgars, or Servants of God, numbered 100,000 men. Many of these "soldiers" died at the hands of the British rather than resorting to violence. In doing so, they contributed enormously to the breaking of the imperial power's will.

Though we've often heard lately that the British and the Soviet empires both came to grief in Afghanistan, the fact is that the British ruled the region they called the Northwest Frontier for more than a century. Their reign was always uneasy—the Pashtun, or the Pathans as the British called them, were tough, and the

British were nasty. The commander of the Punjab Frontier Force sent this dispatch back to London in 1859:

> *To have to carry destruction, if not destitution, into the homes of some hundreds of families is the great drawback of border warfare, but with savage tribes, to whom there is no right but might, the only course open as regards humanity as well as policy, is to make all suffer.* . . . *In short, civilized warfare is inapplicable.*

Punitive expedition after expedition burned valley after valley, year after year, but never managed to stamp out resistance.

This was the world into which Ghaffar Khan was born. His father, though devout, sent him to a Christian mission school, where the boy did well. The young Khan was about to join the Pathan Guides, an elite infantry corps with long history of service to the Empire. In short, he was going to attain the highest position he could in his colonial world. But the day before his enlistment, according to his biographer, Eknath Easwaran, he heard a British officer insult one of the enlisted Pathans, disrespect he could not tolerate. He also decided against traveling to England to study engineering, turning down a scholarship offer from the missionaries. Instead, he opened a small school in his village, farmed his family land, and began to circulate in progressive Muslim circles, meeting with others who wanted to modernize Pashtun life.

Evading British checkpoints and patrols, he began wandering in the hills to the north—a district under such strict military rule that any Pathan who didn't bow low enough before an Englishman was locked in stocks. He walked from town to town, reopening schools closed by the British, meeting always with village elders and with the poorest people in town. Easwaran also insists that at sometime in these years, after a period of fasting in an isolated mosque, he had some kind of religious experience akin to Francis's awakening at San Damiano:

Islam! Inside him the word began to explode with meaning.
Islam! Submit! Surrender to the Lord and know His strength.

Something gave him enormous drive. Between 1915 and 1918, he visited each of the five hundred villages in the settled districts of the frontier. As he learned more about the nonviolent campaign that Gandhi had begun in India, he began to see his work as a campaign for freedom as well as moral and material uplift. And just as the Hindus had begun to call Gandhi "Mahatma," the Muslims of the frontier started to proclaim Ghaffar the "Badshah Khan," or "King of Khans." Thus it wasn't long before the British arrested him for the first time, a practice they continued throughout the next decades with predictable results: with each release, his reputation grew greater.

By 1929, he had met Gandhi for the first time and heard him speak about the need for a "nonviolence of the strong." Khan returned home to urge more social reforms on his fellow Pashtun. "You have all heard of America and Europe," he told them. "The people in those countries may not be very religious, but they have a sense of patriotism, love for their nation, and social progress. And look at the progress that has been made there. Then take a look at ourselves! We have hardly learned to stand on our own feet yet!" But those could have been the words of any reforming nationalist politician of the age. Khan was much more—a deeply spiritual man who thought Gandhi's nonviolence resonated strongly with his own Islam, especially the Orthodox understanding of a *jihad* against one's own weaknesses and temptations. To his mind, the great weakness of the Pashtun was their obsessive attention to honor and revenge between different clans, producing an endless cycle of revenge killing that the British easily exploited. In response, Khan formed the Khudai Khidmatgars—a real army, with uniforms and officers and flags and even a bagpipe corps, and perhaps the strangest oath any army had ever taken:

I promise to refrain from violence and taking revenge.
I promise to forgive those who oppress me or treat me with
    cruelty.

They began by wearing simple white overshirts, but drilling and marching soon dirtied them. The residue from the local tannery turned out to be perfect for turning shirts a deep brick red, however, and so the Red Shirts, as the British called them, were born. Aside from being unpaid, the army's members also pledged to volunteer at least two hours a day building schools and helping with community projects. Women joined as well as men. Units took long treks into the hills, and as they marched they sang:

We are the army of God,
By death or wealth unmoved.
We march, our leader and we,
Ready to die.

As it turned out, they had organized just in time, for in 1930 Gandhi touched off history's most massive campaign of civil disobedience when he made salt at the beach in Dandi. Almost immediately, people across the subcontinent joined the salt satyagraha, a Boston Tea Party multiplied by a million. The British went berserk at this open contempt for their rule—they arrested a hundred thousand people, eventually including Gandhi, shut down newspapers, raided Congress Party offices, beat unarmed crowds. But in the Northwest Frontier, far from the attention of the world, things were darker still.

In April, Ghaffar Khan, in a mass meeting in his hometown, urged Pashtuns to join in the civil resistance sweeping India. He set off for Peshawar to make the same plea but was arrested en route. Thousands of demonstrators surrounded the jail, remaining nonviolent while their leader was sent off to a three-year jail sentence in India.

Khan's lieutenants in Peshawar were arrested as well, and again a large crowd formed there too, in the Kissa Khani bazaar. According to all accounts, they had begun to drift away when two or three British armored cars arrived and drove into the throng, killing several. Instead of dispersing, the protesters paused to gather their dead. Annoyed, the British began firing. Gene Sharp, a longtime nonviolence researcher at Harvard's Center for International Affairs, perhaps tells the story best:

> When those in front fell down wounded by the shots, those behind came forward with their breasts bared and exposed themselves to the fire, so much so that some people got as many as twenty-one bullet wounds in their bodies, and all the people stood their ground without getting into a panic. . . . The crowd kept standing at the spot facing the soldiers and were fired at from time to time, until there were heaps of wounded and dying lying about. This state of things continued from eleven till five o'clock in the evening. When the number of corpses became too many the ambulance cars of the government took them away and burned them.

Imagine Kent State, but not just for thirty seconds. For the whole damn day. And remember that this restraint came after a lifetime of savage repression by the British—year after year of fear and humiliation on a scale that we can hardly imagine, even in the wake of September 11.

At one point, the British ordered native soldiers, the Garhwal Rifles, to open fire. When these crack troops refused to shoot unarmed people, the entire platoon was court-martialed—and a chill went down the spine of the Empire, for the system could not tolerate mutiny of that sort. The British themselves had fewer scruples and set themselves to breaking the nonviolent campaign with a series of fierce provocations, carried out in complete secrecy since all journalists had been banned from the province.

The same commander who had opened fire in the bazaar led 800 troops on Khan's hometown, where they beat the nonresisting Khidmatgars and then stripped the red shirts off their bodies before burning and looting the village. In Easwaran's account, after all the volunteers had been beaten and arrested, the commander bellowed, "Any more Red Shirts?" One old man ran home, daubed paint on his clothes, and ran back into the street. "Here's one," he shouted. And he was not alone. By summer's end almost a hundred thousand had taken the oath, even though they were routinely flogged, stripped, even tossed into cesspools. An American tourist who passed through noted that "gunning the Red Shirts" was a popular pastime for the officers.

And yet the nonviolence held as it did throughout India, and against it, British will quickly crumbled. In a matter of months, the colonial authorities officially recognized Gandhi and his movement for the first time, inviting him in for negotiations that led to the Gandhi-Irwin Pact. (In the words of Winston Churchill, it was "the nauseating and humiliating spectacle of this . . . seditious fakir striding half-naked up the steps of the viceroy's palace, there to negotiate and to parley on equal terms with the representative of the king-emperor.") Among other concessions, this agreement granted a limited self-rule to the frontier for the first time; in retrospect, the pact really began the decade-long countdown to independence for all of British India.

That decade gave Khan and Gandhi time to become close friends. Whenever the British, who remained very much in power, exiled him from the frontier, Khan would settle at Gandhi's ashram. Picture after picture shows them sitting side by side, Gandhi chanting from the Gita at prayer meetings, Khan following with passages from the Koran, sometimes borrowing Gandhi's glasses when he had forgotten his own. And in a period of relative calm, when the British allowed it, first Nehru and then Gandhi came to visit Khan beneath the Khyber Pass.

Gandhi, in fact, recalled his visit as one of the most moving trips of his life, for instead of the thronging, screaming crowds that greeted him in India, tens of thousands of Pashtuns lined the streets of Peshawar in their red shirts, smiling but absolutely silent. In talk after talk he urged them to carry their nonviolence even further. He told them not just to control their anger but to aim for "the complete eradication of anger from the heart," adding, "A person who has known God will be incapable of harboring anger or fear within him, no matter how overpowering the cause for it may be."

It is hard to imagine this tiny Hindu exhorting the Pashtun to even greater toughness, but then the whole business is hard to imagine. Clearly Gandhi felt as if he was among the few people in the world able even to begin to absorb his message, and the fact that they were from different civilizations seemed to matter little. At each stop, says Easwaran, "some Pathan would stand before the assembly, red-shirted and eager, and tell the Mahatma what he meant to the Pathan nation. 'We can never forget the debt we owe to you,' one burly Pathan said at Mardan, 'for having stood with us in our stricken plight. We are ignorant, we are poor—but we lack nothing because you have taught us the lesson of nonviolence.'"

Their nonviolence did not flag in the last years before independence, not even when Khan was beaten and arrested one last time. In some ways, the greatest tests came as the end of British rule drew near and communal violence wracked the country. Gandhi and Khan wandered the entire subcontinent, sometimes apart and sometimes together, pleading with people to stop the killing. In India's Bihar province, they drove from village to village, Gandhi napping with his feet on Khan's lap. At prayer meetings they would read from each other's scriptures—locally it worked to suppress the hatred, but everywhere around them violence kept flaring up.

And when independence arrived, partition came with it. Both Gandhi and Khan boycotted the celebrations; for them, the price of freedom was too high. Pakistan, for Gandhi, meant an end to his dream of Muslim-Hindu unity. For Khan it meant not only that, it meant that the Pathans had traded British rule for rule from Karachi. Their territory was divided between Pakistan and Afghanistan, despite his pleas for some kind of Pashtun autonomy. Within a few years, the new authorities had placed him in jail; indeed, by the time he died, in 1988 at the age of ninety-seven, he'd spent as many years in Pakistani jails as British ones.

I have no idea what residue remains of the Khudai Khidmatgars; it's even harder to spot from a distance than the residue of Gandhi's life in the politics of India. Certainly Khan's ideas on the emancipation of women—"In the Holy Koran you have an equal share with men. You are today oppressed because we men have ignored the commands of God and the Prophet. . . . If we achieve success we solemnly promise you that you will get your rights"— seem to have withered instead of grown. The nonviolent creed didn't survive the Soviet incursion or the other events of the years that followed.

Khan and the Khudai Kidmatgars may all be mere anomaly, suggesting nothing in the way of strategy or approach. "That such men would have laid down their arms and accepted nonviolence as the superior weapon sounds almost like a fairy tale," wrote Gandhi once. And yet it did happen. It is, at the least, a curious piece of data to add to our stock about Islam, about Afghanistan and Pakistan, and perhaps about human nature as well.

W. S. MERWIN

To the Words

from *The New Yorker*

When it happens you are not there

oh you beyond numbers
beyond recollection
passed on from breath to breath
given again
from day to day from age
to age
charged with knowledge
knowing nothing

indifferent elders
indispensable and sleepless

keepers of our names
before ever we came
to be called by them

you that were
formed to begin with
you that were cried out
you that were spoken
to begin with
to say what could not be said

ancient precious
and helpless ones

say it

Prayer

from *The New Yorker*

Approaching ninety, and still with a hope
That I could tell it, say it, blurt it out.

If not before people, at least before You,
Who nourished me with honey and wormwood.

I am ashamed, for I must believe You protected me,
As if I had for You some particular merit.

I was like those in the gulags who fashioned a cross from twigs
And prayed to it at night in the barracks.

I made a plea and You deigned to answer it,
So that I could see how unreasonable it was.

But when out of pity for others I begged a miracle,
The sky and the earth were silent, as always.

Morally suspect because of my belief in You,
I admired unbelievers for their simple persistence.

What sort of adorer of Majesty am I,
If I consider religion good only for the weak like myself?

The least normal person in Father Chomski's class,
I had already fixed my sights on the swirling vortex of a destiny.

Now You are closing down my five senses, slowly,
And I am an old man lying in darkness.

Delivered to that thing which has oppressed me
So that I always ran forward, composing my poems.

Liberate me from guilt, real and imagined.
Give me certainty that I toiled for Your glory.

In the hour of the agony of death, help me with Your suffering
Which cannot save the world from pain.

(*Translated from the Polish by the author and Robert Hass*)

TONI MORRISON

The Dead of September 11

from *Vanity Fair*

Some have God's words; others have songs of comfort for the bereaved. If I can pluck courage here, I would like to speak directly to the dead—the September dead. Those children of ancestors born in every continent on the planet: Asia, Europe, Africa, the Americas . . . ; born of ancestors who wore kilts, obis, saris, gèlès, wide straw hats, yarmulkes, goatskin, wooden shoes, feathers and cloths to cover their hair. But I would not say a word until I could set aside all I know or believe about nations, war, leaders, the governed and ungovernable; all I suspect about armor and entrails. First I would freshen my tongue, abandon sentences crafted to know evil—wanton or studied; explosive or quietly sinister; whether born of a sated appetite or hunger; of vengeance or the simple compulsion to stand up before falling down. I would purge my language of hyperbole; of its eagerness to analyze the levels of wickedness; ranking them; calculating their higher or lower status among others of its kind.

Speaking to the broken and the dead is too difficult for a mouth full of blood. Too holy an act for impure thoughts. Because the dead are free, absolute; they cannot be seduced by blitz.

To speak to you, the dead of September, I must not claim false intimacy or summon an overheated heart glazed just in time for a camera. I must be steady and I must be clear, knowing all the time that I have nothing to say—no words stronger than the steel that pressed you into itself; no scripture older or more elegant than the ancient atoms you have become.

And I have nothing to give either—except this gesture, this thread thrown between your humanity and mine: *I want to hold you in my arms* and as your soul got shot of its box of flesh to understand, as you have done, the wit of eternity: its gift of unhinged release tearing through the darkness of its knell.

ALICIA OSTRIKER

The Kiss of Judas

from *The Atlantic Monthly*

Among many, one panel:
Perhaps it catches the eye
Owing to its symmetry
Or its subject, betrayal.

Giotto is simple.
What does "simple" mean?
Soldiers, torches, a friendship,
Money, a kiss.

Two profiles: One looks upward,
Lips protrude with intention,
Brow slightly frowns.
And one receptive, brunette,

Eyes almost Byzantine,
Grave if not solemn,
His neck remains bare
To show absence of fear.

Judas wears a cloak
To reveal that he's hidden.
His embrace also hides
The other man's body.

Could Judas wish to become
Joined with his Lord's body?
Giotto has painted him
Like almost everyone else

In the Scrovegni Chapel,
Slightly rounded, short,
Not too far from being
A dog or a bird.

Isn't it hard, though, to leave?
Pope Leo liked them. We, too,
Those tender Giotto blues,
Those rose tints, those ash greens.

We were never in a church
More comforting than this one.
Imagine if women's wombs
Had paintings like this one.

All of us would be born
Wise and good, then.

SUSAN POLLACK

The Wives of Gloucester

from *Orion*

The turquoise-robed statue of St. Peter leads the midnight procession down narrow streets running to the harbor and sea. Eight young fishermen, their muscles straining beneath tight T-shirts, shoulder the seven-hundred-pound icon. Arms linked, several hundred of us follow, chanting, "*Viva San Pietro, Viva San Pietro.*" Our voices rise over the whirring of industrial refrigerators and compressors as we pass a cluster of fish processing plants, an icehouse, and docks heaped with nets and lobster traps, the gear gritty with fish blood and scales. Modern-day pilgrims, to honor the fishermen's patron saint and to ask for prosperous fishing, we carry flashlights as well as candles, and wave tubes of green Cyalume in the night sky. Old women wave at the glowing procession from the stoops of their clapboard houses; children and grandchildren lean out the windows and shower us with thick clouds of red, white, green, and orange and yellow confetti.

It is June 28 and the annual St. Peter's fiesta is coming to a close in Gloucester, Massachusetts. Over the long weekend, several thousand celebrants crowded into this sea-girded city, America's oldest fishing port. All have gone home now, except this small group of late-night marchers, most of them from Sicilian-American fishing families like my friends Angela and John Sanfilippo, who are striding through the streets arm in arm. Gloucester lies along the rocky coast of Cape Ann, only forty miles from my home in Boston, but it seems a world away. We are walking now through a section of town known as the Fort, a neighborhood that has long housed immigrant fishing families, most recently the Sicilians, who began arriving in Gloucester in the early 1900s. In the Fort, the streets always smell of fish, even now on a Sunday when the processing plants are shuttered. Wind moans through the rigging of steel fishing trawlers docked nearby, and when fog rolls in, the distant foghorn bellows through the alleys.

This port city is permeated by the sea, by a unique history, and by a long roster of ghosts—the spirits of fishermen, schooner captains, and dorymen lost offshore—and also of the Gloucester-women who never saw the legendary fishing grounds of North Atlantic waters—Georges Bank, the Scotian Shelf, Grand Banks. The women knew the fertile grounds only as a litany of names, words uttered with hope and promise, and spoken again before the clanging of funeral bells. The wives, sisters, and mothers of Gloucester's maritime world are the "anxious worried women" in T. S. Eliot's poem "The Dry Salvages," in which this community figures so prominently. Between 1716 and the present day some 5,368 Gloucestermen died at sea. All that history, loss, and human affection presses into the present celebration.

In a town like Gloucester, the fishing way of life is found not only on the boats and docks, not only in stories and songs, but in the everyday rituals of food—which, after all, is what commercial fishing is all about. The ethos of this community is evident in the central place given to the *fruits de mer,* to good food in all its glory. Over the past twenty years, I have celebrated many feast days with the Sanfilippos. These annual feasts are as rich in tradition, as sustaining and glorious as an opera, and yet, this evening I sense an ominous undertow. The reality behind the festivities is grim as this once astoundingly rich fishery continues to decline. Codfish was long the mainstay of the Gloucester fishery. The first European settlers marveled at its abundance: "He is a very bad fisher, [who] cannot kill in one day with his hooke and line, one, two, or three hundred Cod," enthused Captain John Smith in his 1616 *A Description of New England*. So central to the Massachusetts economy was the cod that a five-foot-long hand-carved "Sacred Cod" dominates the chambers of the statehouse.

When I was a girl in the early 1960s, my mother had a dozen recipes to dress up the plain-Jane cod, a species so abundant that it was served breaded and baked for school lunch every Friday. The trouble began not long after, when a fleet of European factory trawlers launched a massive fish hunt off the East Coast. In 1977, the United States extended its jurisdiction out to two hundred miles, and with the foreign ships gone, the cod rebounded. But the U.S. government failed to control its own greatly expanding fleet. By the mid-1980s, a battle was raging over how best to conserve New England groundfish, particularly cod. Fishermen, who were at last making money again, did not want cutbacks; scientists were warning of a stock failure, and government fishery regulators were immobilized.

Today, codfish remain scarce, despite stringent but belated conservation efforts. The populations of haddock and yellowtail flounder, two other staples of the region's groundfishery, have recently shown some signs of recovery, although, they, too, remain low. Even the most resourceful families, like the Sanfilippos, struggle to catch enough fish simply to pay their bills. Over lunch this afternoon, John attempted to make light of his predicament, asking, "If fishing's poor are you still supposed to pin dollar bills on St. Peter?" His question spurred a lively argument in Sicilian, which a niece translated for me. At last year's fiesta, at this very same table, the Sanfilippos had sat around worrying about their son, Dominic, forced by the dearth of cod to travel to far Alaska to fish. And since then, Dominic has had to give up on fishing, as have many other Gloucestermen. Since 1995, nearly eighty New England fishing families, many from

Gloucester, have sold their boats to the government as part of a $25 million federal buyout.

The loss of cod threatens the survival of this celebrated fishing port, along with its centuries-old fishing traditions and the culture of its fishing families—from England, Ireland, Nova Scotia, Newfoundland, the Azores, and Sicily. If Gloucester's fishing way of life perishes, so will a vision of the common good, something all too rare in our self-absorbed American society. I have seen too many fishing communities fail—in Newfoundland, Long Island, Chesapeake Bay—and I don't want to see this happen to Gloucester.

As this year's midnight procession continues, I slip my arm through Angela's. It is easy to feel the strength of her arm, the determination in her stride. For a quarter century now, the women of Gloucester have been a political force, banding together to successfully fight offshore oil drilling, and going on to wage numerous other battles, sometimes with the help of a spiral-bound cookbook they sell at seafood festivals and by special order. It is up to Angela and the other fishermen's wives to hold the community together until the cod come back. To sustain themselves, they call on all their resources, including Old World traditions like the fiesta. As we walk along now, Angela concedes she is worried, then turns confident again, leaning over and whispering, "No one will ever break our spirit, no matter what."

For Angela, the fiesta is a political as well as spiritual occasion. This morning, she stood in Gloucester's large waterfront piazza waiting for Cardinal Bernard Law of the Boston archdiocese to arrive. An animated woman with a black beehive hairdo, high heels, and red dress, Angela walked back and forth across Gloucester's St. Peter Square in front of a high white and gold altar. Old Sicilian men and women in bright shirts and white trousers slowly filled the piazza; they sat in rows of folding chairs and held umbrellas to shield themselves from the blistering midmorning sun. A band

played an Arthur Murray version of "When the Saints Go Marching In." A Ferris wheel spun high over the altar beside concessions
selling Rita's Fried Dough and John's Famous Pizza. By 10:30, dizzy
and dehydrated, I bought a lemonade and took shelter under Rita's
fluorescent pink awning. But Angela continued pacing. She knows
Cardinal Law well; they have worked together on projects aimed
at sustaining fishing families through these difficult times. The
Gloucester Fishermen's Wives Association and the archdiocese,
with Senator Edward Kennedy's help, launched a program to offer
affordable health insurance to fishermen, their wives, and children. This year the church leader was late because he had just
flown in from Rome. He stepped out of a black air-conditioned
car and greeted Angela's husband, "Hello, Mr. Thatcher, (ha, ha),"
then turned toward Angela, who kissed his hand. Only Angela and
Cardinal Law were dressed in red, and they greeted each other like
two bright songbirds.

Over the years, the church leader has used his fiesta sermons to
make passionate appeals on behalf of Gloucester fishing families.
"The people who fish," he has said, "know how to protect the environment better than anyone else." And he has advocated pre-
serving the port as a working waterfront—in the face of
skyrocketing development pressures. Every time a hard-pressed
fish house or dock or a factory goes out of business, Gloucester is
flooded with applications for waterfront condominiums. Angela
and the other women of the Gloucester Fishermen's Wives Association have emerged as an unmistakable power in this and other
battles that will determine Gloucester's future.

I first met Angela in 1978, while reporting on the campaign by fishermen and conservationists to prevent offshore oil drilling on the
Georges Bank fishing grounds. Her charisma and youth impressed
me—she was then in her late twenties, a leader of the Fishermen's

Wives, and a powerful presence. So were the other Wives: women like Lena Novella, Angela's predecessor, who had fought successfully for passage of the U.S.'s two-hundred-mile limit law. The Wives, they are always called, like an archetypal force, which, of course, they are. More recently, under Angela's leadership, the Wives have helped bring about an impressive set of accomplishments. They include improved safety standards on U.S. vessels; the end of ocean dumping; a ban on destructive factory trawlers; the creation of a marine sanctuary at Stellwagen Bank; further moratoria on oil drilling at Georges Bank, and the first subsidized health plan for fishermen. Locally, they have fought for the working waterfront and launched a program to help hard-pressed fishermen find other jobs. Today if she believes a federal restriction will hurt fishermen, she picks up the phone and calls Ted Kennedy.

I have lived by the ocean all of my life, wading through marshes in hip boots and sailing in every kind of wind. I love going out in a small boat to crew for a fellow sailor or to help a fisherman lift nets. I've delighted in watching the winter sun rise over the back deck of a fishing trawler one hundred miles offshore, and I've thanked luck or grace for bringing me through more than one close call. Yet I have little interest in catching fish and less in the increasingly sophisticated equipment used to do this. What has always drawn me to commercial fishing is the culture—that remarkable mix of language, story, and tradition. I am fascinated by the ethos that causes a fisherman to sacrifice a day's work—to risk his own life, even—to assist another fisher, a man he might not even speak to at the dock. And I have marveled every time I've seen a macaroni casserole or platter of spaghetti appear on the doorstep of a neighbor who is sick, elderly, or has lost someone at sea.

On Gloucester's food pyramid, spaghetti is an essential building block, a food group unto itself. The appreciation for pasta is obvious. I've never experienced anything like the hush that comes over a meal when the pasta is served. So I was honored when, the first time I celebrated St. Anthony's feast day with Angela, she and her mother taught me how to make their sauce—with the freshest tomatoes, garlic, basil, and olive oil. That spaghetti dinner concluded a week-plus novena in which Angela and her mother, Angela's daughters, Mary Ann and Giovanna, and several dozen other fishermen's wives, daughters, and sisters had offered special prayers and songs to the popular saint. I confess I was moved less by the recitation of Anthony's miracles than by witnessing a still-intact community in action. I was immediately aware that in Gloucester, I had entered a world quite different from my own original community. In this maritime enclave, women still sing and cook pasta together and help care for one another's children. Here I saw children buoyed by an extended sense of family, unknown in my childhood—an upper-middle-class world in which adults struggled individually for renown and worried about their children getting into Ivy League colleges.

I found a place in Angela's world—as a peeler of garlic. Moments after the women blew out the altar candles at their novena, we headed downstairs, where Angela promptly handed me an apron and a knife. While I peeled, Angela washed basil and tomatoes, and other women filled vats of water and placed them on the stove to boil, all the while conversing in their native Sicilian. If I looked up, someone stopped to translate, but mostly the women kept on talking, rapidly, expressively, animating the tiny kitchen with their words. Their resulting spaghetti has both the bite of raw garlic and the distinctive sweetness of vine-ripened tomatoes.

That taste is with me still, as are the sounds of the women singing—slow lyrical songs and rousing ones with folk melodies, songs they had known since they were girls. Later I began to reflect on how much the novena reminds me of the Passover seder and my own, only half-remembered heritage. Like the seder, the novena of the Wives links generations and honors the spiritual resources to weather hard times. The Gloucester ceremony calls for an expression of gratitude, not a tasting of bitter herbs, yet in coming together the women remember. Angela began offering the novena in 1976, during another fishing crisis. Then, Gloucester fishermen were facing the ravages of overfishing by foreign vessels and John was on the verge of bankruptcy. Angela called on St. Anthony, asking him to intervene. When John was rewarded with a bountiful swordfish catch, Angela vowed to hold this annual novena, continuing the tradition of her Sicilian family.

I stand in awe of the fortitude of these women, of their good cheer and strong faith. How fitting it is that they should pray to St. Anthony, the once-timid saint who found his voice. It was Anthony who preached to the fish, who caused them to lift their heads out of the water to listen, and it was Anthony's sermons that led to social change, as the hungry were fed, debts absolved, and prisoners freed.

Driving home from Cape Ann to Boston that year, after the novena, I felt flooded with new life yet also tugged by a sadness, a curious sense of loss. It had been many years since I had felt so moved by a people or place. An abiding love for the dunes and potato fields of eastern Long Island launched me on this unlikely career writing about fishing communities and the sea. As a reporter for the *East Hampton Star,* I had tried to capture the fishermen's voices in a regular column and to influence editorial policy on everything from water pollution to factory ships and the need for tougher waterfront zoning. When at last I left East Hampton it was to work in Maine as the staff writer for *National Fisherman.* For that gig, I traveled extensively along the Eastern Atlantic Coast, reporting on boats, fisheries, and life at sea. But when not traveling, I felt almost adrift in the affluent Maine coastal town that was my new home. I missed watching the fishermen mending their nets outside my window, hearing their pickup trucks at dawn, and finding gifts of fresh-caught fish and scallops in my refrigerator when I returned home from work. Only after leaving East Hampton did I come to understand how deeply I had been touched by the people there and the sense of community itself. From the isolation of Maine, I began to think with increasing regularity about what we mean by community, and why it matters so much to us.

Leaving Angela's that day of the feast, I felt called to tell what I could of Gloucester's story, hoping that my words might help keep one fishing community alive. And with that, my own creative life suddenly had meaning again.

Now, nearly a decade later, on a bright but frigid November morning, as I walk from the Gloucester railroad station to the harbor, I wonder what will happen to this community if the cod do not come back. It's been five months since I last visited Gloucester, and with the streets swept clean of all vestiges of fiesta, I spot new signs of gentrification—a boutique and an upscale restaurant, a bed-and-breakfast. Things *are* changing in town, and I wonder what this means for the fishing community. If, as I hope, the fishery does finally rebound, what kind of community will survive in Gloucester? Will Gloucester become like so many other American communities—a collection of individuals simply living in the same geography? Or will people continue to be bound by their concern for one another?

Arriving at the harbor, I'm assaulted by a bitter wind that whips across the water. Yet the sky is so clear that from the landmark weathered bronze statue of the fisherman at the wheel, I can see well beyond Ten Pound Island and the lighthouse at Eastern Point. I am here to attend yet another meeting of the New England Fishery Management Council, the group responsible for writing U.S. codfish regulations. Today's session, in a glassy building just beyond the fishermen's statue, follows the release of another gloomy scientific report: The cod population at the Georges Bank fishing grounds has not recovered. Tightening restrictions have saved some cod, but the adult fish have failed to produce enough young. Things look even worse closer to shore, in the Gulf of Maine, where John Sanfilippo works. Fishermen simply are catching too many cod to sustain a healthy population.

This is devastating news to Angela and the roomful of fishermen who have been hit by one cutback after another. Angela, like most fishing leaders, fights increasing restrictions because she sees the traumatic human effects—fishermen forced to sell their boats. Angela does not win all the battles. And I don't always agree with her. She has a strong commitment to the environment, but when it is pitted against fishermen's lives, she will always chose the latter. Because of this, I hesitate to share with her my growing uneasiness that something dramatic—such as shutting down the codfishery completely for a few years—may be necessary to save it.

Yet Angela can see another point of view. At a heated public meeting several years ago, when fishermen, angry over new regulations, blamed environmentalists, she rose and challenged the fathers, sons, and grandfathers of her port. She told the men that they were wrong to view environmentalists as enemies. They had been, she said, true friends to fishermen ever since the battle against offshore oil, and it was important to work together. Today, however, Angela and the Wives have thrown in their hats with the mayor of Gloucester and a coastwide coalition of fishing groups challenging the scientific study and seeking to buy time from the new regulations. The fishers' distrust of such a study is nothing new; it marks an increasingly troublesome rift between those who study the oceans and those who fish it. While fishery council members debate procedural minutiae, fishing representatives wait patiently to speak. As we wait, I recall Angela's often-repeated words: "The Lord provides the fish to catch."

Usually Angela is surrounded a phalanx of fashionably dressed, energetic, and well-spoken fishermen's wives. It's likely you'll spot Mary Brancaleone, the Wives Association's clerk, Rosalie Vitale, its treasurer, Sefatia Romeo, its young vice president, or activists Mary Costanza or her daughter Josephine Taormina, dressed in pantsuits and gold earrings, traveling to Boston or even Washington, D.C., for a public hearing, ladling out chowder at a seafood festival, or sipping tea with the director of Harvard's Schlesinger Library, the repository of the Wives' Association papers. Today a few women stop in briefly to confer with Angela or David Bergeron, the Wives Association's staff secretary. The Wives usually leave the public speaking to Angela. At these times, she reveals the orator's gift. It is as if St. Anthony's tongue had been passed on to her during all those novenas. Angela's ability to articulate a vision of the common good is clearly one reason the Wives enjoy broad public support. Over the years, she and the Wives not only have worked to help sustain their special Gloucester community, they also have worked hard to build bridges to others.

The Wives were not raised to be activists. They grew up in a world that revolved around the family boat. Lena Novella remembers her father telling her, "With a boat you can buy a house, but with a house, you cannot buy a boat." Often Gloucester fishermen continue speaking Sicilian on the boats long after their children have forgotten the dialect they learned from their grandparents. It is the women who learn English and assimilate, in a startling reversal of the traditional immigrant experience. At the state-funded Gloucester Fishermen and Families Assistance Center, for example, Nina Groppo serves as a bilingual job training counselor, Jean Gallo as training coordinator, Rosandra Brancaleone (Mary's daughter) as receptionist, and Angela as project manager. At the eight-year-old center, the Wives work to help fishermen and their families find employment outside fishing, even as the women continue to fight politically to save Gloucester's fishing industry.

At today's meeting, Angela raises concern about a proposed rule, arcane in its wording, that she fears may cause fishermen to take undue risks by staying offshore when the weather turns bad. She makes a short, impassioned appeal to regulators to pay more attention to safety concerns. Fishing, currently, is the most dangerous profession in America, more hazardous even than coal mining or logging. A fisherman working at sea can slip, fall on a wet deck, lose a finger or an eye, mangle his arm in a winch, or get washed overboard. Not long ago, a heavy rubber float struck John Sanfilippo in the head as he was hauling back his net. Since then he's worn a helmet when working on deck. "It's not just bad weather, anything can happen on the boats," says Angela. She worries especially now that John fishes alone. He used to fish with their son, Dominic, but the catch did not support two families.

On a chilly March morning, hours after John has gone fishing, I catch up with Angela in the "product development" kitchen that the fishermen's wives operate in downtown Gloucester. Here around a large table and professional stove, the women prepare seasoned, breaded, ready-to-bake fish fillets, squid salads, and fish chowders to sell at seafood festivals. They argue in Sicilian about how their booth should look at the Boston Seafood Show, and they test recipes for new editions of their cookbook, *A Taste of Gloucester: A Fisherman's Wife Cooks,* which they sell for ten dollars.

Last summer the community bestowed a long-overdue honor on its women. A fishermen's wives' memorial was dedicated at the harbor's edge, not far from the famous fisherman's statue. The memorial depicts a woman looking seaward, holding the hand of one child and cradling another in her arms. Whenever I think of the Wives, however, I picture a constellation of women making pasta, arguing in Sicilian, and walking arm in arm with their husbands at the end of one fiesta, following the fishermen's saint back into town. The piazza, where Angela had stood earlier in her high heels and red dress, lies empty, save for a few stragglers. The altar is still ablaze with light, and a Ferris wheel illuminates the sky. The procession of fishermen and their wives moves up the hill to the St. Peter's Club. The young fishermen lower the turquoise-robed saint, and we all huddle closer. A brass band strikes up "God Bless America," and again people lean out their windows and drench us in confetti. In the harbor, below us, fishermen are already starting up their boats and heading out to sea.

The feast is over. Soon the Wives will be on their own again, left to tend to their families and community.

Born of a Rib

Genesis 21:21–22

from Orion

Maybe it was actually from the delicate
rib of a piñon mouse put to a deep
sleep just for this purpose in his bed
of shredded juniper bark, or from
the steadfast bone of a snoring boar,
that chest stave as tough and stone-
mandatory as one of his searing tusks.

Sometimes it seems the making
must have originated in the edifying
rib of a fern leaflet drowsy
before dawn, because the satiating
taste of its earth-subtle sap
still lingers in the mouth. Yet
there is evidence that the forming
came from the marrow blood of a blue
whale's rib, because the regular
thunder of his near heart remains
permanent and dictatorial in the sound
of time passing in its orbits.

There are moments when I could imagine
emerging, gyring and firmament-rounded,

made soaring by the hollow bone
of a broad-winged hawk in his element,
or being turned upside down, born
subterranean, sun-denying and recalcitrant
from the dormant rib of a brown bat
in his cave hibernation.

Everything might be different today,
we could agree, if the rib chosen
had been taken from the shell
of the somnolent rosy cockle,
so steadfastly sculpted, so smoothly
sea-polished, so stoically pure,
or if the insistent, violet rib
of the rainbow had been the one selected,
or if the false, transparent rib
of the night's vaulted sleep had been
the one extracted for the purpose.

But in truth—remember—from whatever
spine of creature, plant, or sky-cage
the said material rib was stolen,
to that alone must belong forever,
all the blessing, all the blame.

Screwtape Instructs Scrapetooth

from beliefnet.com

My dear Scrapetooth,

You may wonder at receiving a communication from someone of my Abysmal Seniority. The truth is, I was on an errand in the Second Circle and happened to pass by the student notice boards, where the new patient assignments are posted. Permit me to congratulate you on being assigned a television anchorman. I look forward to seeing what you do with him. The task is significant and complicated enough to have attracted considerable attention Below; you may consider it a chance to show your paces and impress prominent diabolical figures, among whom I number myself. You may think I refer to the importance of tempting a subject who, if properly turned, can help mislead, confuse, and ultimately recruit to our side the many millions of additional souls in his viewing audience. Not so! Or, at least, not primarily. One can attain brilliant successes and deep professional satisfaction through the corruption of a completely private person. (And one can fail abjectly . . . ah, that miserable, delicious Wormwood! But I digress.) What makes this particular task truly noteworthy is the combination of a private person of limited gifts with a powerful and outsized public persona. Purely from a gastronomic perspective, the potential rewards are awesome. Such twistings and turnings of insecurity and self-justification, such excellent and succulent depths of self-deception! Some of us already have begun to salivate. Do not disappoint us. Many interesting tactical choices lie before you—for instance, whether to let your man become progressively more entranced with the power and influence of his position, and more committed to enhancing that status at any cost, or whether instead to whip him with the sense that what he does is "only" journalism, a game of surfaces and hurried deadlines, and let him lose himself in reveries of someday doing something more "serious." The first strategy will gradually render him unbearably arrogant and unreachable by normal scruples. The second will prevent genuine engagement with the task before him, with the attendant career stagnation, frustration, and hostility. Either dish can be satisfying; it is really a matter of personal taste.

Feel free to call upon me any time. We have not met much, but I am still a senior devil and as such command my small degree of influence Down Here.

Your affectionate third cousin twice removed,

Screwtape

My dear Scrapetooth,

You ask how I come by what you call my special knowledge of TV journalists, yours in particular. Dear boy, I hope I did not mislead. I have no direct knowledge of the creature who is under your supervision. I merely extended to him the observations I have made of the hapless members of his profession who have found their way here before him. (A habit you ought to practice, by the way. Relegation of the individual case to a general category based on under-informed assumption is an essential skill to master if you wish to descend the ladder of Nether Administration.) But back to my supposed expertise regarding your patient. The explanation is simple. Novice devils are not generally aware that here and there in the nether regions—specifically, in portions of the Fourth, Fifth and Eighth Circles, on the southerly side—it is possible to pick up a steady stream of terrestrial television signals. You would be surprised how many devils while away their time between shifts decoding and imbibing these emissions, especially the all-news channels. They are not as satisfying to the appetite as the direct draughts of human fear, anguish, and confusion that we enjoy in the course of our duties, but they serve well as a snack between meals and as a reminder of those ultimate pleasures. We are led to believe that television reception is even better in the Other Place but that its denizens do not share our interest in it.

My direct impressions of your man have been—of necessity—superficial, but a few thoughts present themselves. He reads the news slowly and sonorously, plainly enamored of his own voice. This affords you opportunities to feed his vanity, encouraging him to concentrate more on the figure he cuts doing his job than on the satisfactions of the job itself. And that is essential if you are to block any chance of his striving to use his influential position for good deeds. The more you can enhance his feeling that he enjoys special status, the likelier you will be, in any given situation, to persuade him that on this occasion it is better to keep his powder dry—after all, he is a very important man; he ought to husband his influence and save it for a time when it will do the most good. With a little work on your part, you can make sure that that time will never come.

Your cousin,

Screwtape

My dear Scrapetooth,

You and your patient gave me quite a scare yesterday evening. Watching him host his special in-depth program on the future of public assistance, I was distressed to hear him delve at length into questions of what human creatures at the moment are pleased to call "ethics." At one particularly alarming moment—I need not remind you of it, surely—he turned those well-known deep-set eyes directly toward the camera, furrowed that striking brow, and asked, "We know this will balance the budget. But is it the right thing to do?"

For an awful second I feared you had already lost control of your subject. I feared for your continued well-being. Had the man developed the habit—the rare, noxious habit—of weighing the morality of everything that passed his lips? The phenomenon has been known to occur, even among journalists. Generally it means some devil has relaxed his vigilance in elementary matters. Over the last few generations we have been highly successful in limiting the damage done by the popularity of ethical codes in private life—the humans' unaccountable attraction to, if not success at, being truthful, faithful, loving, and so forth. We have done this by gradually inculcating the unexamined idea that those codes must be interpreted differently, at any rate less literally, when one is going about the business that furnishes one's livelihood. How many exemplary cases have I seen who, while committed firmly to the Enemy's service at home and on the weekends, spend their working hours telling the untruths known fashionably today as "spin" or advancing policies or projects whose likely bad effects they studiously avoid thinking about on the grounds that an employee's foremost ethical obligation is to advance the interests of the company! What a surprise for them when they discover their real home is with us. Journalists—did you wonder when I would return to the business at hand?—suffer a special, rather subtle case of this confusion, and as a result they must be handled with delicacy. As a rule they do not simply suspend their moral codes while working but, rather, consider their work to be subject to an ethical code of its own that is different from the everyday one but just as rigorous. A primary feature of this professional code is the insistence that the journalist should not think too much about the likely consequences of publishing his story or about whom it will hurt or help. This is called being objective. It is asserted that a focus on the (unknowable) consequences of reporting a news story would make it impossible for stories to be reported fairly or effectively.

I cannot claim that this potentially useful element of your patient's professional formation is the work of our Research Department. No, it bears some of the Enemy's hallmarks—I believe he has some notion of getting the creatures to focus their attention on the parts of their lives they can control and deemphasizing those they cannot. Nonetheless it is a tool we have been able in many cases to turn to our purposes. The first step is to heighten the patient's sense that, since his work falls under the jurisdiction of its own code of ethics, it exists in some real way separate from ordinary life and its "ordinary" rules. The second step is to enhance that feeling of being outside the rules until it begins to color all his nonwork life as well.

I have known cases where this sense of journalistic detachment was so successfully advanced that the patient declined in private life to make contributions to charitable causes, to perform routine community obligations such as volunteering for his children's school events, to develop opinions on the great political issues of his day—even, in one case, to vote in national elections. All to maintain the status of journalistic observer in its most pristine form! This is excellent; this is ideal.

So you can imagine my concern on hearing your patient express, first, a direct ethical concern about the contents of his story, and second, an implied solidarity with ordinary citizens' interest in the morality of public programs. My concern gnaws at me; it pains me. I await with tense eagerness any explanation you can offer.

Your very impatient, very distant cousin,

Screwtape

My dear Scrapetooth,

The calm audacity of your reply amazes me. You assert in unruffled tones (a trifle too unruffled, in truth, to address someone of my Depth in the administration) that you have the situation well under control. The man, you say, is not becoming moral at all; he is merely going with the fashion. Yes, among the humans of today, a dip into morality is now considered the latest thing! The temper of the times, you say, is against the journalistic presumption of objectivity; in the patient's city and in the circles within which he moves, not so much his colleagues but his confidential sources and high official contacts, one's credibility is enhanced by being "born again." You claim to have impressed laboriously on your patient's mind the disadvantage he suffers from not being thus newly "born again," his lack of access to the inner circles of power, their shared language, their bible study classes and men's fellowships and prayer breakfasts.

You point with pride to your success in keeping him away from any notion that he might actually join this world by converting. Rather, under the influence of the drumming envy and discontent you inflicted, he conceived the notion of presenting himself as a sort of morally struggling, questing figure—not just different from his journalistic colleagues but in active contrast to them.

If this tale of yours is true, I must express my admiration. I have not seen so neat a spot of moral jujitsu since an episode in my own early career, when, faced by a patient being importuned to embrace the Enemy's service, I realized that a pretended conversion for social gain would mire my man in a lifetime of hypocrisy while also giving him endless hours of fear and anxiety lest he be found out. It sounds as if you have had a similar brainstorm. In allowing your patient to salt his broadcasts with moral-sounding but empty verbal gestures, a sort of surface moral vocabulary, all for the purpose of signaling his membership in a select peer group, you are using the Enemy's dearest tools in the service of mere snobbism. This is delightful, and it promises more gains in future. Moral postures struck for the purpose of keeping up with the fashion are not necessarily disqualifying for the Enemy—he, our Intelligence Service tells us, clings in such cases to the chance that outward habit will inculcate inward purpose—but there is no doubt that they are at least initially corrupting. And moral postures struck in the plain sight of several million news viewers, most of whom will take the posturing at face value, exert a uniquely corrosive effect on the man's other professional values.

But how can we be sure in the long run that the surface posturing will not become the real thing? For that matter, my dear Scrapetooth, how can I be sure that this explanation on your part is true and is not just a highly original way to cover an impending disaster? No doubt we will know soon enough: I, for one, intend to watch assiduously whether the patient's moral posturing helps his immediate career prospects, as he expects it to, and what use he makes of any advancement. A large new dose of responsibility has been known unaccountably to sober up its holder and turn him to serious thoughts, of the sort that endanger our project. On the other hand, it can serve merely as a bigger and faster car with which he can drive himself where he was going anyway.

As I compose these sentences I note a broadcast announcement that your man will soon anchor an hour-long special on how ordinary citizens can combat the moral vacuity of everyday life. It looks as if his, and your, career strategy is paying off smartly: He is being given a chance to fill a journalistic niche as Moral Philosopher. How will he handle this initial foray—with continued superficiality or, perish the idea, with sincerity and thoughtfulness? The stakes, my dear Scrapetooth, are high for you also.

Your urgently interested cousin,

Screwtape

Well, well, my newly promoted colleague, my dear, esteemed Scrapetooth,

I cannot be the first to congratulate you—others in the structure of authority Down Here are too quick for that. But I hope I may add my voice in admiration for the way in which your patient acquitted himself. And so soon after his elevation to the moral philosopher role he craved, with the assignment of hosting a series of taped specials on moral conundrums! It is true he is not safe in Our House yet—that must await his departure from the mortal world. Still, certain actions taken during the taping of his latest show point him firmly in our direction. It would require a real contravention of what he is pleased to call the Moral Law for him to end up traveling any other way.

It was delicious, was it not? He had just gone on air to engage two pundits and a research scientist in a discussion of what the government could do to help families whose children suffer from some dread disease. (I forget the particulars already; physical suffering is always welcome, but its details bore us.) Earlier in the show he had convened another panel of families involved, tragic figures struggling to save their children from agonized untimely death. One of these desperate parents after going off the air had asked him to broker an introduction between themselves and the second panel's research scientist—nothing dramatic, nothing to catch a devil's eye, just one of those tiny insidious actions from which some good might result. And what was our patient's response? He forgot to do it. He had no particular reason to make or not to make this small connection; the thing merely slipped his mind.

Such a result, my dear Scrapetooth, testifies to your alert presence at your patient's elbow and to the finesse with which you had previously worked him over. It proves beyond a doubt that your analysis of his moral state all along was correct. The honors now being heaped upon you are well deserved, and your future success seems guaranteed. As you progress Downward I sincerely hope you will spare a thought for those of us who offered you advice along the way. And one other thing: Your continued close relationship with your patient ought to put you in a good position to recommend guests for future specials. Tell me, if a senior devil such as I—experienced, authoritative, photogenic—were to obtain the necessary clearances from Below, do you think your patient would be interested in putting him on TV?

Your attentive and sympathetic third cousin,

Screwtape

GARY SMITH

Higher Education

from *Sports Illustrated*

This is a story about a man, and a place where magic happened. It was magic so powerful that the people there can't stop going back over it, trying to figure out who the man was and what happened right in front of their eyes, and how it'll change the time left to them on earth.

See them coming into town to work, or for their cup of coffee at Boyd & Wurthmann, or to make a deposit at Killbuck Savings? One mention of his name is all it takes for everything else to stop, for it all to begin tumbling out. . . .

"I'm afraid we can't explain what he meant to us. I'm afraid it's so deep we can't bring it into words."

"It was almost like he was an angel."

"He was looked on as God."

There's Willie Mast. He's the one to start with. It's funny, he'll tell you, his eyes misting, he was so sure they'd all been hoodwinked that he almost did what's unthinkable now—run that man out of town before the magic had a chance.

All Willie had meant to do was bring some buzz to Berlin, Ohio, something to look forward to on a Friday night, for goodness' sake, in a town without high school football or a fast-food restaurant, without a traffic light or even a place to drink a beer, a town dozing in the heart of the largest Amish settlement in the world. Willie had been raised Amish, but he'd walked out on the religion at twenty-four—no, he'd peeled out, in an eight-cylinder roar, when he just couldn't bear it anymore, trying to get somewhere in life without a set of wheels or even a telephone to call for a ride.

He'd jumped the fence, as folks here called it, become a Mennonite and started a trucking company, of all things, his tractor-trailers roaring past all those horses and buggies, moving cattle and cold meat over half the country. But his greatest glory was that day back in 1982 when he hopped into one of his semis and moved a legend, Charlie Huggins, into town. Charlie, the coach who'd won two Ohio state basketball championships with Indian Valley South and one with Strasburg-Franklin, was coming to tiny Hiland High. Willie, one of the school's biggest hoops boosters, had banged the drum for Charlie for months.

And yes, Charlie turned everything around in those winters of '82 and '83, exactly as Willie had promised, and yes, the hoops talk was warmer and stronger than the coffee for the first time in twenty years at Willie's table of regulars in the Berlin House restaurant. They didn't much like it that second year when Charlie brought in an assistant—a man who'd helped him in his summer camps and lost his job when the Catholic school where he coached went belly-up—who was black. But Charlie was the best dang high school coach in three states; he must've known something that they didn't. Nor were they thrilled by the fact that the black man was a Catholic, in a community whose children grew up reading tales of how their ancestors were burned at the stake by Catholics during the Reformation in Europe more than four hundred years ago. But Charlie was a genius. Nor did they cherish the fact that the Catholic black was a loser, sixty-six times in eighty-three games with those hapless kids at Guernsey Catholic High near Cambridge. But Charlie . . .

Charlie quit. Quit in disgust at an administration that wouldn't let players out of their last class ten minutes early to dress for practice. But he kept the news to himself until right before the '84 school year began, too late to conduct a proper search for a proper coach. Willie Mast swallowed hard. It was almost as if his man, Charlie, had pulled a fast one. Berlin's new basketball coach, the man with the most important position in a community that had dug in its heels against change, was an unmarried black Catholic loser. The *only* black man in eastern Holmes County.

It wasn't that Willie hated black people. He'd hardly known any. "All I'd heard about them," he'll tell you, "was riots and lazy." Few had ever strayed into these parts, and fewer still after that black stuffed dummy got strung up on the town square in Millersburg, just up the road, after the Civil War. Maybe twice a year, back in the 1940s and '50s, a Jewish rag man had come rattling down Route 39 in a rickety truck, scavenging for scrap metal and rags to sell to filling stations thirty miles northeast in Canton or sixty miles north in Cleveland, and brought along a black man for the heavy lifting. People stared at him as if he were green. Kids played Catch the Nigger in their schoolyards without a pang, and when a handful of adults saw the color of a couple of Newcomerstown High's players a few years before, you know what word was ringing in those players' ears as they left the court.

Now, suddenly, this black man in his early thirties was standing in the middle of a gym jammed with a thousand whites, pulling their sons by the jerseys until their nostrils and his were an inch apart, screaming at *them*. Screaming, "Don't wanna hear your shoulda-coulda-wouldas! Get your head outta your butt!" How dare he?

Worse yet, the black man hadn't finished his college education, couldn't even teach at Hiland High. Why, he was working at Berlin Wood Products, the job Charlie had arranged for him, making little red wagons till 2 P.M. each day. "This nigger doesn't know how to coach," a regular at the Berlin House growled.

Willie agreed. "If he wins, it's because of what Charlie built here," he said. "What does he know about basketball?"

But what could be done? Plenty of folks in town seemed to treat the man with dignity. Sure, they were insular, but they were some of the most decent and generous people on earth. The man's Amish coworkers at the wood factory loved him, after they finally got done staring holes in the back of his head. They slammed Ping-Pong balls with him on lunch hour, volleyed theology during breaks, and dubbed him the Original Black Amishman. The Hiland High players seemed to feel the same way.

He was a strange cat, this black man. He had never said a word when his first apartment in Berlin fell through—the landlord who had agreed to a lease on the telephone saw the man's skin and suddenly remembered that he rented only to families. The man had kept silent about the cars that pulled up to the little white house on South Market Street that he moved into instead, about the screams in the darkness, the voices threatening him on his telephone and the false rumors that he was dating their women. "They might not like us French Canadians here," was all he'd say, with a little smile, when he walked into a place and felt it turn to ice.

Finally, the ice broke. Willie and a few pals invited the man to dinner at a fish joint up in Canton. They had some food and beers and laughs with him, sent him on his merry way, and then . . . what a coincidence: The blue lights flashed in the black man's rearview mirror. DUI.

Willie's phone rang the next morning, but instead of it being a caller with news of the school board's action against the new coach, it was *him.* Perry Reese Jr. Just letting Willie know that he knew exactly what had happened the night before. And that he wouldn't go away. The school board, which had caught wind of the plot, never made a peep. Who *was* this man?

Some people honestly believed that the coach was a spy—sent

by the feds to keep an eye on the Amish—or the vanguard of a plot to bring blacks into Holmes County. Yet he walked around town looking people in the eyes, smiling and teasing with easy assurance. He never showed a trace of the loneliness he must have felt. When he had a problem with someone, he went straight to its source. Straight to Willie Mast in the school parking lot one night. "So you're not too sure about me because I'm black," he said, and he laid everything out in front of Willie, about racism and how the two of them needed to get things straight.

Willie blinked. He couldn't help but ask himself the question folks all over town would soon begin to ask: Could I do, or even dream of doing, what the coach is doing? Willie couldn't help but nod when the black man invited him along to scout an opponent and stop for a bite to eat, and couldn't help but feel good when the man said he appreciated Willie because he didn't double-talk when confronted—because Willie, he said, was real. Couldn't help but howl as the Hiland Hawks kept winning, forty-nine times in fifty-three games those first two years, storming to the 1986 Division IV state semifinal.

Winning, that's what bought the black man time, what gave the magic a chance to wisp and curl through town and the rolling fields around it. That's what gave him the lard to live through that frigid winter of '87. That was the school year when he finally had his degree and began teaching history and current events in a way they'd never been taught in eastern Holmes County, the year the Hawks went 3–18 and the vermin came crawling back out of the baseboards. Damn if Willie wasn't the first at the ramparts to defend him, and damn if that black Catholic loser didn't turn things right back around the next season and never knew a losing one again.

How? By pouring Charlie Huggins's molasses offense down the drain. By runnin' and gunnin', chucking up threes, full-court pressing from buzzer to buzzer—with an annual litter of runts, of spindly, short, close-cropped Mennonites! That's what most of his players were: the children, grandchildren, and great-grand-children of Amish who, like Willie, had jumped the fence and endured the ostracism that went with it. Mennonites believed in many of the same shall-nots as the Amish: A man shall not be baptized until he's old enough to choose it, nor resort to violence even if his government demands it, nor turn his back on com-munity, family, humility, discipline, and orderliness. But the Mennonites had decided that unlike the Amish, they could con-tinue schooling past the eighth grade, turn on a light switch or a car ignition, pick up a phone, and even, except the most conserv-ative of them, pull on a pair of shorts and beat the pants off an opponent on the hardwood court without drifting into the devil's embrace.

The Hawks' Nest, Hiland's tiny old gym, became what Willie had always dreamed it would be: a loony bin, the one place a Mennonite could go to sweat and shriek and squeal; sold out year after year, with fans jamming the hallway and snaking out the door as they waited for the gym to open, then stampeding for the best seats an hour before the six o'clock jayvee game; reporters and visiting coaches and scouts sardined above them in wooden lofts they had to scale ladders to reach; spillover pouring into the auditorium beside the gym to watch on a video feed as noise thundered through the wall. A few dozen teenage Amish boys, taking advantage of the one time in their lives when elders al-lowed them to behold the modern world, and sixteen-year-old cheerleaders' legs, would be packed shoulder to shoulder in two corners of the gym at the school they weren't permitted to attend. Even a few Amish men, Lord save their souls, would tie up the horses and buggies across the street at Yoder's Lumber and slink into the Nest. And plenty more at home would tell the missus that they'd just remembered a task in the barn, then click on a radio stashed in the hay and catch the game on WKLM.

Something had dawned on Willie, sitting in his front-row seat, and on everyone else in town. The black man's values were virtually the same as theirs. Humility? No coach ever moved so fast to duck praise or bolt outside the frame of a team picture. Unselfishness? The principal might as well have taken the coach's salary to pep rallies and flung it in the air—most of it ended up in the kids' hands anyway. Reverence? No congregation ever huddled and sang out the Lord's Prayer with the crispness and cadence that the Hawks did before and after every game. Family? When Chester Mullet, Hiland's star guard in '96, only hugged his mom on parents' night, Perry gave him a choice: Kiss her or take a seat on the bench. Work ethic? The day and season never seemed to end, from 6 A.M. practices to 10 P.M. curfews, from puke buckets and running drills in autumn to two-a-days in early winter to camps and leagues and an open gym every summer day. He out-Amished the Amish, out-Mennonited the Mennonites, and everyone, even those who'd never sniffed a locker in their lives, took to calling the black man Coach.

Ask Willie. "Most of the petty divisions around here disappeared because of Coach," he'll tell you. "He pulled us all together. Some folks didn't like me, but I was respected more because he respected me. When my dad died, Coach was right there, kneeling beside the coffin, crossing himself. He put his arm right around my mom—she's Amish—and she couldn't get over that. When she died, he was the first one there. He did that for all sorts of folks. I came to realize that color's not a big deal. I took him for my best friend."

And that man in Willie's coffee clan who'd held out longest, the one given to calling Coach a nigger? By Coach's fifth year, the man's son was a Hawk, the Hawks were on another roll, and the man had seen firsthand the effect Coach had on kids. He cleared his throat one morning at the Berlin House; he had something to say.

"He's not a nigger anymore."

The magic didn't stop with a nigger turning into a man and a man into a best friend. It kept widening and deepening. Kevin Troyer won't cry when he tells you about it, as the others do. They were brought up to hold that back, but maybe his training was better. He just lays out the story, beginning that autumn day ten years ago when he was sixteen, and Coach sat him in the front seat of his Jeep, looked in his eyes, and said, "Tell me the truth."

Someone had broken into Candles Hardware and R&R Sports and stolen merchandise. Whispers around town shocked even the whisperers: that the culprits were their heroes, kids who could walk into any restaurant in Berlin and never have to pay. They'd denied it over and over, and Coach had come to their defense . . . but now even he had begun to wonder.

A priest. That's what he'd told a few friends he would be if he weren't a coach. That's whose eyes Kevin felt boring into him. How could you keep lying to the man who stood in the lobby each morning, greeting the entire student body, searching everyone's eyes to see who needed a headlock, who needed lunch money, who needed love? "Don't know what you did today, princess," he'd sing out to a plump or unpopular girl, "but whatever it is, keep it up. You look great."

He'd show up wearing a cat's grin and the shirt you'd gotten for Christmas—how'd he get into your bedroom closet?—or carrying the pillow he'd snagged right from under your head on one of his Saturday morning sorties, when he slipped like smoke into players' rooms, woke them with a pop on the chest, then ran, cackling, out the door. Sometimes those visits came on the heels of the 1 A.M. raids he called Ninja Runs, when he rang doorbells and cawed "Gotcha!" tumbling one family after another downstairs in pajamas and robes to laugh and talk and relish the privilege of being targeted by Coach. He annihilated what people here had been brought up to keep: the space between each other.

His door was never locked. Everyone, boy or girl, was welcome to wade through those half dozen stray cats on the porch that Coach gruffly denied feeding till his stash of cat food was found, and open the fridge, grab a soda, have a seat, eat some pizza, watch a game, play cards or Ping-Pong or Nintendo . . . and talk. About race and religion and relationships and teenage trouble, about stuff that wouldn't surface at Kevin Troyer's dinner table in a million years. Coach listened the way other folks couldn't, listened clean without jumping ahead in his mind to what he'd say next, or to what the Bible said. When he finally spoke, he might play devil's advocate or might offer a second or third alternative to a kid who'd seen only one or might say the very thing Kevin didn't want to hear. But Kevin could bet his mother's savings that the conversations wouldn't leave that house.

Coach's home became the students' hangout, a place where they could sleep over without their parents' thinking twice . . . as long as they didn't mind bolting awake to a blast of AC/DC and a 9 A.M. noogie. There was no more guard to drop. Parents trusted Coach completely, relied on him to sow their values.

He sowed those, and a few more. He took Kevin and the other Hawks to two-room Amish schools to read and shoot hoops with wide-eyed children who might never get to see them play, took the players to one another's churches and then to his own, St. Peter, in Millersburg. He introduced them to Malcolm X, five-alarm chili, Martin Luther King Jr., B. B. King, crawfish, Cajun wings, John Lee Hooker, Tabasco sauce, trash-talk fishing, Muhammad Ali.

And *possibility.* That's what Coach stood for, just by virtue of his presence in Berlin: possibility, no matter how high the odds were stacked against you, no matter how whittled your options seemed in a community whose beliefs had barely budged in two hundred years, whose mailboxes still carried the names of the same Amish families that had come in wagons out of Pennsylvania in the early 1800s—Yoders and Troyers and Stutzmans and Schlabachs and Hostetlers and Millers and Mullets and Masts. A place where kids, for decades, had graduated, married their prom dates, and stepped into their daddies' farming or carpentry or lumber businesses without regard for the fact that Hiland High's graduating classes of sixty ranked in the top ten in Ohio proficiency tests nearly every year. Kevin Troyer's parents didn't seem to care if he went to college. Coach's voice was the one that kept saying, "It's *your* life. There's so much more out there for you to see. Go places. Do things. Get a degree. Reach out. You have to take a chance."

The kids did, more and more, but not before Coach loaded them with laundry baskets full of items they'd need away from home, and they were never out of reach of those 6 A.M. phone calls. "I'm up," he'd say. "Now you are too. Remember, I'm always here for you."

He managed all that without raising red flags. He smuggled it under the warm coat of all that winning, up the sleeve of all that humility and humor. Everyone was too busy bubbling over the eleven conference titles and five state semifinals. Having too much fun volunteering to be henchmen for his latest prank, shoving Mr. Pratt's desk to the middle of his English classroom, removing the ladder to maroon the radio play-by-play man up in the Hawks' Nest loft, toilet-papering the school superintendent's yard and then watching Coach, the most honest guy in town, lie right through all thirty-two teeth. He was a bootlegger, that's what he was. A bootlegger priest.

"Kevin . . . tell the truth."

Kevin's insides trembled. How could he cash in his five team-mates, bring down the wrath of a community in which the Ten Commandments were still stone, own up to the man whose explosions made the Hawks' Nest shudder? How could he explain something that was full of feeling and empty of logic—that somehow, as decent as his parents were, as warm as it felt to grow up in a place where you could count on a neighbor at any hour, it all felt suffocating? All the restrictions of a Conservative Mennonite church that forbade members to watch TV, to go to movies, to dance. All the emotions he'd choked back in a home ruled by a father and mother who'd been raised to react to problems by saying, "What will people think?" All the expectations of playing for the same team that his All-State brother, Keith, had carried to its first state semi in twenty-four years, back in 1986. Somehow, busting into those stores in the summer of '91 felt like the fist Kevin could never quite ball up and smash into all that.

"I . . . I did it, Coach. We . . . "

The sweetest thing eastern Holmes County had ever known was ruined. Teammate Randy Troyer, no relation to Kevin, disappeared when word got out. The community gasped—those six boys could never wear a Hawks uniform again. Coach? He resigned. He'd betrayed the town's trust and failed his responsibility, he told his superiors. His "sons" had turned to crime.

The administration begged him to stay. Who else was respected enough by family court judges, storekeepers, ministers, and parents to find resolution and justice? Coach stared across the pond he fished behind his house. He came up with a solution both harder and softer than the town's. He would take Randy Troyer under his own roof, now that the boy had slunk back after two weeks of holing up in Florida motels. He'd be accountable for Randy's behavior. He'd have the six boys locked up in detention centers for two weeks, to know what jail tasted and smelled like.

But he would let them back on the team. Let them feel lucky to be playing basketball when they'd really be taking a crash course in accountability.

Kevin found himself staring at the cinder-block wall of his cell, as lonely as a Mennonite boy could be. But there was Coach, making his rounds to all six lost souls. There was that lung-bursting bear hug, and another earful about not following others, about believing in yourself and being a man.

The Berlin Six returned. Randy Troyer lived in Coach's home for four months. Kevin walked to the microphone at the first pep rally, sick with nerves, and apologized to the school and the town.

Redemption isn't easy with a 5' 11" center, but how tight that 1991–92 team became, players piling into Coach's car every Thursday after practice, gathering around a long table at a sports bar a half hour away in Dover and setting upon giant cookie sheets heaped with five hundred hot wings. And how those boys could run and shoot. Every time a twenty-footer left the hands of Kevin Troyer or one of the Mishler twins, Nevin and Kevin, or the Hawks' star, Jr. Raber, Hiland's students rose, twirling when the ball hit twine and flashing the big red 3's on their T-shirts' backs.

Someday, perhaps in a generation or two, some Berliner might not remember every detail of that postseason march. Against Lakeland in the district championship, the Hawks came out comatose and fell behind 20–5, Coach too stubborn to call a timeout—the man could never bear to show a wisp of doubt. At halftime he slammed the locker-room door so hard that it came off its hinges, then he kicked a crater in a trash can, sent water bottles flying, grabbed jerseys, and screamed so loud that the echoes peeled paint. Kevin and his mates did what all Hawks did: gazed straight into Coach's eyes and nodded. They knew in their bones how small his wrath was, held up against his love. They burst from that locker room like jackals, tore Lakeland to bits, and handily won the next two games to reach the state semis. The world came to a halt in Berlin.

How far can a bellyful of hunger and a chestful of mission take a team before reality steps in and stops it? In the state semifinal in Columbus, against a Lima Central Catholic bunch loaded with kids quicker and thicker and taller and darker, led by the rattlesnake-sudden Hutchins brothers, Aaron and all-stater Anthony, the Hawks were cooked. They trailed 62–55 with thirty-eight seconds left as Hiland fans trickled out in despair and Lima's surged to the box-office windows to snatch up tickets for the final. Lima called time-out to dot its *i*'s and cross its *t*'s, and there stood Coach in the Hiland huddle, gazing down at a dozen forlorn boys. He spoke more calmly than they'd ever heard him, and the fear and hopelessness leaked out of them as they stared into his eyes and drank in his plan. What happened next made you know that everything the bootlegger priest stood for—bucking the tide, believing in yourself and possibility—had worked its way from inside him to inside them.

Nevin Mishler, who would sit around the campfire in Coach's backyard talking about life till 2 A.M. on Friday nights, dropped in a rainbow three with twenty-seven seconds left to cut the deficit to four. Time-out, calm words, quick foul. Lima's Anthony Hutchins blew the front end of a one-and-one.

Eleven seconds left. Jr. Raber, whose wish as a boy was to be black, just like Coach, banked in a driving, leaning bucket and was fouled. He drained the free throw. Lima's lead was down to one. Time-out, calm words, quick foul. Aaron Hutchins missed another one-and-one.

Nine ticks left. Kevin Troyer, who would end up going to college and becoming a teacher and coach because of Coach, tore down the rebound and threw the outlet to Nevin Mishler.

Seven seconds left. Nevin turned to dribble, only to be ambushed before half-court by Aaron Hutchins, the wounded rattler, who struck and smacked away the ball.

Five seconds left, the ball and the season and salvation skittering away as Nevin, who cared more about letting down Coach than letting down his parents, hurled his body across the wood and swatted the ball back toward Kevin Troyer. Kevin, who almost never hit the floor, who had been pushed by Coach for years to give more, lunged and collided with Anthony Hutchins, then spun and heaved the ball behind his back to Jr. Raber as Kevin fell to the floor.

Three seconds left. Jr. took three dribbles and heaved up the impossible, an off-balance thirty-five-footer with two defenders in his face, a shot that fell far short at the buzzer . . . *but he was fouled.* He swished all three free throws, and the Hawks won, they *won*—no matter how many times Lima fans waiting outside for tickets insisted to Hiland fans that it couldn't be true—and two days later won the only state title in school history, by three points over Gilmour Academy, on fumes, pure fumes.

In the aisles, people danced who were forbidden to dance. The plaque commemorating the crowning achievement of Coach's life went straight into the hands of Joe Workman, a water and towel boy. Kevin Troyer and his teammates jumped Coach before he could sneak off, hugging him and kissing him and rubbing his head, but he had the last laugh. The 9 A.M. noogies would hurt even more those next nine years, dang that championship ring.

Someone would come and steal the magic. Some big-cheese high school or college would take Coach away—they knew it, they just knew it. It all seems so silly now, Steve Mullet says. It might take Steve the last half of his life to finish that slow, dazed shake of his head.

Berlin, you see, was a secret no more by the mid-1990s. Too much winning by Coach, too many tourists pouring in to peer at the men in black hats and black buggies. Two traffic lights had gone up, along with a Burger King and a couple dozen gift shops, and God knows how many restaurants and inns with the word *Dutch* on their shingles to reel in the rubberneckers. Even the Berlin House, where Willie Mast and the boys gathered, was now the Dutch Country Kitchen.

Here they came, the city slickers. Offering Coach big raises and the chance to hush that whisper in his head: Why keep working with disciplined, two-parent white kids when children of his own race were being devoured by drugs and despair for want of someone like him? Akron Hoban wanted him. So did Canton McKinley, the biggest school in the city where Coach had grown up, and Canton Timken, the high school he attended. They wanted to take the man who'd transformed Steve Mullet's family, turned it into something a simple and sincere country fellow had never dreamed it might be. His first two sons were in college, thanks to Coach, and his third one, another guard at Hiland, would likely soon be too. Didn't Steve owe it to that third boy, Carlos, to keep Coach here? Didn't he owe it to all the fathers of all the little boys around Berlin?

Coach had a way of stirring Steve's anxiety and the stew of rumors. He would walk slow and wounded through each April after he'd driven another team of runts to a conference crown, won two or three postseason games, and then yielded to the facts of the matter, to some school with nearly twice as many students and a couple of 6' 5" studs. "It's time for a change," he'd sigh. "You guys don't need me anymore."

Maybe all missionaries are restless souls, one eye on the horizon, looking for who needs them most. Perhaps Coach was trying to smoke out even the slightest trace of misgivings about him, so he could be sure to leave before he was ever asked to. But Steve Mullet and eastern Holmes County couldn't take that chance. They had to act. Steve, a dairy farmer most of his life, knew about fencing. But how do you fence in a man when no one really understands why he's there, or what he came from?

Who was Coach's family? What about his past? Why did praise and attention make him so uneasy? The whole community wondered, but in Berlin it was disrespectful to pry. Canton was only a forty-five-minute hop away, yet Steve had never seen a parent or a sibling of Coach's, a girlfriend or even a childhood pal. The bootlegger priest was a man of mystery and moods as well as a wide-open door. He'd ask you how your grandma, sister, and uncle were every time you met, but you weren't supposed to inquire about his—you just sensed it. His birthday? He wouldn't say. His age? Who knew? It changed every time he was asked. But his loneliness, that at last began to show.

There were whispers, of course. Some claimed he'd nearly married a flight attendant, then beat a cold-footed retreat. A black woman appeared in the stands once, set the grapevine sizzling, then was never glimpsed again. Steve and his pals loved to tease Coach whenever they all made the twenty-mile drive to Dinofo's, a pizza and pasta joint in Dover, and came face-to-face with that wild black waitress, Rosie. "When you gonna give it up?" she'd yelp at Coach. "When you gonna let me have it?"

He'd grin and shake his head, tell her it would be so good it would spoil her for life. Perhaps it was too scary, for a man who gave so much to so many, to carve it down to one. Maybe Jeff Pratt, the Hiland English teacher, had it right. Loving with detachment, he called it. So many people could be close to him, because no one was allowed too close.

A circle of women in Berlin looked on him almost as a brother—women such as Nancy Mishler, mother of the twins from the '92 title team, and Peg Brand, the school secretary, and Shelly Miller, wife of the booster club's president, Alan. They came to count on Coach's teasing and advice, on his cards and flowers and prayers when their loved ones were sick or their children had them at wit's end, and they did what they could to keep him in town. "I wish we could find a way to make you feel this is your family, that this is where you belong," Peg wrote him. "If you leave," she'd say, "who's going to make our kids think?" The women left groceries and gifts on his porch, homemade chocolate-chip cookies on his kitchen table, invited him to their homes on Sundays and holidays no matter how often he begged off, never wanting to impose.

But they all had to do more, Steve decided, picking up his phone to mobilize the men. For God's sake, Coach made only $28,000 a year. In the grand tradition of Mennonites and Amish, they rushed to answer the community call. They paid his rent, one month per donor; it was so easy to find volunteers that they had a waiting list. They replaced his garage when a leaf fire sent it up in flames; it sent him up a wall when he couldn't learn the charity's source. They passed the hat for that sparkling new gym at Hiland, and they didn't stop till the hat was stuffed with 1.6 million bucks. Steve Mullet eventually had Coach move into a big old farmhouse he owned. But first Steve and Willie Mast had another brainstorm: road trip. Why not give Coach a couple of days' escape from their cornfields and his sainthood, and show him how much they cared?

That's how Steve, a Conservative Mennonite in his midforties, married to a woman who didn't stick her head out in public unless it was beneath a prayer veil, found himself on Bourbon Street in New Orleans. Standing beside Willie and behind Coach, his heartbeat rising and stomach fluttering as he watched Coach suck down a Hurricane and cock his head outside a string of bars, listening for the chord that would pull him inside.

Coach nodded. This was the one. This blues bar. He pushed open the door. Music and smoke and beer musk belched out. Steve looked at Willie. You could go to hell for this, from everything they'd both been taught. Willie just nodded.

They wedged into a whorl of colors and types of humanity. When Steve was a boy, he'd seen blacks only after his parents jumped the fence, became Mennonites, and took the family in their car each summer to a city zoo. Nothing cruel about blacks was ever said. Steve's parents simply pulled him closer when they were near, filled him with a feeling: Our kind and theirs don't mix. Now there were blacks pressed against his shoulders, blacks on microphones screaming lust and heartache into Steve's ears, blacks pounding rhythm through the floorboards and up into his knees. People touching, people gyrating their hips. You could go to hell for this. Steve looked at Willie as Coach headed to the bathroom. "I can't take this," Steve said.

"It's Coach's time, bub," Willie said.

Coach came back, smelled Steve's uneasiness, and knew what to do. "Liven up," he barked and grinned. They got some beers, and it was just like the Hawks' radio play-by-play man, Mark Lonsinger, always said: Coach stood out in a room the instant he walked in, even though he did everything to deflect it. Soon Coach had the folks nearby convinced that he was Black Amish, a highly obscure sect, and Steve, swallowing his laughter, sealing the deal with a few timely bursts of Pennsylvania Dutch, had them believing the three of them had made it to New Orleans from Ohio in a buggy. Before you knew it, it was nearly midnight, and Steve's head was bobbing, his feet tapping, his funk found deep beneath all those layers of mashed potatoes. You know what, he was telling Willie, this Bourbon Street and this blues music really aren't so bad, and isn't it nice, too, how those folks found out that Mennonites aren't Martians?

When they pulled back into Coach's driveway after days filled with laughter and camaraderie, Steve glanced at Willie and sighed, "Well, now we return to our wives."

"You're the lucky ones," said Coach. "Don't you ever forget that."

Steve realized something when they returned from the road: It wasn't the road to ruin. He felt more space inside himself, plenty enough room for the black friends his sons began bringing home from college for the weekend. He realized it again the next year, when they returned to Bourbon Street, and the next, when they went once more, and the one after that as well. "Some things that I was taught were strictly no-nos . . . they're not sins," Steve will tell you. "All I know is that it all seemed right to do with him."

Funny how far that feeling had fanned, how many old, deep lines had blurred in Berlin, and what occurred in a dry community when Coach overdid it one night four years ago and tried one last time to leave. "I screwed up," he told school superintendent Gary Sterrett after he got that second DUI, fourteen miles up the road in Sugar Creek. "You need to take my job."

What happened was sort of like what happened the time the ball rolled toward the Hawks' bench in a game they were fumbling away that year at Garaway High, and Coach pulled back his leg and kicked the ball so hard that it hissed past a referee's ear and slammed off the wall, the gym hushing in anticipation of the technical foul and the ejection. But nothing happened. The two refs had such enormous respect for Coach, they pretended it away.

He apologized to every player and to every player's parents for the DUI. Steve never mentioned it. The community never said a word. It was pretended away.

They've combed through the events a thousand times, lain in bed at night tearing themselves and God to shreds. There were clues, after all, and it was their job to notice things Coach was too stubborn to admit. They thought, when he holed up in his motel room for three days in Columbus last March, that it was merely one of his postseason moods, darker than ever after falling one game shy, for the third straight year, of playing for the state title. They thought he was still brooding two months later when, preoccupied and suffering from a cold he couldn't shake, he started scrambling names and dates and getting lost on country roads.

It all came to a head one Saturday last June, when he climbed into another rented tux because Phil Mishler, just like fifty or sixty kids before him, had to have Coach in his wedding party. At the reception, Coach offered his hand to Tom Mullet and said, "I'm Perry Reese Jr., Hiland High basketball coach." Tom Mullet had been Hiland's assistant athletic director for ten years.

Phone lines buzzed that Sunday. People began comparing notes, discovering new oddities. On Monday night two of Coach's best friends, Dave Schlabach and Brian Hummel, headed to Mount Hope and the old farmhouse Coach had moved into just outside Berlin, the only house with lights in a community of Amish. They found him shivering in a blanket, glassy-eyed and mumbling nonsense.

Their worst possible fears . . . well, it went beyond all of them. Brain tumor. Malignant. Inoperable. Four to eight months to live, the doctors at Canton's Aultman Hospital said. You can't bring down a sledgehammer faster than that.

Jason Mishler, Coach's starting point guard the past two years, was the first kid to find out. He stationed himself in the chair beside Coach's bed, wouldn't budge all night and most of the next day. His cousin Kevin Mishler, from the state championship team, dropped his vacation on Hilton Head Island, S.C., and flew back. Dave Jaberg, who had played for Hiland a few years before that, dropped the bonds he was trading in Chicago and drove for six hours. Jr. Raber was on the first plane from Atlanta. Think a moment. How many teachers or coaches would you do that for?

The nurses and doctors were stupefied—didn't folks know you couldn't fit a town inside a hospital room? Coach's friends filled the lobby, the elevator, the halls, and the waiting room. It was like a Hiland basketball game, only everyone was crying. Coach kept fading in and out, blinking up at another set of teary eyes and croaking, "What's new?"

What do people pray for when doctors don't give them a prayer? They swung for the fences. The Big M, a miracle. Some begged for it. Some demanded it. A thousand people attended a prayer vigil in the gym and took turns on the microphone. Never had so much anger and anguish risen from Berlin and gone straight at God.

Steroids shrank the tumor enough for Coach to return home, where another throng of folks waited, each telling the other tales of what Coach had done to change his life, each shocked to find how many considered him their best friend. When he walked through his front door and saw the wheelchair, the portable commode, the hospital bed, and the chart Peg Brand had made, dividing the community's twenty-four-hour care for Coach into six-hour shifts, he sobbed. The giving was finished. Now all he could do was take.

Go home, he ordered them. Go back to your families and lives. He called them names. They knew him well enough to know how loathsome it was for him to be the center of attention, the needy one. But they also knew what he would do if one of them were dying. They decided to keep coming anyway. They were family. Even more in his dying than in his living, they were fused.

They cooked for him, planned a trip to New York City he'd always dreamed of making, prayed and cried themselves to sleep. They fired off e-mails to churches across the country, recruited

entire congregations who'd never heard of Coach to pray for the
Big M. Louise Conway, grandmother of a player named Jared
Coblentz, woke up three or four times a night, her heart thump-
ing so hard that she had to drop to her knees and chew God's ear
about Coach before she could drop back to sleep. People combed
the Internet for little-known treatments. They were going to hoist
a three at the buzzer and get fouled.

Coach? He did the strangest thing. He took two radiation
treatments and stopped. He refused the alternative treatments, no
matter how much people cried and begged and flung his own
lessons in his face. Two other doctors had confirmed his fate, and
damned if he was going to be helpless for long if he could help it.
"Don't you understand?" he told a buddy, Doug Klar. "It's O.K.
This is how it's supposed to be."

He finally had a plan, one that would make his death like his
life, one that would mean the giving wasn't finished. He initiated
a foundation, a college scholarship fund for those in need, started
it rolling with his $30,000 life savings, and, after swallowing hard,
allowed it to be named after him on one condition: that it be kept
secret until he was dead.

He had no way to keep all the puzzle pieces of his life in boxes
now; dying shook them out. Folks found out, for instance, that
he turned forty-eight last August. They were shocked to meet two
half sisters they'd never heard of. They were glad finally to see
Coach's younger sister, Audrey Johnson, whose picture was on his
refrigerator door and who was studying to be a social worker, and
his younger brother, Chris, who helps run group homes for people who can't fend for themselves and who took a leave of absence
to care for Coach.

It turned out that Audrey had made a couple of quiet visits a
year to Coach and that the family had gathered for a few hours on

holidays; there were no dark or splintering secrets. He came from two strict parents who'd died in the '80s—his dad had worked in a Canton steel mill—and had a mixed-race aunt on one side of the family and a white grandfather on the other. But there were never quite enough pieces of the puzzle for anyone to put them together on a table and get a clean picture.

Coach's family was shocked to learn a few things too. Like how many conservative rural white folks had taken a black man into their hearts. "Amazing," said Jennifer Bethà, his half sister, a supervisor for Head Start. "And so many loving, respectful, well-mannered children around him. They were like miniature Perrys! Our family was the independent sort, all kind of went our own ways. I never realized how easy it is to get to Berlin from Canton, how close it is. What a waste. Why didn't we come before?"

Coach had two good months, thanks to the steroids. Berlin people spent them believing that God had heard them and that the miracle had come. Coach spent the months telling hundreds of visitors how much he cared about them, making one last 1 A.M. Ninja Run and packing his life into ten neat cardboard boxes.

The first week of August, he defied doctors' orders not to drive and slipped into the empty school. Gerald Miller, his buddy and old boss at the wagon factory, found him later that day at home, tears streaming down his cheeks. "Worst day of my life," Coach said. "Worse than finding out about this thing in my head. I cleaned out my desk. I can't believe it. I'm not gonna teach anymore. I'm done."

In early September the tumor finally had its way. He began slurring words, falling down, losing the use of his right hand and leg, then his eyesight. "How are you doing?" he kept asking his visitors, on blind instinct. "Is there anything I can do for *you?*"

Till the end he heard the door open and close, open and close, and felt the hands, wrapped around his, doing that too.

On the day he died, November 22, just over a week before the Hawks' first basketball game and seventeen years after he first walked through their doors, Hiland looked like one of those schools in the news in which a kid has walked through the halls with an automatic weapon. Six ministers and three counselors walked around hugging and whispering to children who were huddled in the hallway crying or staring into space, to teachers sobbing in the bathrooms, to secretaries who couldn't bear it and had to run out the door.

An old nettle digs at most every human heart: the urge to give oneself to the world rather than to only a few close people. In the end, unable to bear the personal cost, most of us find a way to ignore the prickle, comforting ourselves that so little can be changed by one woman or one man anyway.

How much, in the end, was changed by this one man? In Berlin, they're still tallying that one up. Jared Coblentz, who might have been the Hawks' sixth man this year, quit because he couldn't play for anyone other than Coach. Jason Mishler was so furious that he quit going to church for months, then figured out that it might be greedy to demand a miracle when you've been looking at one all your life. Tattoo parlors added Mennonites to their clientele. Jr. Raber stares at the R.I.P. with a P beneath it on his chest every morning when he looks into the mirror of his apartment in Atlanta. Jason Mishler rubs the image of Coach's face on the top of his left arm during the national anthem before every game he plays at West Liberty (W.Va.) State.

The scholarship fund has begun to swell. Half the schools Hiland has played this season have chipped in checks of $500 or

$600, while refs for the girls' basketball games frequently hand back their $55 checks for the pot.

Then there's the bigger stuff. Kevin Troyer has decided that someday, rather than teach and coach around Berlin, he'll reverse Coach's path and do it with black kids up in Canton. Funny, the question he asked himself that led to his decision was the same one that so many in Berlin ask themselves when they confront a dilemma: What would Coach do? Hard to believe, an outsider becoming the moral compass of a people with all those rules on how to live right.

And the even bigger stuff. Like Shelly and Alan Miller adopting a biracial boy ten years ago over in Walnut Creek, a boy that Coach had taken under his wing. And the Keims over in Charm adopting two black boys, and the Schrocks in Berlin adopting four black girls, and the Masts just west of town adopting two black girls, and Chris Miller in Walnut Creek adopting a black girl. Who knows? Maybe some of them would have done it had there never been a Perry Reese Jr., but none of them would have been too sure that it was *possible*.

"When refugees came to America," the town psychologist, Elvin Coblentz, says, "the first thing they saw was the Statue of Liberty. It did something to them—became a memory and a goal to strive for your best, to give your all, because everything's possible. That's what Coach is to us."

At the funeral, just before Communion, Father Ron Aubry gazed across St. Peter, Coach's Catholic church in Millersburg. The priest knew that what he wanted to do wasn't allowed, and that he could get in trouble. But he knew Coach too. So he did it: invited everyone up to receive the holy wafer.

Steve Mullet glanced at his wife, in her simple clothing and veil. "Why not?" she whispered. After all, the service wasn't the bizarre ritual they had been led to believe it was, wasn't all that different from their own. Still, Steve hesitated. He glanced at Willie Mast. "Would Coach want us to?" Steve whispered.

"You got 'er, bub," said Willie.

So they rose and joined all the black Baptists and white Catholics pouring toward the altar, all the basketball players, all the Mennonites young and old. Busting laws left and right, busting straight into the kingdom of heaven.

GEORGE STEINER

Of Larger Darkness

from *Harper's Magazine*

We have no more beginnings. *Incipit,* that proud Latin word signaling the start, survives in our dusty *inception.* The medieval scribe marks the opening line, the new chapter, with an illuminated capital. In its golden or carmine vortex the illuminator of manuscripts sets heraldic beasts, dragons at morning, singers and prophets. The initial, where this term signifies beginning and primacy, acts as a fanfare. It declares Plato's maxim—by no means self-evident—whereby in all things natural and human the origin is the most excellent. Today, in Western orientations—observe the muted presence of morning light in that word—the reflexes, turns of perception, are those of afternoon, of twilight.

There have been previous senses of ending and fascinations with sundown in Western culture. Philosophic witness, the arts, historians of feeling, report on "closing-times in the gardens of the West" during the crises of the Roman imperial order, during the apocalyptic fears at the approach of the first millennium A.D., in the wake of the Black Death and the Thirty Years' War. Motions of decay, of autumn and failing light, have always attached to men and women's awareness of physical ruin, of common mortality. Moralists, even prior to Montaigne, pointed out that the newborn infant is old enough to die. There is in the most confident metaphysical construct, in the most affirmative work of art, a memento mori, a labor, implicit or explicit, to hold at bay the seepage of fatal time, of entropy into each and every living form. It is from this wrestling match that philosophic discourse and the generation of art derive their informing stress, the unresolved tautness of which logic and beauty are formal modes. The cry "the great god Pan is dead" haunts even those societies with which we associate, perhaps too conventionally, the gusto of optimism.

Nevertheless, there is, I think, in the climate of spirit at the end of the twentieth century, a core-tiredness. The inward chronometry, the contracts with time that so largely determine our consciousness, point to late afternoon in ways that are ontological—this is to say, of the essence, of the fabric of being. We are, or feel ourselves to be, latecomers. The shadows lengthen. We seem to bend earthward and toward the night as do heliotropic plants.

Inhumanity is, so far as we have historical evidence, perennial. There have been no utopias, no communities of justice or forgiveness. Our current alarms—at the violence in our streets, at the famines in the so-called Third World, at regressions into barbaric ethnic conflicts, at the possibility of pandemic disease—must be seen against the backdrop of a quite exceptional moment. Roughly from the time of Waterloo to that of the massacres on the Western Front in 1915–16, the European bourgeoisie experienced a privileged season, an armistice with history. Underwritten by the exploitation of industrial labor at home and colonial rule abroad, Europeans knew a century of progress, of liberal dispensations, of reasonable hope. It is in the afterglow, no doubt idealized, of this exceptional calendar—note the constant comparison of the years prior to August 1914 to a "long summer"— that we suffer our present discomforts.

We have not yet begun to gauge the damage to man—as a species, as one entitling himself *sapiens*—inflicted by events since 1914. We do not yet begin to grasp the coexistence in time and in space, a coexistence sharpened by the immediacy of graphic and verbal presentation in the global mass media, of Western superfluity, and the starvation, the destitution, the infant mortality, that now batten on some three-fifths of mankind. There is a dynamic of clear-sighted lunacy in our waste of what is left of natural resources, of fauna and flora. The south col of Everest is a garbage dump. Forty years after Auschwitz, the Khmer Rouge bury alive an estimated hundred thousand innocent human beings. The rest of the world, fully apprised of the fact, does nothing. New weapons soon start flowing from our factories to the killing fields. To repeat: violence, oppression, economic enslavement, and social irrationality have been endemic in history, whether tribal or metropolitan. But this century has given despair a new warrant. It has raised the distinct possibility of a reversal of evolution, of a systematic turnabout toward bestialization. It is this that makes Kafka's *Metamorphosis* the key fable of modernity.

What I want to consider briefly is the impact of this darkened condition on grammar—where I take grammar to mean the articulate organization of perception, reflection, and experience, the nerve structure of consciousness when it communicates with itself and with others. I intuit (these are, of course, almost wholly conjectural domains) that the future tense came relatively late into human speech. It may have developed as late as the end of the last ice age, together with the "futurities" entailed by food storage, by the making and preservation of tools beyond immediate need, and by the very gradual discovery of animal breeding and agriculture. In some "meta-" or prelinguistic register, animals would appear to know presentness and, one supposes, a measure of remembrance. The future tense, the ability to discuss possible events on the day after one's funeral or in space a million years hence, looks to be specific to *Homo sapiens*. As does the use of the subjunctive and of counterfactual modes that are themselves kindred, as it were, to future tenses. It is only man, so far as we can conceive, who has the means of altering his world by resort to "if" clauses, who can generate clauses such as: "If Caesar had not gone to the Capitol that day." It seems to me that this fantastic, formally incommensurable "grammatology" of verb futures, of subjunctives and optatives, proved indispensable to the survival, to the evolution, of the "language animal," confronted, as we were and are, by the scandal, by the incomprehensibility of individual death. There is a sense in which every human use of the future tense of the verb *to be* is a negation, however limited, of mortality. Even as every use of an "if" sentence tells of a refusal of the brute inevitability, of the despotism of the fact. *Shall, will,* and *if,* circling in intricate fields of semantic force around a hidden center or nucleus of potentiality, are the passwords to hope.

Hope and fear are supreme fictions empowered by syntax. They are as indivisible from each other as they are from grammar. Hope encloses a fear of unfulfillment. Fear has in it a mustard seed of hope, the intimation of overcoming. It is the status of hope today that is problematic.

Out of Mosaic and prophetic Judaism grew two major branches or "heresies." The first is Christianity, with its promise of God's kingdom to come, of reparation for unjust suffering, of a Last Judgment and an eternity of love through the Son. The future tense of the verb inhabits nearly every saying of Jesus. He is, for his followers, hope made flesh. The second branch, again Jewish in its theoreticians and early proponents, is utopian socialism and, most signally, Marxism. Here the claims on transcendence are made immanent, the kingdom of justice and equality, of peace and prosperity, is proclaimed to be of this world. With the voice of Amos, socialist idealism and Marxist-Leninist communism cry anathema on selfish wealth, on social oppression, on the crippling of countless common lives by insensate greed. The desert marches on the city. After the bitter struggle (after Golgotha) comes "the exchange of love for love, of justice for justice."

The twentieth century has put in doubt the theological, the philosophical, and the political-material insurance for hope. It queries the rationale and credibility of future tenses. It makes understandable Kafka's statement that "there is abundance of hope, but none for us."

It is not the cant phrase "the death of God," which predated Nietzsche and to which I am unable to assign any arguable meaning, that is pertinent. The determinant of our current situation is more embracing. I would call it "the eclipse of the messianic." In Western religions, the messianic, whether personalized or metaphoric, has signified renovation, the end of historical temporality, and the coming in glory of an afterworld. Over and again, the future tense of hope has sought to date this event (the year 1000 or 1666 or, among present-day chiliastic sects, the turn of our millennium). In a literal sense, hope has sprung eternal. Western faiths are redemption narratives. But the messianic is no less instrumental in secular programs. For anarchist and Marxist imaginings of the future, it will be represented by the "withering away of the state." Behind this figure lies Kant's argument on universal peace and the Hegelian thesis of an end to history. In a paradoxical regard, the messianic can be independent of any postulate of God: it stands for man's access to perfectibility, to a higher and, presumably, enduring condition of reason and of justice.

Future tenses are an idiom of the messianic. Take away energizing anticipation, the luminous imperative of waiting, and these tenses will be end-stopped. "Life expectancy" is, then, no longer a messianic-utopian projection but an actuarial statistic. Such pressures on the incipience of meaning and communication in the individual and collective subconscious, on the means of articulate speech, are gradual. Figures of daily discourse, totally devoid of concrete truth—"sunrise," for example—will persist like domestic ghosts. Except with masters of poetry and of speculative thought, language is conservative and opaque to nascent intuitions (hence the need for mathematical and logically formal codes in the swiftly moving sciences). But just as the almost imperceptible tectonic movements in the deeps of the earth sever and reshape continents, so the forces emanating from the eclipse of the messianic will find manifest expression. Grammars of nihilism flicker on the horizon. Emily Dickinson put it succinctly. Unless I misread, ours are "Those Evenings of the Brain."

Valedictions look backward. In our age of transition to new mappings, to new ways of telling the story, the natural and the "human" sciences present a spiraling motion. It is that of which Nietzsche's "eternal return" and Yeats's "great gyres" are images. Knowledge proceeds forward technically, in its methods, in the ground it covers. But it seeks out origins. It would identify and grasp the source. In this movement toward "primacy," different sciences, different bodies of systematic inquiry, draw strikingly close to one another.

Cosmology and astrophysics are proposing models of the birth of our universe with a scenic sweep and speculative flight that are far closer to ancient or "primitive" creation myths than they are to mechanistic positivism. Just now, the hypothesis of "continuous creation," of the provenance of matter out of interstellar "dark matter" or nothingness, is out of favor. Some kind of "big bang" is thought to have detonated our cosmos around fifteen billion years ago. Background radiation and the compaction of "lumps" in new galaxies are held to be spoors of this *incipit*. In a sovereign paradox, the farther the horizon of radio astronomy, of the observation of nebulae at the "edge of the universe," the deeper our descent into the temporal abyss, into the primordial past in which expansion began. The crux is indeed the concept of a beginning. Our current magi tell us that it is, *stricto sensu,* absurd, without meaning, to ask what was before the initial nanoseconds of the "bang." There was nothing. Nothingness excludes temporality. Time and the coming into being of being are quintessentially one (exactly as St. Augustine taught). The present of the verb *to be,* the first *is,* creates and is created by the fact of existence. Although the conditions of "strangeness" and "singularity"—terms that reach as probingly into metaphysics or poetics as they do into the physics of cosmology—during the initial particle of time may still escape our computations, late-twentieth-century science is now "within three seconds" of the start of the universe. The creation story can be told as never before.

In this story, the evolution of organic life comes late. Here also the energies of insight press on origination. The question as to the origin and evolution of self-replicating molecular structures occupies paleontology, biochemistry, physical chemistry, and genetics. Life-forms more and more rudimentary, nearer and nearer to the threshold of the inorganic, are being discovered or modeled. The study of DNA (where the double helix is itself an icon of the spiraling pattern in today's sciences and systems of sensibility) leads back to the inception of ordered vitality, of the encoding of developmental possibilities. This "re-duction," or leading backward, has brought with it the likelihood that genetic material, capable of self-reproduction, will be created in the laboratory. The Adamic act and the making of the golem are rationally conceivable.

The quest for point zero in astrophysics, for the ultimate foundation of organic life in molecular biology, has its counterpart in the investigations of the human psyche. In progressive interplay, neurophysiology, genetics, neurochemistry, the study of artificial intelligence, and psychology, analytic and clinical, are edging toward the earliest sediments of mental being. The subconscious, even, conceivably, the outlying regions of the unconscious—of that first long night in us—are being drawn toward observation. This rising out of chaos is mimed perfectly in the celebrated initial chord of Wagner's *Ring,* whose resonance, simultaneously radiant and ominous, poses the question: As we comb the deeps, what monsters are we trawling?

Arrestingly, as on a spiral staircase, descent into the past and the ascent of knowledge meet in ambiguous intimacy. Archaic religious-mythological figurations reemerge, barely concealed. Marx's 1844 manuscripts infer some catastrophic event in the genesis of society that provoked the deployment of class enmity, of social exploitation and the cash-nexus. In the Freudian legend of the structuring of the human psyche, familial and social relations arise from the primal murder of the father by the horde of his sons. In the anthropology of Lévi-Strauss, the domestication of fire makes man "transgress" into culture; it severs him from nature and impels him toward the solitude of history. Quite obviously, these scenarios of explanation are borrowed from that of Original Sin, of the Fall of Man out of the sphere of innocent grace into that tragic knowingness or historicity. As we seek out the "lost" beginnings of our universe, of our organicity, of our psychic identity and social context, of our language and historical temporality, this search, this "long day's journey into night," is not neutral. It tells, as Hegel famously taught, of twilight. It adumbrates intuitions of some primal error. It manifests what is, as I have tried to suggest, the most deep-seated of the many crises or revolutions we are experiencing: that of the future tense. The utopian, messianic, positivist-meliorist "futures" presumed, blueprinted in the Western legacy from Plato to Lenin, from the Prophets to Leibniz, may no longer be available to our syntax. We now look back at them. They are monuments for remembrance, as obstinately haunting as Easter Island stone faces, on the journey into our outset. We now remember the futures that were.

What Kind of Errand?

from *Parabola*

The author and his stepbrother Nicky, a Buddhist photographer, have been traveling through the Colombian jungle, recording the clash between modernity and tradition in its villages. After six weeks, they come into contact with someone who knows of an Indian shaman who is both accessible and willing to be photographed.

Don Juan and Carlos [Castaneda]'s adventures were fresh in my head on the morning when Nicky and I—after the usual endless bus rides and a final journey by hired Jeep through a vast, anonymous stretch of lowland jungle—stood before a primitive, one-room house in a remote village. It turned out that the owner of the house—a tiny man with a broad, pleasant face dressed in worn blue dungarees and a T-shirt—was not the shaman we were looking for but a friend of his. This was not too surprising, as I knew that when Carlos was looking for sorcerers without Don Juan's help, it was always a long process of driving here and there and back again, talking to one person and another and another. To find a genuine Adult Unlike Other Adults in one step, you usually had to have one of them along with you; otherwise, plenty of patience was necessary.

Nicky and our driver worked out some more details about the real shaman's whereabouts, and we got back in the Jeep and traveled deeper into the jungle. After another long, bumpy drive through moist air and an endless expanse of surplus-store green, the Jeep brought us to another village, this one even smaller and sleepier than the first. At first nobody seemed to be around. There weren't even any of the thin, skittish dogs that were so depressingly common in most of the towns and villages. After our driver turned off the Jeep's engine, however, I realized we were not alone after all. Noise was coming from the house the driver had stopped in front of—in fact, quite a bit of it. The three of us hopped out and approached the house's single, half-open doorway. Considering the remoteness of the location, I found it odd that no one had come out to greet the sound of the Jeep, and it now became clear that our presence had gone unnoticed because something really hilarious was going on inside. The little house—again composed of only a single room—seemed almost to shake with wild laughter.

Our guide entered, and Nicky and I, ducking our heads, followed. It was quite dark, but I could see well enough to notice that the place was strangely short on furniture. The only major object in the room was a long wooden bench set against one wall. The floor was dirt, with a space of a few inches open between it and the walls all the way around. The walls themselves were free of decoration save for the one opposite the bench, at the center of which hung a page that looked like it had been torn from an American magazine. The face in the picture was familiar, but it took a moment for me to figure out who it was: Shaun Cassidy—the younger brother of *Partridge Family* star David, who had recently had a hit on the charts in the States. What was Shaun Cassidy's face doing here, on the wall of this house, in the heart of this sweaty, anonymous jungle? I didn't have time to ponder the question, for there were more details to take in and analyze. Perhaps the most suggestive and troublesome of these was the sweet yet nasty smell that filled the place—a smell I identified, after a moment, as oxidizing alcohol.

On the bench sat two men, somewhere in their fifties or sixties, dressed, as the man in the previous village had been, in dungarees and T-shirts. Both held small plastic cups in their hands, and on

the ground before them was a bottle of something called Aguardi-
ente. I recognized the stuff because I had seen it everywhere on
our trips. Made from pressed sugar cane and exceptionally inex-
pensive, the stuff was Tres Esquinas's only real competition for
Colombia's alcoholic beverage of choice. On the side of the room
opposite the two men, seated cross-legged on the dirt floor with a
cup of her own, was a woman dressed in a plain, somewhat
grubby cotton shift who looked a little older, and a little drunker,
than the men. The three of them stared over at us, the subject of
their laughter seemingly forgotten. There was a moment of awkward silence. Finally the woman, pointing to us, said something
in a loud, raspy, incomprehensible Spanish to her two friends.
Then the three of them exploded into laughter again.

When it had died down a bit, our guide engaged one of the
men in conversation. I tried to follow what was going on but soon
gave up. Nicky, however, was listening carefully, and in a moment
he spoke to me in a low voice.

"He's telling them why we're here. That one on the left is the
shaman."

The shaman, who, Zen acceptance or no Zen acceptance, didn't
look at all the way I had wanted him to, listened as our guide
spoke his piece. Then he nodded his head slowly and gravely and
barked out a few sentences. Again the guide turned and spoke to
Nicky, and Nicky spoke to me.

"Maybe we can take his picture," Nicky said, "but we have to
sit with them first for a while, so they can get to know us."

"Get to know us! They're not even going to remember we were
here by tomorrow morning. Let's just get out of here."

As if he hadn't heard me at all, Nicky went over and sat down
between the two men. I considered my options but realized I didn't
have many, as the old woman was now gesturing for me to come
sit by her. Slowly but surely getting more angry, I walked over and

plunked down on the ground next to her, whereupon she gave me a friendly whack on the back and offered me a drink from her plastic cup. I smiled weakly and shook my head. She then embarked on a dense and extraordinarily rapid monologue, not a word of which could I understand.

Over on the bench Nicky was getting the same treatment from the two men, but he was clearly having a better time of it than I was, thanks, as usual, to his infuriating Buddhist patience. If up until now Nicky's ability to be in the Moment without succumbing to judgment or scorn was something I had regarded with puzzled respect, I now felt suddenly quite ready to strangle him for it. To hell with him, I thought to myself. To hell with being in the Moment, and to hell with the Buddha, and Zen, and the camera in the Jeep outside, and this whole lousy, tragic, stupid, worn-out, broken-down, irritating, garbage-filled world we were dragging it through. To hell with it all. For some mysterious reason, my disappointed expectations were producing a sensation of self-loathing that was just as strong as the one I felt for everything and everyone else. What a spoiled, naïve jerk I had been, expecting to find some romantic Man of Knowledge waiting for me here in this all-too-ordinary jungle.

Nicky's Spanish was fairly good, and in response to this or that statement he would nod his head, smile patiently, and say a few words in reply. Perhaps to escape from the still all-but-overpowering smell of alcohol, our guide had stepped back out of the hut and into the overcast daylight. Through the doorway I could see him, standing by the Jeep, smoking a Pielroja. Though completely one-sided save for the occasional nod or "*no comprendo*" from me, my conversation with the old woman ground on for a good fifteen minutes. Occasionally I would attempt a withering glance over at Nicky, but he either didn't want to acknowledge me or was actually caught up in the conversation he was having with the two men. At long last, the three of them got to their feet and I took the opportunity to get up too.

"What's going on?"

"He's agreed to let me photograph him," Nicky said, even-toned and again completely devoid of sarcasm.

"That's terrific. Anthropologists around the world are going to be grateful for your efforts."

Again Nicky said nothing in return but exited the house behind the two men. Meanwhile, the woman, who had moved over to the bench the men had left, refilled her plastic cup and gestured for me to join her. I smiled and motioned apologetically to the doorway, suggesting that my efforts were needed outside. When I stepped out into the light, Nicky and the guide were unloading our gear from the Jeep, the shaman's Indian friend was standing and watching them vacantly, and the shaman himself was nowhere to be seen. A few children, dressed in the usual brightly colored Western textiles, had emerged from the other huts, and I realized the little village hadn't been so empty after all.

"Where's the shaman?" I said.

"Over there in one of those huts," said Nicky, passing the main camera bag to me. "He needs to change into his costume. Do you have the cash I gave you this morning?"

"Yeah. Why?"

"We need to pay him."

"Pay him! Oh come on. Don't tell me you're really considering giving this guy money too?"

Nicky remained maddeningly unwilling to share in or even acknowledge my irritation. He really was riding this stupid nonjudgment horse to the end of the race. I found the cash and gave it to him, and in a few moments more the shaman emerged from a nearby hut. Though still drunk, he was now dressed up in a surprisingly dramatic native outfit, including an elaborate feather headdress and what seemed to be a sort of magician's staff, also outfitted with a couple of feathers. Even though I continued to despise him, I had to admit he looked pretty impressive. Nicky directed him to stand over by the house, and we commenced our usual camera-setup drill. As we did so, ever more villagers, adults and children, appeared from here and there and watched the process.

Nicky's camera worked best with long exposures, and he now explained the need to hold very still to the shaman, who cooperated as best he could, staring ferociously at Nicky's lens and trying not to sway back and forth too much. Occasionally, as if to help himself stay in character, he produced a short, angry grunt and shook his magician's staff menacingly.

I stood in my usual spot behind Nicky as he hunched under the old-fashioned black photographer's cloak and fiddled with the knobs of his complicated camera. There before us, in one neat package, stood the whole Life Manual problem. It was a problem I had now become fairly good at reading and thinking about, but that I was not a whit better at approaching and actually dealing with in real life than I had been when I first started addressing it more than a year before. The world, said my Life Manuals, was not what I wanted it to be. In fact, it was quite often just about the absolute opposite of that, down to the smallest detail. But if I was to take the basic Life Manual program of action seriously, I was not to be put off by this fact. Instead, I was to learn how to see the world as perfect and lacking for nothing, even for all that it might not seem to be so. In order to do this, I needed to apply the Brillo pad of nonjudgment to all my accustomed habits and perceptions. I needed to act, to work, to think, and to observe, and I needed to do so without ever asking things to be other than just as they were. If I did this long enough—and perhaps even if I did it for just a short while—the world, or my perception of it, would eventually change. I would see, to my great joy and surprise, that everything really *was* just as it was supposed to be, and always had been.

In a few minutes Nicky was satisfied and we packed up the camera. After a little more conversation and the passing over of some money, we got back in the Jeep and drove away, with the shaman and his friend and some of the other villagers waving us off. Nicky had the shots he wanted—shots not of ideal, romanticized reality, but of the flawed, frustrating, determinedly ordinary reality that life specializes in. If I was ever to be happy with that reality, it was clear that I still had plenty more work to do.

One Man on a Tractor Far Away

from *Christianity Today*

APRIL 28, 1995

I've opened a small suitcase on the bed. The window shades are pulled. They usually are, night and day. Their white translucence, though, allows a fine spring light in the bedroom; and as I move from the closet to the dresser, gathering clothes for packing, I feel glad anticipations about the weekend.

It's Friday. Early afternoon. In forty-five minutes I will leave town for Wheaton College in Illinois where one of my stories is to receive its first public performance. As good as that—better than that, actually—I'm to meet one of my best friends there, whose full-length play will also be performed. His piece is the real feature of Wheaton's theater festival; mine's a private excitement.

My friend's name is David McFadzean. The director at Wheaton is Jim Young, soft-spoken, with talent as deep as tree roots.

I'm going to drive. I'll be back on Sunday.

So, then: two clean shirts, fresh underwear, a pair of dark slacks; my shaving kit is in the bathroom. . . .

Just as I burst from the bathroom, Thanne appears at the top of the stairs. She lets me rush past her, then follows into the bedroom. She's moving slowly. Thanne will often suspend her work while I get ready for some extended trip. She'll say good-bye in the driveway.

"You think I'll need my raincoat?"

She doesn't answer.

"Thanne?"

I glance at her. No, her slowness now is not a preparation for "good-bye." She hasn't sat. My wife is gazing at the window shades as if they were open and the world lay visible before her. Her head is drawn back. There are small bunches of flesh at the corners of her lips.

"Thanne?"

For a moment she stands unmoving. The shades are pulled; there is no world before her. There's nothing to see. Her face is illuminated by a diffusion of light. I stuff the shaving kit into my suitcase. I will say her name again, with greater emphasis—but then she speaks in a dreaming murmur: "Wally."

"Yes? What?"

Now Thanne turns and turns on me the same wondering gaze she gave the window shade.

"Dad's gone," she says.

"Ah."

There is no explanation for this, but I understand the sense of her words immediately, completely. I don't ask her to elaborate. There is no compulsion in me toward surprise or shock. Rather, I scrutinize the woman carefully, to see how she is herself responding to this . . . this, what? Act of God?

Dad's gone.

But she stands as erect as first I ever saw her, and the cast of her neck and head make her seem a Grecian column to hold the roofs of temples. Except for the line between her eyebrows, her countenance is composed.

"Thanne?"

I'm asking after her state of being. I would add, How are you?—except she thinks I'm asking for details, and answers first.

Softly, as if all this were a wonder to her, Thanne draws me the picture in her mind. "Mom says it was just after lunch. They'd come back to their rooms. Dad had shifted himself from the wheelchair into his TV chair. Mom wasn't paying any attention. She was just about to sit, when Dad took three quick breaths . . . and then he was gone."

I step toward her now. I gather the woman into my arms. I take her face against my throat, and we stand still. She is not crying. She is deeply quiet.

My wife's father, Martin Bohlmann, has just died. This is the first of our four parents to go.

Softly, still with that note of awe-ful wonder, Thanne adds one more detail.

"Mom's says it's a good thing Dad took those three breaths, and that they were loud. Otherwise she'd have talked to a dead man till suppertime."

SPRING, 1967

The farmer was not a talky man. Not ever, I suppose—though when I first met him I assumed that the size and the noise of his family didn't permit him time to talk.

At the age of twenty-three I drove west from Ohio to the flat, black farmland of eastern Illinois, there to visit the Bohlmann farm, to seek approval of the Bohlmann parents, and to court the Bohlmann daughter named Ruthanne.

On a Friday evening we sat down to supper in the spacious kitchen. The day had been balmy. I remember that the kitchen door stood open to the porch, so that breezes stole in behind me. The air was warm and rich and loamy. Jonquils and daffodils were in bloom, the tulip beds about to pop, the ground as yet uncultivated. I'd been a city boy all my life. I wanted to weep for the perfect sense of sufficiency this world provided me.

There were eight of us at the table, though it could accommodate fifteen at least. Martin and Gertrude had brought forth fourteen children. They buried one in infancy and now had watched nearly all the others depart for college. Ruthanne was the tenth child born to them, the fifth from the last.

The farmer bowed his head. "Come!" he said with surprising force, then lowered his voice for the rest of the prayer: "*Come, Lord Jesus, be our guest. . . .*"

I soon learned that the first word was something like a gong, alerting the rest of his huge family to the sacred duty now begun.

Apart from that commanding *Come,* Martin's praying and his manner both were mild. His hair, on the other hand—aimed at me from the bowed head at the other end of the table—constituted a fierce aggression. It never would comb down, but stood up and stabbed like bayonets in defiance.

As soon as the prayer was done, a hard, clattering silence overtook the table, while all the Bohlmanns concentrated on filling up their plates.

Potatoes and vegetables had been raised in the kitchen garden. Popcorn, too. Milk came from Bohlmann cows. There'd been a time when the hog was hung up on a chilly autumn morning and butchered in the barn door, giving cracklings to the family, hams and chops and sausages and lard. Gertrude used the lard for the wedding cakes she baked to earn spending money. The Bohlmanns owned neither the land they worked nor the house they slept in. They rented. They never paid income tax, since their annual income never approached a taxable figure. For them it was a short distance from the earth to their stomachs—and back to earth again. Thanne recalls the cold two-holer on snowy winter mornings.

Martin ate that meal mostly in silence. But so did he eat all his meals, and so did he live most of his life: in silence.

When he was done, he slipped a toothpick into the corner of his mouth, read aloud a brief devotion for our general benefit, pushed back his chair, stood up, and walked outside.

I followed him. I think I thought I'd talk with him, persuade him of the honor of my intentions. But Martin moved in the sort of solitude that, it seemed to my young self, admitted no foolish intrusions. And once outside, he kept on walking. So I lingered in the yard and watched, following no farther than that.

In twilight the farmer, clad in clean coveralls, strolled westward into the field immediately beyond the yard. He paused. He stood in silhouette, the deep green sky framing his body with such precision that I could see the toothpick twiddling between his lips. His hair was as stiff and wild as a thicket, the great blade of his nose majestic.

Soon Martin knelt on one knee. He reached down and gathered a handful of dirt. He lifted it, then sifted the lumpish dust through his fingers onto the palm of his other hand. Suddenly he brought both hands to his face and inhaled. The toothpick got switched to the side; Martin touched the tip of his tongue to the earth. Then he rose again. He softly clapped his two hands clean, then slipped them behind the bib of his coveralls, and there he stood, straight up, gazing across the field, his form as black as iron in the gloaming, his elbows forming the joints of folded wings—and I thought: How peaceful! How completely peaceful is this man.

It caused in me a sort of sadness, a nameless elemental yearning.

APRIL 29, 1995

I am in Wheaton with David McFadzean, sitting at a small table in the college snack bar. I drove my little pickup here, while Thanne drove the mini-van south into the Illinois farm country of her childhood. She's with her mother and her siblings in Watseka, arranging for her father's funeral, which has been scheduled for Monday. Thanne has already contacted our own children, to see which will be able to attend the funeral. They will all be there—at least for the wake on Sunday.

Since there's little I can do for Martin now, and since Thanne herself is surrounded by a small city of Bohlmanns, we decided I should keep my appointments after all. And I have. But I move as something of an alien here. I'm morbidly conscious of my body, the thing I live in, as if it were a bunting concealing my truer self. No, that's not quite accurate: rather, my body is the heavy thing I bear wherever I go, as if it were a prison of severe limitations. And here's the irony: to lose it or to leave it is to die.

Last night the Wheaton College Theater Department performed my story, "One In A Velvet Gown." It's a melancholy piece, based on personal boyhood experience. Watching it, I became a watcher of my past, departed self.

We're going to watch David's play tonight. He tells me it's still a work in progress. He grins, suddenly conscious of what he's doing. He's preparing the both of us to forgive the flaws he fears we'll see.

"How's Thanne," he says. This is a running joke: "I'd rather be talking to her, not you!" His eyes blink flat with a false sincerity.

I swallow coffee and surprise myself by saying, "He can't be gone."

"What?" David tucks his chin into his neck and curls a lip of wry query: "Whaaat?" He thinks I'm giving him joke for joke.

I say, "Thanne's dad died yesterday," and then I feel terrible. It's a crude, stupid way to announce such a thing. But this is how separate I feel: when David snaps to a confused sobriety, I don't apologize. I don't say anything. I don't even acknowledge his gestures of sympathy—or if I do, I don't know that I do.

For as soon as I uttered that sentence of death out loud, I realized I meant much more than Martin's physical departure. I meant the man's entire way of life, his perfect peace in the universe. And now my spirit is breathless at so tremendous a loss. For if these are gone, then the world has become a dangerous place altogether.

What? And shall all my fears return again, making me an alien wherever I go?

1900–1950

Martin Bohlmann was born with the century. His relationship to the earth, therefore, was established long before society developed its ever more complex technologies for separating human creatures from the rest of creation.

Throughout his young manhood, farming was largely the labor of muscle and bone, hoof and hand. The very first successful gasoline tractor was not manufactured until 1892. In 1907 there were a mere six hundred tractors in the entire United States.

Thanne can remember the years before her father purchased his first John Deere in the late forties. She watched him plowing behind draft horses, steady beasts with hooves the size of the little girl's head.

"Prince," the farmer called them, and "Silver."

Often it was Ruthanne's task to lead them to water. And this is why she remembers the time and the chore so well: it frightened the child to walk between two such massive motors of rolling hide, her head below their necks. The quicker she went, the quicker they took their mighty paces, until she thought she could never stop them, and they would fly headlong into the pond, all three!

Her father, however, commanded them mutely with a gesture, with a cluck and a tap of the bridle. Silent farmer. Silent, stolid horses. They were for him a living, companionable power. And when Martin and his horses spent days plowing fields—moving with huffs and clomps and the ringing of chains, but with no explosions of liquid fuel—their wordless communication became community. The farmer never worked alone. He was never isolated. And if the dog named Rex ran beside them, then there were four who could read and obey the rhythms of creation, four creatures, therefore, who dwelt in communion with their Creator.

Ah, what a woven whole that world was! How the picture stirs my yearning—and my sadness too, if I could not enter the peace the farmer knows!

Horses plowed. ("Walk on, Silver. Walk on!") Horses mowed. Horses pulled the rake that laid the alfalfa in windrows to dry, giving Martin's fields the long, strong lines of a darker green that looked, from the road, like emotion wreathed in an ancient face.

And when the hay was dry, horses pulled a flat wagon slowly by the windrows while one man forked the hay up to another who stood on the wagon. This second man caught the bundles neatly on his own fork, then flicked them into an intricate cross-arrangement on the wagon, building the hay higher and tighter, climbing his work as he did, climbing so high that when the horses pulled the wagon to the barn, the man on his haystack could stare dead-level into the second-story windows of the farmhouse. Then horses pulled the rope that, over a metal wheel, hoisted the hay to the loft in the barn.

Martin and his neighbors made hayricks of the overflow. They thatched the tops against rain and the snow to come. The work caused a gritty dust, and the dust caused a fearful itch on a summer's day. But the work and the hay—fodder for the fall and the winter ahead—were a faithful obedience to the seasons and the beasts, Adam and Eve responsible for Eden. Martin Bohlmann knew that!

He milked the cows before sunrise. There was a time when he sat on a stool with his cheek against their warm flanks in winter. Cows would swing their heads around to gaze at him. He pinched the teats in the joint of his thumb and squeezed with the rest of his hand, shooting a needle spritz into the pail between his ankles. He rose. He lifted the full pail and sloshed its blue milk into the can; then he carried the cans, two by two, outside.

The winter air had a bite. His boots squeaked on the crusted snow as he lugged the cans to the milk house. The dawn was gray at the eastern horizon, the white earth ghostly, the cold air making clouds at the farmer's nostrils—and someone might say that he, alone in his barnyard, was lonely. He wasn't, of course; he was neither lonely nor alone. His boots still steamed with the scent of manure; his cheek kept the oil of the cattle's flanks; the milk and the morning were holy. They were—the very harmony of them was—manifestation of the Creator. And the work was nothing more or less than Martin's obedience. Of which is peace.

1991–1995

When Thanne and I moved from Evansville in the southeast corner of Indiana to Valparaiso in the northeast, I was granted the chance to fulfill a personal yearning—a lifelong yearning, to tell the truth, but one made ever more intense by the farms of eastern Illinois. I wanted in some modest way to live the farmer's life. We sought more than a lot and a house, therefore. Thanne and I went looking for land. Today we own twenty-four acres, fields and woods, a tool shed, a barn.

Martin himself had retired before we moved to this place; but we were closer to him now, could visit and talk with greater frequency. And I could focus my questions upon practical problems and solutions of my own small farm.

I have learned! In these latter years, I've come to understand the thing I once could only admire.

So, then: in the spring of 1992, I became the owner of a John Deere 5000 series farm tractor. It pulls at the power of forty horses, more than enough to handle the work I do, light plowing, disking. I drag timber from the woods to cut and split for firewood; I mow the broader fields, stretch fence, chip tree limbs, grade the ground and haul earth and stone and sand—all with my little Deere. The machine is perfectly suited to the cultivation of our modest crops, berry bushes, hickory and walnut trees, strawberry hills, scattered stands of apple trees, a sizable vegetable garden.

For decades before our relocation north, my family and I had lived in the inner city. We were hedged in on every side. True safety (or so it seemed to me) existed only within the walls of our house. I lived in suspicion of strangers. My children's new friends—the boy-type friends especially—might bring the threat that I could not protect against. After nightfall folks regularly gathered across the street from our house to drink, gamble, smoke dope. I slept tense.

I drove my car with such distracted anxiety that Evansville police officers knew me by sight: the pastor with a rap sheet. Well, I was not felonious, but I'd gathered my share of driving tickets and accident reports.

Once we came to the land, however, and once I'd learned to listen to its rhythms, I felt a dear sense of expansion—yes, and the beginning of peace: now I plant and pick, harrow and harvest generous crops in their due seasons.

My tractor is nothing like the modern behemoths that cut swaths as wide as avenues through dustier fields, machines wearing double tires on every wheel, pulling several gangs of plows and disks and harrows at once, while the operator sits bunkered in an air-conditioned cab, watching the tracks of his tires in a televi-sion monitor.

Me, I take the weather on my head. I mow at the width of six feet. And mine is but a two-bottom plow.

But Martin's wisdom makes of small things true sufficiency.

Summer, the Late 40's

My father-in-law purchased his first tractor—a John Deere ex-actly as green as mine, but smaller and less powerful—at the only price he could afford, something less that two hundred dollars.

"Billig," he judged the sale, which could be translated from the German as *"cheap,"* but that in his mouth meant, *"Such a deal!"* He bought the tractor used from one of his neighbors. The ma-chine wasn't even two years old, but it kept stalling, driving the neighbor crazy. In the barnyard, in the field, pulling a wagon or plowing, the tractor would quit and refuse to produce the spark for starting again, however hard the poor man cranked.

That farmer figured he was selling aggravation.

Martin, on the other hand, sought to buy a sturdy servant, not only with his cash but also with his spirit. The dollars bought the cold equipment; but patience and peace bought time to examine it with complete attention, his mind untroubled; and mother-wit brought the tool to life again.

In those days tractors used a magneto generator. My father-in-law opened it and discovered a loose washer inside. The washer had shifted whenever the tractor bumped over rough ground, shorting the coils and killing the engine. Martin simply removed that washer. Thereafter he had a dependable tool for as long as ever he farmed. It was there when I came courting his daughter. It was there when he finally retired at the age of seventy and was forced to auction off his farming equipment.

AUTUMN, 1993

Near the western boundary of my acreage, the land descends to a low draw through which my neighbor's fields drain their runoff waters. For several years, the only way I could get back to the woods—and to the writing studio I'd built there—was through that draw. But every spring the thaw and the thunderstorms turned it into a wide stretch of sucking mud.

In order to correct my problem (to me it was a problem) I laid a culvert east-and-west over the lowest section of the draw, then hired a man with a diesel earth shovel to dig a pond on the east side, then to pile that dirt over my culvert. I built a high bank, a dry pathway wide enough to take the weight of my tractor. I seeded it with grass, and the grass grew rich and green. Had God given us dominion over the earth? Well, I congratulated myself for having dominated this little bit of earth.

Congratulated myself and used this elevated path, that is, until the following spring, when severe storms caused such floods that the earth broke and my metal culvert was washed backward and submerged in the pond.

I tried again. I paid several college students to help me reset the culvert, redig and repile the earth upon it. I walled the mouth of the culvert with rock and stone in order to teach the water where to go. I reseeded the whole—and during the summer months watched miserably as little runnels of water found their ways beneath the culvert. By spring these runnels had scoured out caves, and the caves caused the culvert to slump, so that my draw returned to its first state as if it had never been anything else: primal mud.

When Martin came to visit, I showed him my new John Deere. He described for me the pattern for efficient plowing then told me the story I've recounted above, about his own first tractor.

We walked slowly across my back field. I took him to my failed culvert. That's what I called it while we stood by soupy pond: *"Failed."*

Martin turned bodily and looked at the fields west of mine. Even in old age his cheeks still bunched beneath his eyes. He seemed ever to maintain a private smiling. And his nose! That wondrous blade looked Navaho, though the man was German, through and through.

He turned back again and looked down at the flood-torn earth at our feet.

"Take your time," he said to me as if the last two years had been no time at all. *"You've got the time,"* he said. Martin himself was ninety-three years old and I but forty-nine. Yes, from his vantage I had whole quantities of time.

Finally he raised his eyes to mine and said, *"Ask the water what she wants, then give her a new way to do it."*

My John Deere 5000 makes a low muttering sound. At full throttle it emits a commanding growl. But its voice is muffled, modern.

Martin's first tractor uttered that steady pop-pop-pop-pop that, when it called across the fields to the farmhouse, revealed the essential vastness of the earth and all skies.

Pop-pop-pop-pop! Thanne recalls how she would step outside the farmhouse with her father's lunch, cock her eye and listen for that pop-pop, then follow the sound to find the farmer. She ran between cornstalks as high as her waist, the flat leaves nodding, whispering, slapping her legs as she passed them by. In the lunch box were thick beef sandwiches, some cookies, coffee and two toothpicks. Always the toothpicks for her father at the end of his meals.

Pop-pop-pop-pop, and suddenly the child would come out on high ground and catch sight of her father in the distance, mowing between the solitary cottonwoods, creeping on low and golden land beneath the white cumulus giants striding the blue sky above. How tiny, little Ruthanne would think to herself, unable to distinguish her father's features. How little he is: one man on a tractor, far away.

But how peaceful, think I to myself, in spite of Martin's littleness in the universe. How completely peaceful is this man!

For during these last years, I've learned to know the nature of his peace, that it is not in spite of his smallness. It is in fact in the smallness, as long as his is smallness under God.

For Martin Bohlmann, the sweet admission of his personal limitations was ever the beginning of wisdom. Only in knowing oneself as created can one know God as Creator. Otherwise, striving to be in control of our lives, the true Controller must feel like an adversary of massive and terrible force.

I have despised the limits on my own existence, and in that despite have suffered perpetual tensions, seen enemies everywhere. Why, the common act of driving a car can become a contest of mortal consequence. For the streets are battlegrounds, aren't they?

But Martin dwelt in patience and in peace.

Faith and trust and farming were all the same to him. He read the weather as humbly as he read the Bible, seeking what to obey. My father-in-law was an obedient man. This is the crux of the matter: his obedience was the source of his peace, because the one whom he obeyed was God of all, and by obedience Martin became one with all that God had made, as powerful himself and as infinite as the deity with whom he was joined.

Daily the farmer did more than just read and interpret the rhythms of creation (though these he did, for without such readings the farm would fail). As Prince and Silver heeded their master's mute commands, so the farmer also obeyed the natural signs of the Creator, entering into communion with God Almighty.

So here was Martin's peace: not in striving for greatness but in recognizing who is truly great. And this was his peace: by a glad humility to do the will of the Creator.

And so this was Martin's peace as well: to bear the image of God into creation.

Have you not known? Has it not been told you from the beginning? It is he who sits above the circle of the earth, and its inhabitants are like grasshoppers; who stretched out the heavens like a curtain and spreads them like a tent to dwell in. . . .

Lift up your eyes on high and see: who created these? He who brings out their host by number, calling them all by name; by the greatness of his might, and because he is strong in power, not one is missing.

APRIL 30, 1995

But one is missing! Martin is missing. My father-in-law himself. Martin is gone. This man is dead.

I'm driving south on Interstate 57 with a clenched jaw and stark knuckles. Angry. Anxious, really. It's nearly nighttime. South of Kankakee the Illinois farmland stretches east and west of me. More than seeing it, I feel the cultivated earth as a swelling tide, a heaving of massy weight, as of an ocean. It will fall on me soon, and I will drown.

I am about forty-five minutes from the funeral home in Watseka where I will find Thanne and my children. And Martin in a box.

I'm driving at sixty-five miles per hour precisely. The speed limit. Cars rip past me, fire-eyed enemies, each one triumphing over me in my pickup. This particular obedience is not my habit. But I'm torn between desires to be with Thanne and never to be near the casket of my father-in-law. So I'm going at a grim, calculated slowness.

Death and the empty skies consume me now.

I hate this pickup! A beaten '84 Chevy S-10, the seat's too low and too hard. It wasn't made for distance driving. My back is killing me. Oh, God I want to howl! To howl at you!

Because all our human limitations may be made easy in obedience—all but this last one: death!

I gnash my teeth. I roll down my window and weep with the frustration of it all. Martin is not here! I can do nothing about that! This single, final limit makes every other limitation insupportable. And God's infinitude becomes my hell, for it makes my smallness burn like a flesh afire.

I have already left the Interstate. I'm driving east on Highway 24, approaching state Highway 49. The night is hugely black, endlessly empty above my little vehicle, though once I took the farmer's daughter for rides on county roads nearby, and then the nights were filled with delicious mystery.

I had a VW convertible in those days. When the nightwind grew chilly, Ruthanne would draw her knees up to her breast and pull the sweatshirt down to her ankles. That tender gesture stole my heart; her easy intimacy made me a citizen of the night and all that countryside. But there was no death in those days.

The parking lot is full. So I pull out again, park on a side street and walk back. The funeral home spills light from various windows. I can hear a hubbub within.

I enter at the side of the building, artificial light, heat, a human humidity.

In the hallway I hang up my jacket. With slow steps I move to the viewing room. Martin's name and the dates that round his life are on a framed placard: 1900 to 1995. There is a birthday and a deathday.

I shift my sight to the room and look through the doorway. Many people are sitting. I recognize Thanne's sisters, her brothers.

And then, astonishingly, here is Thanne standing directly before me, looking up into my face.

My wife, my wife: are we okay together?

Her countenance wears a pleasant expression. She has not been crying. She touches my cheek. This is how Thanne will remove dried patches of shaving cream. It's also how she indicates to me by feel what she sees by sight: my face does not wear a pleasant expression. Yes. I know how gaunt and anxious I am, my face and my spirit, both.

Thanne takes my hand.

"Come," she says gently. She leads me into the wide viewing room. People glance my way, acknowledge my arrival. They sit on folding chairs all around the walls. Others stand in knots of conversation.

There is the casket, at the far end surrounded by a jungle of flowers. It has the appearance of an altar in church. No one is near it now. We approach, still hand in hand. The room seems (can this be?) to hush a little. I feel a general expectancy. My stomach tightens even more than it was. I don't like to be on display. No emotion could possibly be natural and easy under scrutiny.

But Thanne continues forward to the casket, drawing me with her.

Behind the casket's linen, I see that great sail of a nose rise up. Yes, it is Martin whom I'm coming to see. Yes, and there is his cantankerous hair. Even in death those spikes will not lie down. His eyebrows, too, are great sprouts of hair. His eyes are closed. His bunchy cheeks are slightly rouged.

Suddenly Thanne lets a little giggle escape her lips. The sound of it tingles inside me. She's laughing? But then I see the farmer's mouth, and I understand. Sticking straight up from the corner of his lips, causing a little grin to pool there, is a toothpick, straight, bold, erect.

Thanne tries to whisper in my ear, "The mortician . . ."

But the whisper becomes a squeal: "Oh, Wally," she squeals with perfect clarity, "the mortician is mortified!" And then she can't help it. She breaks out in laughter.

That laughter kills me. I mean, it kills my silly anger; I glance at Thanne's bright, wet eyes and burst into laughter, too.

Martin doesn't move; but his face is not offended by the hilarity, and besides, he was never a talky man. And here are my children, gathering, grinning, all four of them. And now I know what the whole room was anticipating: my taking the last step, my joining them, too.

And so I know exactly what happened after lunch on Friday, April 18, 1995.

Martin Bohlmann, having finished his meal, popped a toothpick into his mouth. He wasn't about to read his devotions. Rather, he was about to do them, devoutly and well.

And though he'd mostly been bound to a wheelchair, the farmer got up nevertheless, and pushed that chair aside and strolled out the door and into the fields west of his dwellings. Twilight. Farther and farther west the old man walked, until he came to a place of pausing. He tucked his hands under the bib of coveralls and gazed extremest west and listened to the deepest rhythms of the universe.

Yes, and I know what happened then. In his own good time, Martin Bohlmann knelt on one knee and scooped up a handful of the black earth and brought it to his face and smelled in it its readiness for plowing and for planting.

A springtime breeze got up and blew. And when at last my father-in-law allowed the soil to sift from his hands into the wind, it was he himself that blew forth, ascending. Here was the dust of his human frame and the lightsome stuff of his spirit.

This, then, I know as well as I know any other thing: even his death was an obedience.

Martin died, therefore, in a perfect peace.

The Oneness of Music

from *Agni*

An Italian doctor I know, who loves music, does research on babies by playing Bartók to them as they grow in their mother's wombs. In the first month after birth, when the *Mikrokosmos* is replayed, their innocent brain impulses undulate on his monitor in bright, active movements of recognition, as bright as when they feel their mother's breast. The doctor's results, which he will continue to explore, say many things that scientists cannot yet sum up about neurology and music's intricate influences. But his work suggests that music is a force whose messages can penetrate the skin, traveling across the earliest tenebrous dark we rock in. In the brain, music finds ground prepared for it, matter primed to receive its marks. We now know the interaction subtly and with individual differences alters the chemistry of our blood.

I came to music very late in life. Except for a strong first encounter at the age of three, I lived outside its illumination until I was nearly fifty. Looking back I wonder how I survived. Both at three, when I was a child listening to a radio, and in 1991 when I was outside Moscow entering a fifteenth-century church, it was the human voice that transported me into music's power. In the first instance, I was waiting in the bathtub for my mother to return from putting my brothers to bed. The black Bakelite radio, resting on a chair, with an electric heater nearby sending out its red bands of heat with their message—you must never under any circumstances touch an electric plug with wet fingers—complete the scene. It was war-weary Wisconsin, winter 1945. As I splashed alone, the radio voice descended into the room and suddenly soared like a winged creature. Its strength, volume, its womanly pouring transfixed me. I thought the bathroom was alive with a goddess from another world. Her authority overwhelmed the heat and danger of the electric coils. I remember trying to mock the voice by covering my ears and singing over it, because it awed and scared me, diving to such sorrow and rising to joy, large and unknown. The voice was Marian Anderson's. At three, I only knew music as nursery songs. But when the radio was switched on sometimes a concert materialized. That night the voice I heard held the power of an annunciation. Its absolute knowledge cried out. The voice not only showed me another world, it threw open the smallness of mine. I could feel drama and pain, unimagined heights. I was touched, even electrified, but had no idea where this invisible world lay.

Then, although I listened to music off and on as I grew up, my interests led me deeper and deeper into words and painting. I don't know if I ever would have discovered music if I had not been seized and taken over by it again outside Moscow in November 1991. I was part of a group of Western writers exchanging ideas with ex-Soviet ones. Snow clamped the ground. Strong winds troubled the days and sleet grizzled out a mean chill. The city itself was under the moleish burrowing of making do, as Muscovites scrambled for firewood, food, and tried to face a future that was all to be born from the collapsed Soviet Union. In most of the writers, we met visions that went no further than fear, lamentation, and uncertainty. They could not rejoice about possible freedom, and little in the word *market* inspired them. Perhaps it was by measuring the strength and dignity in angry and worried faces—some possessed these qualities, some didn't— that I began thinking about the ranges in a human voice. Mine. Others'. Even people's on the streets. Individualism, as we proposed it to the Russians from our recent literature, often felt contorted, insignificant, ego filled. But it, too, had broadened and been renewed by minorities and women adding their voices, turning reality around and altering history. Writers could leave prints or take new samples.

At the Lavra of St. Sergiy, outside Moscow, silence and the crunch of packed snow under our feet met the chill biting the frozen ground. We were nearing the end of two weeks spent in exchanging ideas on art and freedom of speech with Soviet writers who had no knowledge of that dimension in everyday life. Their feelings were anything but brave. The practical problems consumed. As writers, we, too, had soon realized that we were in over our heads. Words were cheap and actions difficult. Writing seemed as soft on our side as it was on the side of Russians who had all but given up trying to challenge areas of truth. We walked pensively, feeling brushed by the gaps in fate and fortune brought about by nationality and history. All around, the Byzantine and Russian Orthodox gold and star-spangled blue domes astounded, even more because of the cold, hard pewter skies. In spite of Soviet policies to destroy churches, this cluster ranging over four centuries had been kept alive, in part for tourism. I stepped into the darkness of the Church of the Life-Giving Trinity appreciative but, in some way, deeply unprepared. As the confusing days quieted in my mind, I slowly came to.

Imagine candles, thin, papery, fine, rising and clinging on chandeliers, candles burning like the hives of God, flames so abundant and busy that they hiss and send up bursts of unmeasurable light in a damp, heavy dark; then feel monks with strong masculine faces and ardent voices and hear other human voices sunk into a darkness so thick and contrasting that the eyes coming in from the outside can barely make out a way in those mystifying contrasts of blaze and dark. Then imagine voices singing the liturgy of centuries. Imagine ancient plainchants that reach back into time, nearly eternal non-Western time, and the embrace of improvising voices that harmonize using polyphonic lines to reveal another melody. The voices swerving and winding their way through the darkness surrounded me and swept me away. I shut my eyes, losing all track and every thread of time as the music grew. Nearly an hour passed as if it were less than a minute. I realized that I had never heard music before. My heart opened to an archaic dawn of human sounds giving shape to a world beyond any single individual. The passionate service in the notes bowed and rose like flames. I remembered, then, Marian Anderson's voice. I remembered my own longing for beauty and how my ears, so tuned to work and responsibility, had forgotten the sounds of sacredness. The harsh closedness of not-listening battered like a wind. I felt the thunderous reverberations of interregnum. The steady voices expressing pain, strength, and hope carried around me and lifted me beyond.

Once home again in Parma, Italy, where I have lived for the past eighteen years, I set aside my inadequate plastic tape recorder and bought a CD player with speakers that could reach even the deaf. Like an addict, I began buying compact discs in stacks. I loved the few folded pages of paper notes that could be pulled from inside the CD'S transparent case. I liked the daguerreotypes, the historical dates explaining the sonata, the ways the melody was led into orchestration, the retrospective inclusive reach of twelve-tone music. And I began to be infused with music. One minute, Shostakovich would shake the chairs with catastrophic disaster and suffering, and in the next Monteverdi would melt the freezing snows. It was my daughter who had me place the CD player in the center of the house, where sounds radiated out into all the rooms: the popular songs she followed then, the sacred music I was learning, the melodies that Mozart shot from his eternal arrows turned the house into a living space with a heart. The black speakers and the black sonoric column became the cairn we stopped at. A long-lost part of our family moved in.

It was in those years that I met Rostropovich. By that time, music had led me into experiences that plunged me deeper into life as well as into understanding a dimension of being an artist. How can I put it? I found knowledge in music that built up around a mighty core: service, faith, rhythm, and energy. He was a neighbor of a dear friend of mine in Switzerland. We were listening to Schubert's *Impromptus* when Rostropovich knocked at the door. He was on his way down to the sauna in the basement. He had his terry cloth robe sashed casually, and his strong pink legs were a shock from the black tuxedoes he usually appeared in. He had stopped in on an impulse. The sea blue couch had room for three. Tea followed, a chat. We might have been sitting on the meadow painted by Giorgione.

The conversation during tea, escaping time, flew like the music in the Russian church. Rostropovich began with charity, how he now often passed on his checks after a concert to groups that needed help. How he'd reached the Berlin Wall by leaving on an impulse on his way to buy his newspaper in Paris. Russia burned in his mind: its mysteries, its artistic dignity, its need to escape from historical shackles. But the afternoon filled up with his new story of Bach's *Six Suites*. Rostropovich's fingers were full of moods and intimacy. When he came back dressed the next day, I asked if I could take his picture. He folded his hands like a curved bridge over a long waterfall. He himself, with his widened middle, looked like an instrument, playing a conversation. He talked about a monastery in Vezelay, France, where he found the strong, severe architecture and arched rhythms that he needed to reinforce patterns he found in the *Suites*. Rostropovich relished the bats that awakened inside the church. He made us see their quivering, quirkish flips exploding in circles as the cello's sounds widened. The concerts would be issued under his own label because they were so personal for him. "Technically I was better thirty years ago, but now I am closer to what's written." He closed his eyes as he said something like, "We are still hundreds of years from playing Bach. We must do our best." I loved that thought, which placed music's transcendental horizon in a time frame so different from any perspective in literature. I asked him who in his opinion had come close to interpreting the *Suites*. "Casals," he said after thinking for a brief second. Then he said, "I think you have to believe in God to be able to play them."

Two years later, his videos came out. His long, animated face, warm, sober, speaks in Russian, while English subtitles run at the bottom of the tapes. The *Suites* follow his explanations, and after many listenings, I find his interpretations difficult but always more moving. I knew Casals's versions well by that time. His *Suites* are warm, caressing. The way Rostropovich plays the pieces, he has reached and risked, suggesting and filling spaces that cannot fit in our minds. They sound quite different from Casals's versions or Yo Yo Ma's, in which the *Suites* are transformed into facets of a perfect diamond. Rostropovich enters and exits, adding pattern to pattern, until we hear melodies unplayed as others play. Powerful solitary searching and strong structural absolutes build into shapes that sometimes cry to be completed in the heart or imagined in forming universes. Sometimes, instead, note after note meets harmonious certainties. In the videos, I see heart-stopping leaps between what he hears and what he plays. This passionate reaching expresses part of his interpretation.

It was not long after those afternoons that I encountered a sound engineer on a train trip between Florence and Milan. At first I judged him. Wearing leather gloves, wireless glasses, the

254 ♦ Wallis Wilde-Menozzi

short-haired young man had large gray earplugs in both ears. I
thought he was an antiseptic creature, perhaps even paranoid,
until he pointed out that I had dropped my wallet, which he returned kindly. He pulled out the plugs with his gloves and started
up a conversation. His slightly rigid face eased as he began talking
about recording. What struck me was his seriousness and sense of
dedication. As he told it, the work goes on day and night in book-
ing agencies, law offices, instrument-makers' shops, in sound
labs, recording studios, plants that manufacture plastics, not to
mention concert halls and churches all over the world. He was
traveling back to Germany and hoped to reach Hamburg in time
to work that night. He had a live recording date in a church; for
these occasions, with soloists, he had to work in the darkest
hours, usually between eleven and three. Music was under siege in
terms of natural environments. It was extremely difficult to find
space that was living and still in consonance with the silence
needed to record soloists. Only a few precious night hours lulled
enough to be used for recording music unmarred by motors and
engines. The darkest part of the night, when silence was rich and
fertile, unlike the silence of insulated studio walls, was a world
worth saving.

Gossip trickled out of him in modest pinches. He had worked
with nearly every famous artist: the arrogant ones, the in-
structable ones, and the geniuses. He said that he lived like a
faithful monk, who must be prepared by study and concentration
to bring back to perfection a straying note. "I'm a conservator,
here to preserve what was written." He was booked up for the
next two years; his family, prominent in the sheet music business
for three generations. He bid me farewell by picking up the plugs
and gently twisting them back into his ears. The young man in
the black leather jacket settled into his own reverie, the score of
black and white notes on his lap. As he trilled time with his fin-

gers, his attitude, even his leather clothing, suggested service to me; that and, in his relationship to darkness, a new kind of knight.

Once my heart opened, music's power to transform revealed its constant, intricate connection to inner and outer worlds. I have little patience for people who see classical music as an activity for elites. It's patrimony that anyone can partake of. I admit that it is a gift, a surprise for those who have no training. But I know (and the Italian doctor with data from many parts of the world won't let me forget) that our brains are ready, whenever, finally, Marian Anderson's voice catches us off guard and buffets us open.

In Fiesole, above Florence on the ancient hills layered by olives and vines, I sometimes sit in the room of a woman who, at ninety-two, seems a wishbone of silence and cosmic laughter. She has been a yogi for nearly fifty years. Her father founded Amici della Musica, which gave Florence its orchestra, and Maggio Musicale. Toscanini stayed in the sun-filled rustic rooms of her estate and did somersaults next to the paths down the hills. One day when guests B. K. S. Iyengar and Yehudi Menuhin were doing yoga, they asked Vanda Scaravelli, if she, the lively woman who speeded in a red Alfa Spider and wore Chanel suits, wished to do some with them. She agreed. Her body, lithe and trained because she was an accomplished concert pianist, found itself released further into life's rhythms. In a matter of months, bending and arching, rooting her feet to the ground, lifting her arms to the skies, she became a yogi. As her energies deepened, her earlier life, except for her love of her children and of music, gradually ended. She began to live an idea of harmony and emotion at another level.

Vanda has instructed me in several unforgettable lessons about the oneness of music and the rhythm of life. Strangely, I have never heard her play. Yet as I wrote about her, it was natural to settle her birdlike body at the keyboard. I believed she was playing

Chopin. Vanda's presence is so harmonious it seems at all times as if clear notes are being struck. I have gathered music flowing from her breathing; from the way her back bends, I see rhythm. Talking with her about Kant, I can hear music's scales and tonal systems. From the bent-eared scores on her piano, I can feel her huge bony hands move with strength and pluck across the keyboard.

Vanda sleeps and lives in one room, bare except for sunlight and moonlight, two mirrors, a daybed, and her piano. The rest of the villa floats unheeded like a lost sunken city. She has few needs but to maintain an intense relationship to the present. "It's so beautiful in that other world, sometimes, it's difficult to come back." In her room, without accepting money, she brings minds and bodies to attention, teaching breathing, yoga positions, and piano to students who ask. There, in black pants and blue sweater, barefoot—her toes long and alive—her often laughing eyes convey relationships beyond words. In the full-length mirror, students furtively check their yoga positions; in the horizontal one, where she smooths her white, wispy hair, her piano fills up the view. Within that concentrated cross of energies and reflected light, Vanda—head, feet, hands—plays, opens up, sends into bodies and out explosions and rhythms, sometimes too beautiful to bear.

By now, it seems impossible that I considered myself alive before music remade my daily way of living. In music I found a language to keep company with a writer's life. In Parma, two colossal musicians figured. Verdi and Toscanini have deep links with the land and its dramatic history. Two forceful men who rarely bent bowed continuously to music's greater power, particularly Toscanini. In videos, he seems incandescent: energy streams through his eyes, arms, and body as he passes on his total recall of a score. This mysterious exchange—transmission and release—how, I wonder, if writers were to be looked at in this sense, would it be measured and expressed? As we write, do our brains alter our body chemistry? As we mature, do we become aware that we are serving gods more powerful than ourselves? Do we bow when the voice passes through us? Yes, I hope; perhaps we do.

Recently, I stood before an open apartment door in Parma, where I was to deliver a translation. I saw a grand piano beyond me; it stood in front of another open door: one that emptied into a terrace with a birch dancing there. I stepped in and asked about it. Signor Calevro, a rather pudgy man in his early forties, beckoned me to sit down around a table rumpled with papers. Instead of discussing the translation, his round eyes misted. He asked me if I believed in invisible things. Without another word, I entered his story. The slow, deliberate progressions felt like the ever-widening circles of beauty and resolution inside the despair of Beethoven's *Moonlight Sonata*. As I write now, the flooding, healing ebbs and flows of that conversation swirl. He had been warned by his agent not to tell the story, but its power pushed him to tell it to me.

The wildly curly headed man held up his rather soft, sensuous hands and explained that the right one became paralyzed in 1983. Not that day, but on another, he asked me to feel the relative strength of his two appendages. His left hand was firm like mine; his right one, when extended with full force, nearly felt like putty. In 1983, Maestro Calevro's lower tendon crushed his radial nerve, bringing his fingers to a limp, dangling weakness in which he could not even make them rise, much less release the black and white keys. The surgeon's knife entered at the elbow two years later in Bern; by 1987, after a terrifying period of darkness and loathing, despair and hatred whenever music reminded him of his loss, Calevro began to feel inchoate tingling in his collapsed hand. Unsuccessful in trying to close off music, he discovered his life still consisted of music's immemorial and inventive activities. He crashed against the bottom and couldn't stay there.

The suffering pianist took up music again, humbly, with one hand, which was all he had. He gave concerts for music written for the left hand, joining history's performers who were often victims of war. He played *Chaconne* by Bach adapted by Brahms, *Studies* by Saint-Saëns. At first, the musical sound seemed bare, empty. Then the middle-aged man realized that one hand was sufficient; the music filled the space the composer had intended. It was a question of playing fully, playing the hand as if it were a violin. Violins gave solos. He kept on, performing but also practicing, using his left hand to teach the right. To swing a finger in a tiny arc, to be a mirror for it, he asked his left hand to instruct his right. Using his left-handed mirror, which played without much concentration, he directed his mind to the right-hand, until the right-hand fingers began to follow. At first they acted like frightening mechanical instruments; slowly they warmed into a living one. Finally Calevro used both hands again, but by then both hands were different, as was he. The story wrapped around us. Music flickered. He would jump up and play examples of right and left passages and of both hands together. It didn't sound that way to me, but he said that when he played with two hands, it was as if he were playing a duet. Each hand had different capacities, one learning from the other. The reflective man, whose eyes are rimmed with sadness that blinks into light, handed me a recent CD, as a sign of health. "I was a good pianist but I didn't really play in the years when I was strong and well. I performed. I've learned now that playing means 'to serve.' I knew that, all musicians do, but I had not imagined that I could learn from my hands and they from me. I'd seen myself, my technical skill and accuracy, as the key to success. Instead, I've been infused by a voice that is perhaps the self, or is the heart speaking. It's a mysterious, beautiful guide, leading the way to an altar we can never quite touch. What can I say? I'm on my knees. I'm at the beginning."

Biographical Notes

John Luther Adams, for the past twenty-five years, has made his home in the boreal forest near Fairbanks, Alaska. From there he has created a unique musical world grounded in the elemental landscapes and indigenous cultures of the North. Adams's music is recorded on the Cold Blue, New World, Mode, and New Albion labels. More information about him and his work is available on the web at www.johnlutheradams.com.

Marvin Barrett is the author of fourteen books. A senior editor and frequent contributor to *Parabola*, he was formerly an editor at *Time* and *Newsweek*. For sixteen years he was a senior lecturer at the Columbia University Graduate School of Journalism. The father of four children, he lives with his wife, the author Mary Ellin Barrett, in New York City.

Wendell Berry is the author of more than thirty books of poetry, essays, and fiction, including *Selected Poems, Life Is a Miracle,* and *Jayber Crow.* He lives in Henry County, Kentucky, with his wife.

Harvey Cox is Thomas Professor of Divinity at Harvard University. His research and teaching interests are in urbanization; theological developments in world Christianity; and the ministry of the church in the global setting, especially Latin America. He is the author of several books including *The Secular City* (1965), *Religion in the Secular City* (1984); *The Silencing of Leonardo Boff: Liberation Theology and the Future of World Christianity* (1988); *Many Mansions: A Christian's Encounter with Other Faiths* (1988); and *Fire from Heaven: The Rise of Pentecostal Spirituality and the Reshaping of Religion in the 21ˢᵗ Century* (1994).

Sara Davidson is the author of the best-selling books *Cowboy* and *Loose Change.* Her writing has appeared in *Rolling Stone, Esquire,* the *Atlantic Monthly,* and the *New York Times Magazine.*

Brian Doyle is the editor of *Portland Magazine* at the University of Portland, in Oregon. He is the author of *Credo,* a collection of essays, and coauthor, with his father, Jim Doyle, of *Two Voices,* a collection of their essays. His essays and poems have appeared in *The American Scholar, The Atlantic Monthly, Harper's Magazine, Orion,* and *Commonweal,* among other periodicals. His essays have been reprinted in The Best Spiritual Writing collections of 1999 and 2001, The

Best American Essays of 1998 and 1999, and in the anthologies *Thoughts of Home* (1995), *Family* (1997), *In Brief* (1998), and *Resurrecting Grace* (2001).

Vincent Druding is assistant editor at *First Things*. He is a graduate of Wabash College and holds an M.A. in Humanities from the University of Chicago.

Robert Eddy founded and edited the journal *Studies in Mystical Literature*. He is the editor of the anthology *Reflections on Multiculturalism* and the author of *Writing Across Cultures*. He is at work on a book of short stories called *Stories from Egypt*.

Joseph Epstein is the author, most recently, of *Snobbery: The American Version*. A collection of his short stories, *Fabulous Small Jews*, will be published in 2003.

Natalie Goldberg is the author of many books, including *Writing Down the Bones, Long Quiet Highway, Living Color, Thunder and Lightning*, and, most recently, a collection of forty poems and twenty paintings entitled *Top of My Lungs*. She is a longtime Zen practitioner.

Seamus Heaney's most recent book of poems is *Electric Light* (2001). A selection of his critical and autobiographical prose entitled *Finders Keepers* has also just appeared. He lives in Dublin.

Patricia Hooper is the author of two books of poetry: *Other Lives*, which was awarded the Poetry Society of America's Norma Farber First Book Award, and *At the Corner of the Eye*. She is also the author of four children's books, including *A Stormy Ride on Noah's Ark*. Her poems have appeared in the *American Scholar*, the *Atlantic Monthly*, the *Hudson Review*, the *Kenyon Review, Ploughshares*, and other magazines.

Leon R. Kass, M.D., is the Addie Clark Harding Professor in the Committee on Social Thought and the College at the University of Chicago, chair of the President's Council on Bioethics, and author of *The Hungry Soul: Eating and the Perfection of Our Nature*.

Heather King has been published in numerous magazines and literary journals. She is a commentator on NPR's "All Things Considered."

Philip Levine's many books include *So Ask: Essays, Conversations, and Interviews; The Bread of Time: Toward an Autobiography; The Mercy;* and *The Simple Truth,* which won the Pulitzer Prize for Poetry in 1995.

Barry Lopez is the author of many books, including *Light Action in the Caribbean: Stories, Crossing Open Ground,* and *About This Life*. The recipient of many literary awards, including the National Book Award for nonfiction, he lives in western Oregon.

Bret Lott is the author of five novels, two story collections, and a memoir. "The Ironic Stance and the Law of Diminishing Returns" is from the forthcoming collection *You Are Not Here Long: On Writing and the Art of Paying Attention.* He teaches at the College of Charleston and is editor of the literary journal *Crazyhorse.*

Bill McKibben is the author of many books, including *The End of Nature; Hundred Dollar Holiday; Hope, Human and Wild;* and *Maybe One.*

W. S. Merwin's books include *The Pupil, The River Sound,* and *The Folding Cliffs.* He was awarded the Pulitzer Prize for Poetry in 1971.

Czeslaw Milosz was awarded the Nobel Prize in Literature in 1980. His recent books include *New and Collected Poems* and *To Begin Where I Am.*

Toni Morrison is the author of *Paradise, Beloved,* and many other books. She was awarded the Nobel Prize for Literature in 1993.

Alicia Ostriker teaches English and creative writing at Rutgers University. She is the author of many books, including *The Volcano Sequence* (2002) and *The Little Space: Poems New and Select* (1998).

Susan Pollack is working on a collection of essays about landscape and imagination, which includes pieces on Virginia Woolf's Sussex, Florentine architecture, and "The Wives of Gloucester." She is an award-winning journalist whose writing has appeared in *Sierra,* the *Boston Globe Sunday Magazine,* the *Amicus Journal, New Age, Mademoiselle,* and *Ms.* She was recently the writer-in-residence at Chatham College. She lives in Cambridge, Massachusetts.

Pattiann Rogers is the author of *Song of the World Becoming, Collected and New Poems, 1981–2001.* Her other books include *The Dream of the Marsh Wren, Writing as Reciprocal Creation,* and *A Convenant of Seasons* (with artist Joellyn Duesberry).

Amy Schwartz is a freelance journalist and a member of the *Washington Post* editorial board.

Gary Smith is a senior writer at *Sports Illustrated* and author of *Beyond the Game: The Collected Sportswriting of Gary Smith.*

George Steiner is the author of *Grammars of Creation, Errata: An Examined Life,* and many other books.

Ptolemy Tompkins is an editor at *Guideposts* and *Angels on Earth* magazines and the author of *This Tree Grows Out of Hell, Paradise Fever,* and, most recently, *The Beaten Path: Field Notes on Getting Wise in a Wisdom-Crazy World.*

Walter Wangerin Jr. teaches theology, English, and creative writing at Valparaiso University. He is the author of *Swallowing the Sacred Stone, Paul,* and many other books.

Wallis Wilde-Menozzi has published widely in North America and Europe. Her memoir *Mother Tongue, An American Life in Italy* has been called "richly absorbing," "a cauldron that burns in the mind." She teaches workshops in Geneva, Milan, and Parma, Italy, where she lives and is presently concluding a novel, *Seven Turns.*

Philip Zaleski is the editor of The Best Spiritual Writing series. His other books include *The Recollected Heart, Gifts of the Spirit* (with Paul Kaufman), and *The Book of Heaven* (with Carol Zaleski). He is currently writing, with Carol Zaleski, a study of prayer and culture entitled *The Language of Paradise.* A senior editor of *Parabola,* to which he contributes a regular column, he also teaches religion at Smith College.

Notable Spiritual Writing of 2001

CHARLOTTE ALLEN
"The Scholars and the Goddess," *The Atlantic Monthly,* January

CHRISTOPHER BAMFORD
"Telling the Rosary," *Parabola,* February

STEPHEN M. BARR
"Anthropic Coincidences," *First Things,* June/July

BENJAMIN BOGIN
"Beyond the End of the Road," *Tricycle,* Fall

ALAN BURDICK
"Now Hear This," *Harper's Magazine,* July

STEPHEN L. CARTER
"Why Rules Rule," *Christianity Today,* September 3

TRACY COCHRAN
"French Lessons," *The Oprah Magazine,* July

STEPHEN V. DOUGHTY
"Adrift," *Weavings,* March/April

TOM DRURY
"First Cut," *Tricycle,* Fall

DIANA ECK
"Afraid of Ourselves," *Harvard Divinity School Bulletin,* Summer/Fall

SARAH E. HINCKLEY
"The Great Beyond," *Christianity Today,* February 3

KRISTEN JOHNSON INGRAM
"The Law of the Vineyard," *Weavings,* September/October

LIN JENSEN
"Swallowing," *Turning Wheel,* Winter

ANNE KLEIN
"The Mantra and the Typist," *Tricycle,* Winter

ARTHUR KRYSTAL
"Why Smart People Believe in God," *The American Scholar,* Autumn

MARK LILLA
"Ignorance and Bliss," the *Wilson Quarterly,* Summer

JOHN LOWE
"Soji-ji," *The American Scholar,* Winter

CATHERINE MADSEN
"Kitsch and Liturgy," *Tikkun,* March/April

KOBUTSU MALONE
"A Roshi on the Row," *Shambhala Sun,* January

JAMES McCONKEY
"Happy Trails to All," *The American Scholar,* Autumn

SUSAN MOON
"I Want to Tell You About Coming Apart," *Shambhala Sun,* November

KEN MYERS
"The Holy and the Weird," *Notre Dame Magazine,* Autumn

ELIZABETH NICKSON
"Where the Bee Sucks," *Harper's Magazine,* January

JEREMY RIFKIN
"The New Genetics Rights Movement," *Lapis,* Summer

DAVID ROTHENBERG
"Music as Nature," *Orion,* Spring

LUCI SHAW
"The Need to Pay Attention," *Weavings,* July/August

PHILIP SIMMONS
"Winter Mind," *UUWorld,* January/February

WOLFGANG SMITH
"Science and Myth: The Hidden Connection," *Sophia,* Summer

HWEE HWEE TAN
"In Search of the Lotus Land," *Image,* Spring

A List of Former Contributors

Lawrence Shainberg
Luci Shaw
Huston Smith
David Steindl-Rast
Ptolemy Tompkins
Janwillem van de Wetering
Terry Tempest Williams

The Best Spiritual Writing 1999

Introduction by Kathleen Norris
Virginia Hamilton Adair
Max Apple
Marvin Barrett
Wendell Berry
S. Paul Burholt
Douglas Burton-Christie
Léonie Caldecott
Tracy Cochran
Robert Cording
Annie Dillard
Brian Doyle
Andre Dubus III
Alma Roberts Giordan
Bernie Glassman
Mary Gordon
Ron Hansen
Seamus Heaney
Edward Hirsch
Pico Iyer
Tom Junod
Philip Levine
Barry Lopez
Anita Mathias
Walt McDonald
Thomas Moore
Louise Rafkin
Pattiann Rogers
Jonathan Rosen
David Rothenberg
Luci Shaw

Eliezer Shore
Louis Simpson
Jack Stewart
Barbara Brown Taylor
Ptolemy Tompkins
Janwillem van de Wetering
Michael Ventura
Paul J. Willis
Larry Woiwode

THE BEST SPIRITUAL WRITING 2000

Introduction by Thomas Moore
Christopher Bamford
Lionel Basney
Wendell Berry
Scott Cairns
Jimmy Carter and Miller Williams
David Chadwick
Robert Cording
Alfred Corn
Harvey Cox
Annie Dillard
Gretel Ehrlich
Frank X. Gaspar
William H. Gass
Natalie Goldberg
Mary Gordon
Deborah Gorlin
Jeanine Hathaway
Linda Hogan
Ann Hood
Andrew Hudgins
Pico Iyer
Philip Levine
Jacques Lusseyran
Anita Mathias
William Maxwell
Bill McKibben
Robert Morgan
Richard John Neuhaus

John Price
Robert Reese
David Rensberger
Pattiann Rogers
Marjorie Sandor
Jim Schley
Roger Shattuck
Kimberley Snow
Anne Stevenson
John Updike
James Van Tholen
Loretta Watts

The Best Spiritual Writing 2001

Introduction by Andre Dubus III
Lorenzo Albacete
Marc Ian Barasch
Wendell Berry
Ben Birnbaum
Robert Cording
Mark Doty
Brian Doyle
David James Duncan
John Landretti
Leah Koncelik Lebec
Bret Lott
Valerie Martin
Alane Salierno Mason
Daphne Merkin
Thomas Moore
Howard Mumma
Sheldon M. Novick
Pattiann Rogers
Floyd Skloot
Joan D. Stamm
George Weigel
Lawrence Weschler
Terry Tempest Williams
Simon Winchester
Charles Wright

Reader's Directory

For more information about or subscriptions to the periodicals represented in The Best Spiritual Writing 2002, please contact:

Agni
Boston University
236 Bay State Road
Boston, MA 02215

The American Scholar
The Phi Beta Kappa Society
1785 Massachusetts Avenue, NW, Fourth Floor
Washington, DC 20036

The Atlantic Monthly
77 North Washington Street, Suite 5
Boston, MA 02114–1908

beliefnet.com
www.beliefnet.com

DoubleTake
55 Davis Square
Somerville, MA 02144

First Things
The Institute on Religion and Public Life
156 Fifth Avenue, Suite 400
New York, NY 10010

Harvard Divinity School Bulletin
Harvard Divinity School
45 Francis Avenue
Cambridge, MA 02138

The Hudson Review
684 Park Avenue
New York, NY 10012

Image
Center for Religious Humanism
3307 Third Avenue West
Seattle, WA 98119

The Kenyon Review
Kenyon College
Gambier, OH 43022

Music *Works*
361-401 Richmond Street
Toronto, ON M5V 3A8

My Generation
780 Third Avenue, 41st Floor
New York, NY 10017

New York Times
229 West 43rd Street
New York, NY 10036

The New Yorker
20 West 43rd Street
New York, NY 10036

Notre Dame Magazine
583 Grace Hall
Notre Dame, IN 46556–5612

Orion
Orion Society
195 Main Street
Great Barrington, MA 01230

Parabola
656 Broadway
New York, NY 10012

Ploughshares
Emerson College
120 Boylston Street
Boston, MA 02116–4624

Sports Illustrated
135 West 50th Street
New York, NY 10020–1201

The Sun
107 North Roberson Street
Chapel Hill, NC 27516

Vanity Fair
4 Times Square
New York, NY 10036–6518

Writing on the Edge
Campus Writing Center
University of California
Davis, CA 95616

Credits